WOODWIND METHODS

An Essential Resource for Educators, Conductors, and Students

CHARLES WEST

Foreword by
Tim Lautzenheiser

Published by
Meredith Music Publications
a division of G.W. Music, Inc.
1584 Estuary Trail, Delray Beach, Florida 33483
http://www.meredithmusic.com

First Edition
September 2015

Text and cover design: Shawn Girsberger

International Standard Book Number: 978–1-57463–436-5
Cataloging-in-Publication Data is on file with the Library of Congress.
Library of Congress Control Number: 2015911004
Printed and bound in U.S.A.

25 24 23 22 21 20 19 18 VLP 3 4 5

CONTENTS

FOREWORD

It is a privilege and an honor to share my thoughts about Dr. Charles "Chuck" West and his latest contribution to the music community: *WOODWIND METHODS: An Essential Resource for Educators, Conductors, and Students*.

By definition, a FOREWORD is usually written by someone who has a personal relationship with the author of the given manuscript. Dr. West is not only a much-respected colleague, but he also is a dear, dear friend. For three years we were teaching colleagues at New Mexico State University. During our mutual tenures "Chuck" became a valuable source of priceless knowledge, a steadfast supporter of the band program, and — above all — a wise-and-trusted mentor/guide in countless ways. In addition to being an innately gifted (and remarkable!) musician, he is THE consummate educator, and — above all — he shares his vast understanding of his well-honed discipline with a sense of purpose and mission.

As I read through the manuscript (word-for-word), I kept thinking, "CHUCK, why didn't you write this great book a few decades ago? This is WONDERFUL! I could have used the newfound understanding on countless occasions!" Despite my selfish wishes, the good news is, it is *now* available and we can all take advantage of what the following pages have to offer; benefits, benefits, and more benefits.

The character of the book is what makes it so magical:

- Here's what to do and this is how it works.
- This is what to do if it doesn't work.
- . . . and now you can make it better by doing this.

The step-by-step, user-friendly instructional dialogue is accessible to anyone/everyone. And, as stated: IT WORKS!

Best of all, it is INCLUSIVE; it offers the answers to all those mysterious inquiries about the various woodwind instruments, and it is written in a fashion that will bring quick resolution to certain challenges that players face along their journeys to musical success. From the posture of an instrumentalist/performer, or a studio teacher, or a band/orchestra director, I would advise having *WOODWIND METHODS* close-at-hand, it is certain-to-be an often-tapped resource.

Is it the message, or is it the messenger that is the key to the book's success? The answer is: YES! Substantive pragmatic information delivered in a tried-and-true style guaranteeing success; SPOT ON!

On a personal note, I have always been (and I will always be) a loyal fan of anything that is sourced by Dr. Charles West. He "walks his talk," and he does it with a sense of EXCELLENCE unknown in common hours. You have in your hands the harvest of A MASTER TEACHER.

— Tim Lautzenheiser
Vice President of Education
Conn-Selmer, Inc.

ACKNOWLEDGMENTS

The list of people to thank for their help and support in the preparation of this book is long. At the top of the list is my wife Mary Jo, who has not only been incredibly supportive, but as an award-winning music teacher and band director at the secondary level, she has been a resource of incalculable value. My colleagues at Virginia Commonwealth University Bruce Hammel, Tabatha Easley, Shawn Welk, Cynthia Donnell and Francile Bilyeu have provided considerable help with proofreading and depth and correctness of information as have Richmond Symphony colleagues Thomas Schneider and Martin Gordon. Richard Killmer at Eastman and Albert Regni of the New York Philharmonic and VCU provided valuable suggestions and caught errors in the fingering charts. VCU administrators Darryl Harper, John Guthmiller, James Frazier and Joseph Seipel were key to providing me the time and freedom to complete the project. Students in my woodwinds class were vigilant about reporting errors and confusions as we "road tested" the book for a semester and other students were kind enough to pose for pictures: Nathan Frost, Michelle Kim, Samantha Hoster, Jacob Bennett, and Jonathan Carr. Fingering charts were beautifully created by VCU Graphics major Susan Liu, Ze Huang provided sketches, and a great deal of help and advice was obtained from Roger Martin, Shelley Jagow, Ed Fraedrich, Jeremy McEntire, Susan Davis, Kathleen Winters, Lauren Sileho, James Gagne and Shawn Girsberger. Finally, to Garwood Whaley my appreciation for his support through the project and for suggesting it in the first place.

INTRODUCTION

This book has two purposes. First, it provides a comprehensive text for future instrumental music teachers in a mixed-instrument college Woodwind Methods class. The second purpose is to provide a reference for professional educators who are already teaching instrumental music. It is meant to be retained on the teacher's bookshelf or desk, and referred to as woodwind challenges arise.

Teaching all five woodwinds at once rather than separately is not only a financial necessity for many colleges and universities, but it provides an unmistakable advantage to students who aspire to teach. By rotating instruments and periodically returning to beginning materials, students have the opportunity to watch the foundational steps as well as to observe common teaching and playing mistakes several times rather than once only. In the process, the accumulation of knowledge and experience makes it possible to gradually involve students in teaching other students, making their mistakes in a safe environment. Furthermore, the heterogeneous environment is considerably closer to the reality that the teacher faces in the band class. Students see and diagnose problems in a diverse environment, and they learn to present information in an orderly, efficient, and effective way.

This text aspires to cover the information that will be necessary to begin playing — assembly, beginning procedures, embouchure, articulation, breath support, common problems and fingerings. It provides an opportunity for future teachers to personally experience a level of performing competence on each instrument while playing music that is interesting, sophisticated and fun to play. Even many of the earliest exercises in this book are harmonized, "leveling the playing field," to allow the challenges presented to students of one instrument to be approximately equal to the challenges presented to students of another. It provides understanding that will be needed as band students advance beyond the teacher's own personal technical level on each instrument, and it presents information that the instrumental teacher needs in the course of a school year—vibrato, alternate fingerings, equipment, methods and etudes and advanced techniques, which can be wildly different form one woodwind to another. Finally, the book seeks to carefully explain the principles behind the information given. This is the focus of the fingering charts especially.

My hope is that the reader will find this book to be uniquely useful and enjoyable.

SECTION 1

WOODWIND METHODS CLASS TEXT

Throughout this book (and generally as standard practice), the fingers are referred to as "Thumb, first, second, third, and fourth fingers," the first being the index finger and not the thumb. Pianists generally refer to the thumb as the "first finger," but woodwind players do not. Thus, "4L" refers to the fourth finger—the "little" or "pinkie" of the left hand.

FLUTE

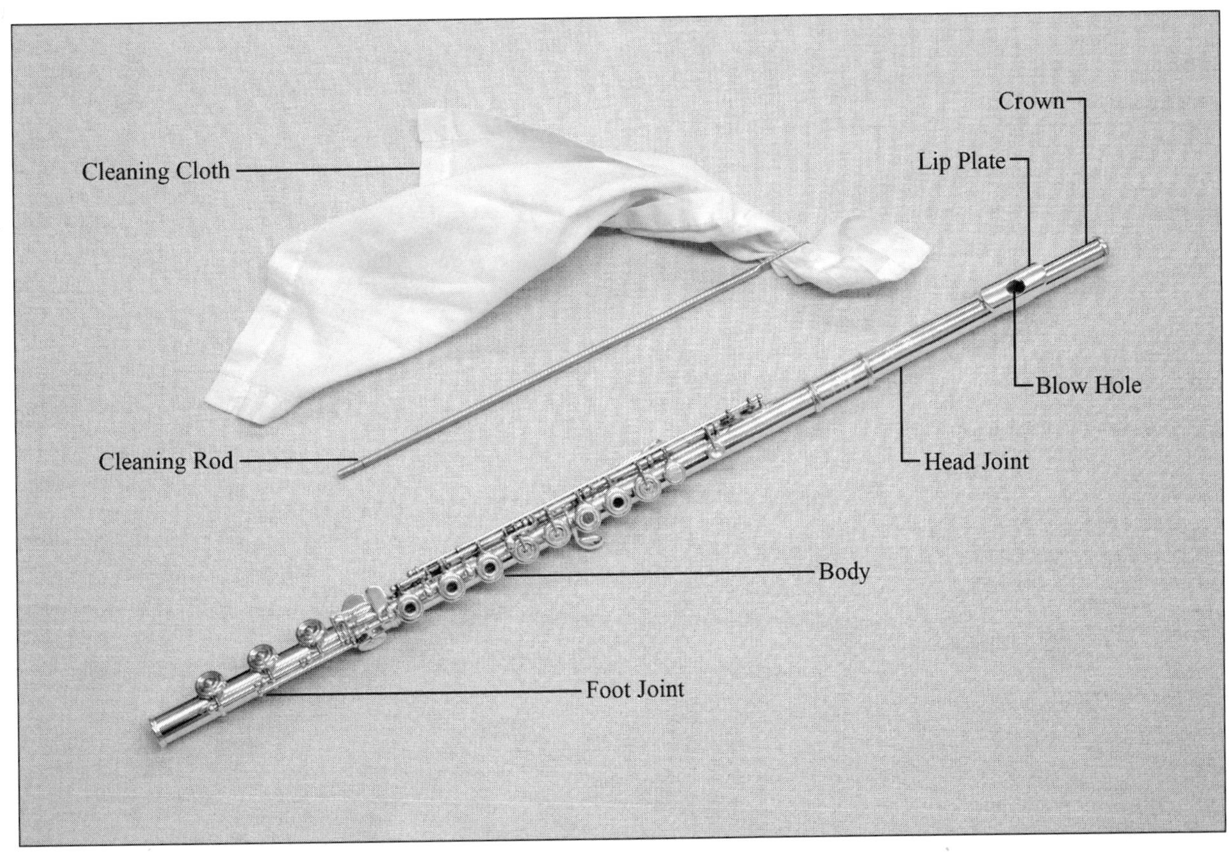

Parts of the flute

Before You Begin

- Do not use cork grease on metal tenons, which simply need to be clean
- Do not grab a joint in such a way that keys that are not designed to be depressed directly by the fingers are being depressed or torqued in the twisting process.
- Generally the less side-to-side pressure one puts on the pads, rods and key cups, the longer the instrument will stay in adjustment.
- The flute should be cleaned (swabbed) with the appropriate swab after playing. Cover the exposed end of the cleaning rod with the cloth to prevent scratching the inside of the instrument.

Assembly

1. Hold the foot joint by the end where there are no keys and hold the body of the flute at the upper end where there are no keys. Carefully twist the two joints together, *lining up the post on the foot joint with the middle of the lowest key on the body* (not in line with the post on the body)

Assembling foot joint and body

2. Holding the flute at the upper end where there are no keys and holding the headjoint below the lip plate, twist the head joint into the body of the flute. Do not push the head joint all the way into the body—leave a small amount of distance (approx 1/4 inch) that could be pushed in if needed.

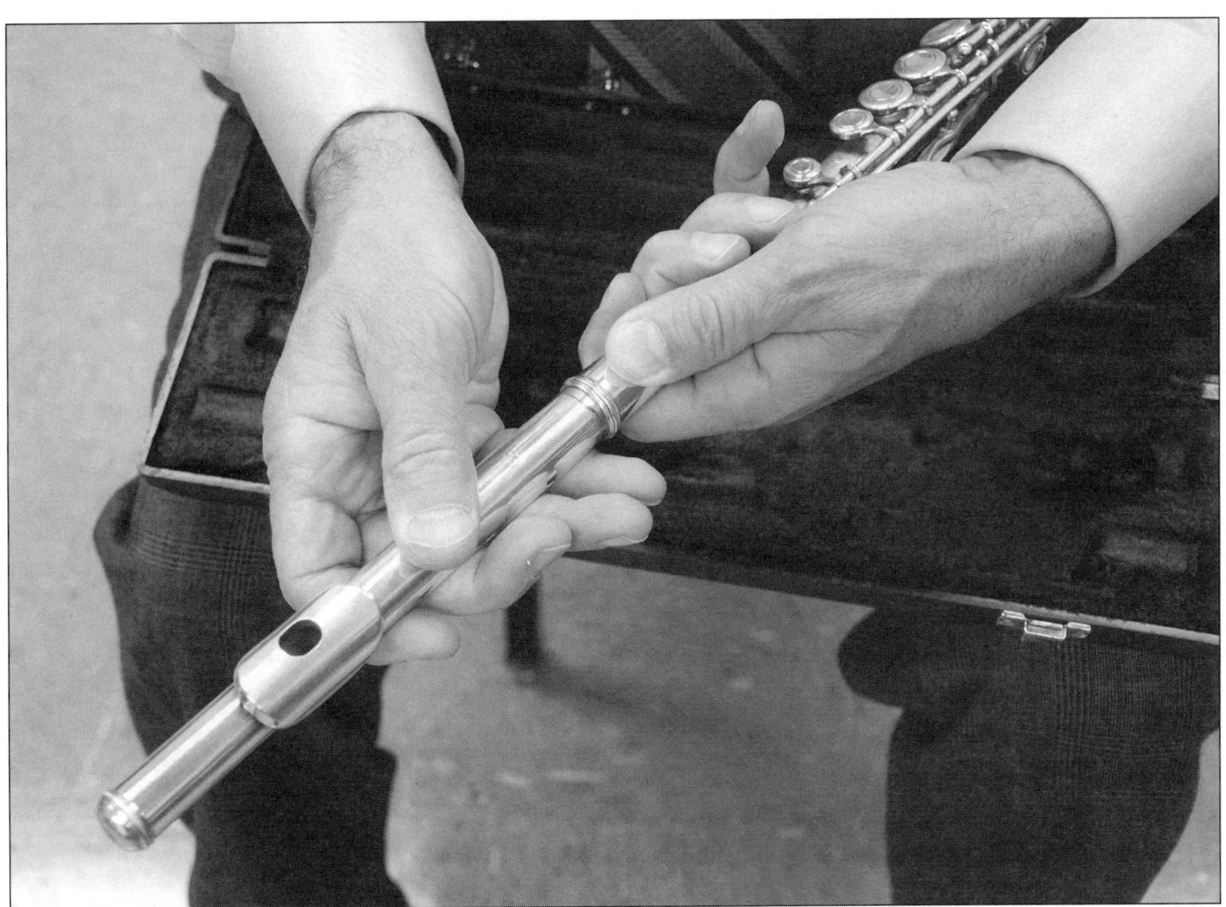

Adding head joint

3. Sighting down the flute from the upper end (the crown), the blowhole in the head joint should be even with or slightly to the right of the top key cup on the body. The ideal configuration will eventually be determined by the way the flute sounds best while balancing in the player's hands, but it would not be surprising if the key cup were at 12:00 and the blowhole were at about 12:30 or perhaps close to 1:00.

■ *Teaching and Learning the First Sounds*

Generally, flute starts most slowly of all the woodwinds because the source of vibration—the air reed—is formed by the lips themselves. The opening in the lips is the *aperture* and the hole in the lip plate of the headjoint is the *blowhole*.

- The aperture in the lips is a slit, not a circle so that a flat "ribbon" of air flows across the blowhole.
- About 1/3 of the blowhole needs to be covered by the lower lip in the lower register, and more for the higher register.
- The lips turn outward so that the air passes over the wet parts of the lips with a maximum amount of lower lip in contact with the lip plate.
- There are three points of balance—the lip, the side of the left index finger, and the right thumb. The instrument should balance without relying upon the right 4th finger. Ideally R4 is only an enhancement to the stability that already exists with the basic three points of balance.

Suggested Beginning Steps for Flute

Blowing a ribbon of air down the index finger

1. Begin by placing the tip of the index finger at the junction where the two colors of lip tissue meet, making a flat (slit-shaped) opening in the lips and blowing a ribbon of air down the index finger.
2. Using the headjoint only, cover about 1/3 of be blowhole with the lower lip and blow the same flat ribbon of air over the blowhole. Ideally you should hear a note sounding. If not, experiment with the position of the blowhole relative to the aperture.
   - The headjoint and the aperture in the lips need to be parallel to each other. A mirror is helpful.
   - Make the steam that condenses on the side of the lip plate opposite the aperture form a "V" shape . If it spills to one side of the other, reposition the headjoint so that the ribbon of air is directed at the far edge of the blowhole.

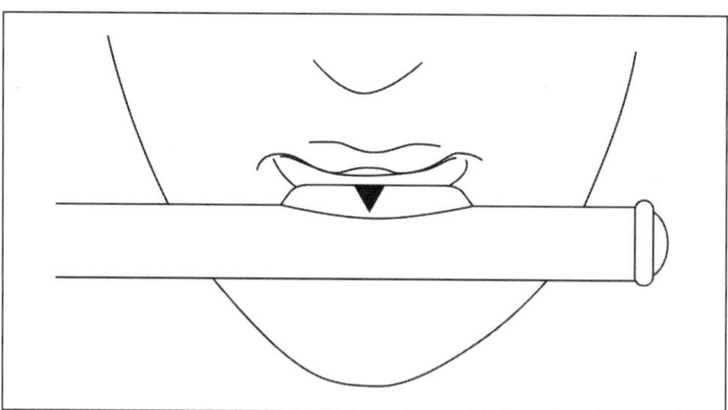
Slit-shaped aperture in lips with V-shaped steam pattern on lip plate

   - You will feel the near edge of the blowhole with the soft tissue of the lower lip.
   - Using the headjoint alone, practice making tones with the bottom end open and with it closed. You will get two notes about an octave apart. Also try inserting one finger varying distances into the open end of the headjoint. One can play "Hot Cross Buns" by simply sliding the finger in and out.
   - Practice removing the headjoint from the lip and replacing it, to find the right "spot" and the right angle on the lips.

- A well-known strategy is to ask the student to "kiss the blowhole," and then roll the flute outward to make a sound. If you try this as a teaching strategy, be sure the blowhole does not end up too high on the lips. Students who begin this way often tend not to break the habit, and when they become older it simply places the flute in the wrong spot.
- Try to make a slight "buzz" or "sizzle" in the sound by keeping the aperture small and the air stream well-aimed.

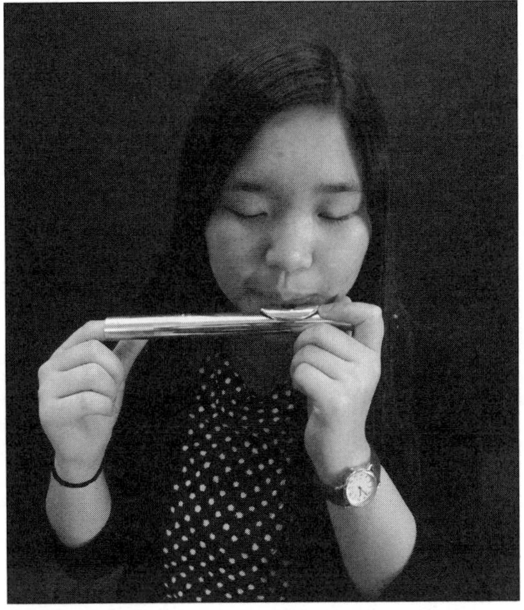

First sounds on headjoint alone

3. Replace the headjoint in the body of the flute as described above.
4. Place the indentation in the lowest bone of the left index finger on the side of the flute above the C key. Making the letter "C" with the right thumb and index finger, place the tip of the right thumb just barely under the body of the flute opposite the first finger pad. These two points plus the lower lip are the *Three Basic points of Balance* of a flute.
5. Place R4 on the E-flat key (See Fingering Chart). Finger R4 will be on that key for almost all notes that you will play on the flute.
6. Your first note will be A-natural, played with the thumb and first two fingers of the left hand down. Note that one pad between L1 and L2 is skipped—not depressed by any finger.

Correct holding position

Articulation

Articulation on flute is relatively uncomplicated. The tongue touches the roof of the mouth, pronouncing the syllable "doo." Higher in the range and on piccolo, the tongue may strike the roof of the mouth slightly farther forward, but this often evolves with reliance on the ear to control one's own playing.

The major problems that one encounters are (1) not tonguing at all, but using a glottal stop or the breath to articulate, (2) supporting the lip with the tongue, and (3) tonguing against the lips instead of the roof of the mouth. In this third instance, you will hear an aspiration sound in the initial attack, and you will likely see a very quick distortion of the embouchure every time the tongue strikes the lips. Speed and multiple tonguing will never develop until this habit is corrected.

As a student develops, multiple articulation becomes a necessity. The flute community is virtually unanimous about double tonguing, which involves the alternation between a stroke with the front of the tongue and a stroke with the back. Thus the syllables "du-gu," or "too-koo" produce the desired articulations. The lasting challenge is to make the articulation produced by the back stroke ("gu") match that of the front stroke ("du"). A common practicing strategy is to play the pattern backwards—rather than putting the "du" on the beat, the "gu" goes on the beat with the "du" on the "and" of the beat. Thinking "goody goody" is helpful to stay mentally organized.

The flute community is somewhat less unanimous about the subject of triple tonguing. While the principle is the same, syllables vary, with "Da ga da Da ga da" being quite common and "Da da ga Da da ga" also enjoying wide acceptance. Still others use a "misplaced" double tongue, using "Da ga da Ga da ga," a pattern which uses duples organized in patterns of three, so that there are never two consecutive front or back strokes. When learned well, this has the best potential to develop the greatest speed.

Common Problems

1. Aperture too large or too high, resulting in an airy, non resonant tone. Aperture should not be a round hole but is a slit in the center of the lips which is no longer than the blowhole itself.
2. Poor holding position, for example:
   - Right index finger resting on the rod to stabilize instrument
   - R4 used as a primary point of balance. *There are three primary points of balance* for the flute—not four.
   - Right arm draped over the back of the chair or hanging down instead of out, causing the flute to roll in too far and thus produce a flat pitch and muffled tone.
   - "Slouching" in the chair, resulting in poor breathing and rolling the flute too far inward.
3. Foot joint and lower joint rods lined up with each other, rather than the foot joint rod being in the center of the bottom key on the body.

4. Covering too much of the blowhole with the lower lip (rolling in too far), causing the sound to be small and the pitch to be flat. At the root of this problem can be (1) the position of the right arm—perhaps over the back of the chair, or in any case the right elbow being too low or (2) a mindset which defines a "good sound" as being "not airy." If "airiness" is the sole benchmark of a quality sound, students will roll inward to eliminate the undesired sound.
5. Too much pressure into the lip. The teacher should be able to tap the flute off of the lip with very little effort. This is especially problematic on piccolo.
6. Using the middle or lower register fingerings in the highest register. While the "wrong" fingerings almost work, the notes produced will sound odd and will likely be out of tune. *This mistake is incredibly common.*
7. Not lifting the left index finger for middle D and E-flat, or less often, leaving it up for E-natural. You will hear a shadow of the lower octave in D and E-flat notes if the first finger is down, and the E natural will be sharp and unfocused if the first finger is up.
8. Flute is out of adjustment. See Equipment Problems and Common Repair Problems sections.
9. Supporting the lip with the tongue. While this may be an easy way to produce a sound at first, it never develops into a characteristic flute sound, and it makes articulation extremely labored.
10. Tonguing between teeth, hitting the lips instead of the roof of the mouth. Sometimes this evolves from misunderstanding the Suzuki method suggestion of "spitting rice."
11. Playing low or middle F# with the R2 (like clarinet and saxophone) and not R3.
12. Overuse of "Thumb B-flat" fingering, resulting in accidentally playing B-flat where there should be a B-natural. Teach Fingering no. 12 (with both index fingers) first so that becomes the default fingering, and add Thumb B-flat to simplify technical passages in flat keys. *Do not use Thumb B-flat when it is adjacent to a B-natural.*
13. Flat at soft dynamics. The flutist must learn to keep the airspeed up and blow more across when playing softly. Always better to sacrifice sound for pitch than to sacrifice pitch for sound.
14. A tab in the middle of the upper lip, distorting the "slit" shape of the aperture that cannot be corrected by exposing the wet inner lip to the air stream. Some flutists play with an "offset" embouchure, usually closing the right side of the mouth and blowing on the left. Playing offset left allows the shoulders and arms to be in a more natural position than offset right. This embouchure develops more slowly than the standard center-aperture embouchure.

Piccolo

1. Too much pressure into the face, especially upper register. Excessive pressure makes high notes much more difficult if not impossible.
2. "Buzzing" the lips on high notes, as a result of tightening rather than changing direction for the upper register. Try "pointing" the upper lip. The piccolo is played higher on the lip and more rolled-in than flute, making the air reed shorter.

■ *Tuning*

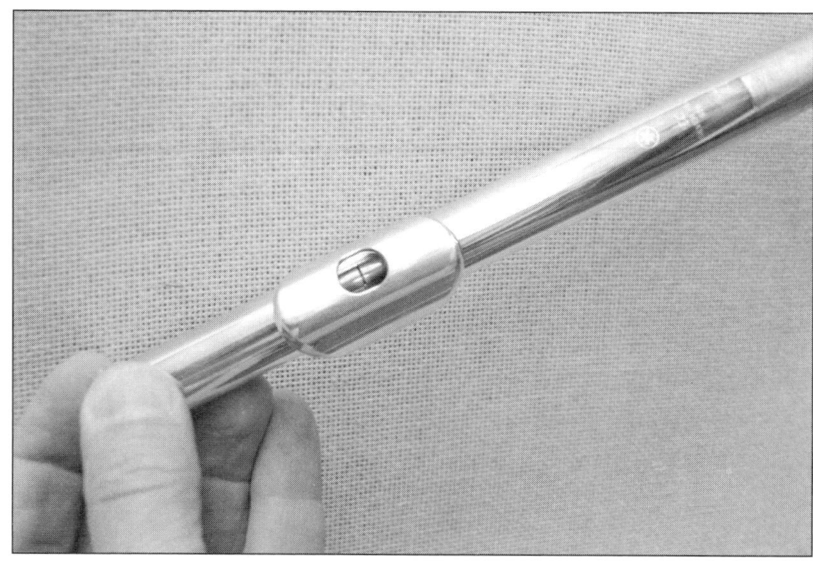

Headjoint with cleaning rod line in the middle of the blowhole

Since "open" C# is sharp on most flutes, flutists should play the instrument with the headjoint pulled out slightly as a matter of habit. The location of the head joint cork is critical to intonation—the line on the end of the cleaning rod needs to be in the dead center or very slightly up the flute (toward the crown) from the center of the blowhole.

The pitch of a flute is remarkably flexible, especially compared to the clarinet. As a rule, about a third of the blowhole should be covered by the lip in the lower register, more for higher registers. Inexperienced flutists often define a "good" sound as one that is "not airy," so they roll the instrument inward, reducing the "airiness" that they perceive as they play. Unfortunately, not only will they play flat as a result, but projection is also compromised. Draping the right arm over the back of the chair or poor posture in general automatically rolls the flute in and flatness results.

Dynamics have a dramatic effect on flute pitch. In contrast to the clarinet, the louder the flute is played the sharper it tends to be, and the pitch flattens at soft dynamics. For this reason, flutists should practice "long tones" while watching a tuner. A loud tone must be blown down into the blowhole, while a soft tone must be blown across the blowhole with fast airspeed and the head kept level. "Ducking" one's head pushes the pitch down and lifting the head lifts the pitch. Developing a habit of lifting the head at the end of a soft phrase and perhaps pushing the lower lip out to blow more across is helpful in counteracting the flatness that one typically hears at the end of the flutist's phrase. Beginnings and ends of phrases are the two places where the airspeed is slowest and thus the pitch tends to be low.

Almost three centuries ago, flutist, composer and author J.J. Quantz advised flutists to "push in" for slow soft movements and "pull out" for loud fast ones. This advice was practical then and remains so today, and it acknowledges the flute's natural pitch-dynamic relationship.

Beyond the above, be vigilant about students using the correct fingerings, remembering that the common error of playing F# with R2 instead of R3 is an automatic intonation problem, as is using lower register fingerings in the third or upper register.

Piccolo

The piccolo is played higher on the lip and is rolled more inward than the flute, and is also commonly played with the headjoint pulled out slightly. Missing any one of these three factors will cause unmanageable sharpness.

Flute Fingering Chart Introduction

Flute fingerings are quite uncomplicated in the lowest two octaves, with most of the second octave fingerings identical to the octave below. As you teach, remember that there are two "first finger up" notes in the second register—the first two above the break, D and E-flat. This differs from the double reeds, which have three half-hole notes in their second registers. If the first finger is left down, you will hear a "shadow" of the lower register in the upper register note, and if 1L is not put down on E-natural, the tone will be sharp, "airy," and "hollow."

The common mistake that students make in the third octave is simply overblowing the fingerings one and two octaves lower. The technique may come more easily this way, but the pitch, response and tone are poor. It only takes one flutist (or worse yet, piccolo player) in a flute section playing the overblown fingerings to cause a very annoying pitch problem in the upper register of an ensemble.

Flute Fingering Chart Commentary

13&27. "Thumb B-flat" is similar to the "Bis" key on saxophone in that in order to move directly to or from B-natural, lateral motion is required. Young players often forget and leave the thumb on the B-flat lever and all B's will be B-flats, whether written or not. For this reason, teach fingerings 12 and 26 first. However, when solidly in a flat key with no B-naturals in sight, Thumb B-flat makes playing in flat keys considerably easier.

31. This is the first fingering of the third octave. Note that this is the third partial of a G fingering and not the fourth partial of a D fingering. From this point upward, the principal fingerings are standard for reasons of pitch and sound—not overblown ones from the lower octave.

33. E-natural is generally sharp and responds poorly on most flutes. A "Split E" mechanism helps this, but is only available on very high-end flutes.

35. Be sure the Thumb B-flat lever is not down, or High F# will be very flat if it responds at all.

39. High B-flat is generally a bit flat. Putting 1L down with the fingering is a common mistake and makes it worse.

41. With a B foot joint, putting the B key down with this fingering stabilizes the tone and aids with response. Most modern B foot joints have a "Gizmo," which is an extension on the low B key to make it more readily accessible with 4R, precisely for this fingering.

Flute Fingering Chart

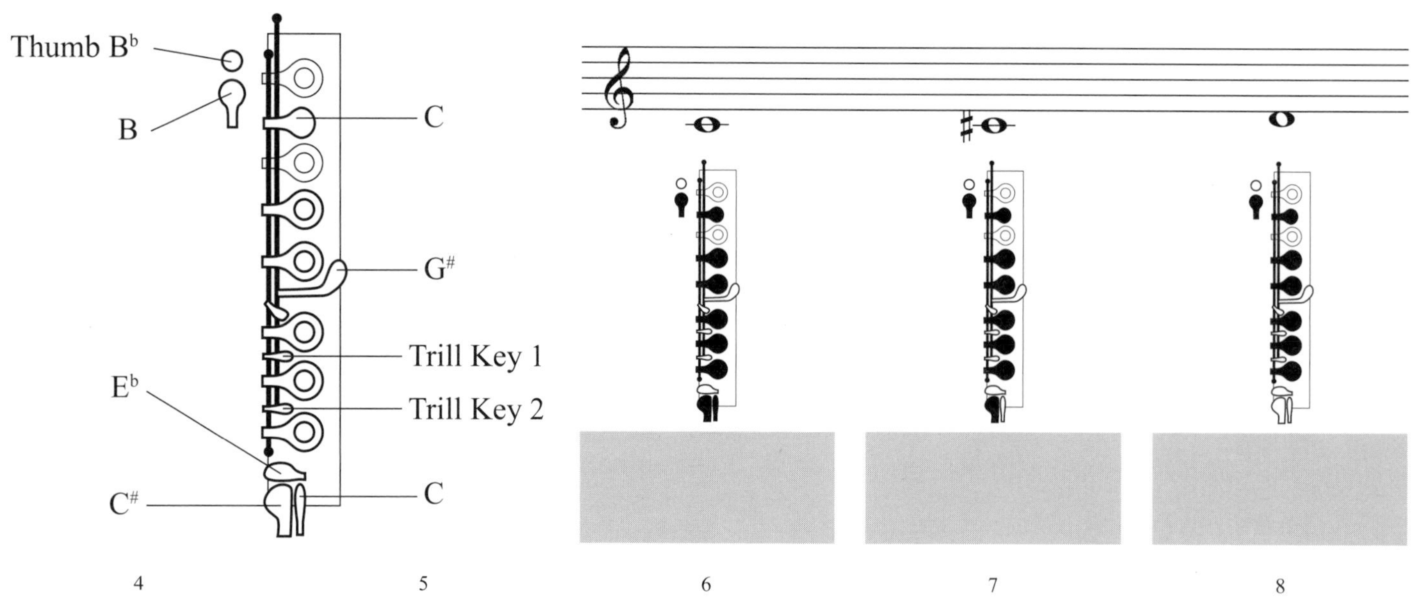

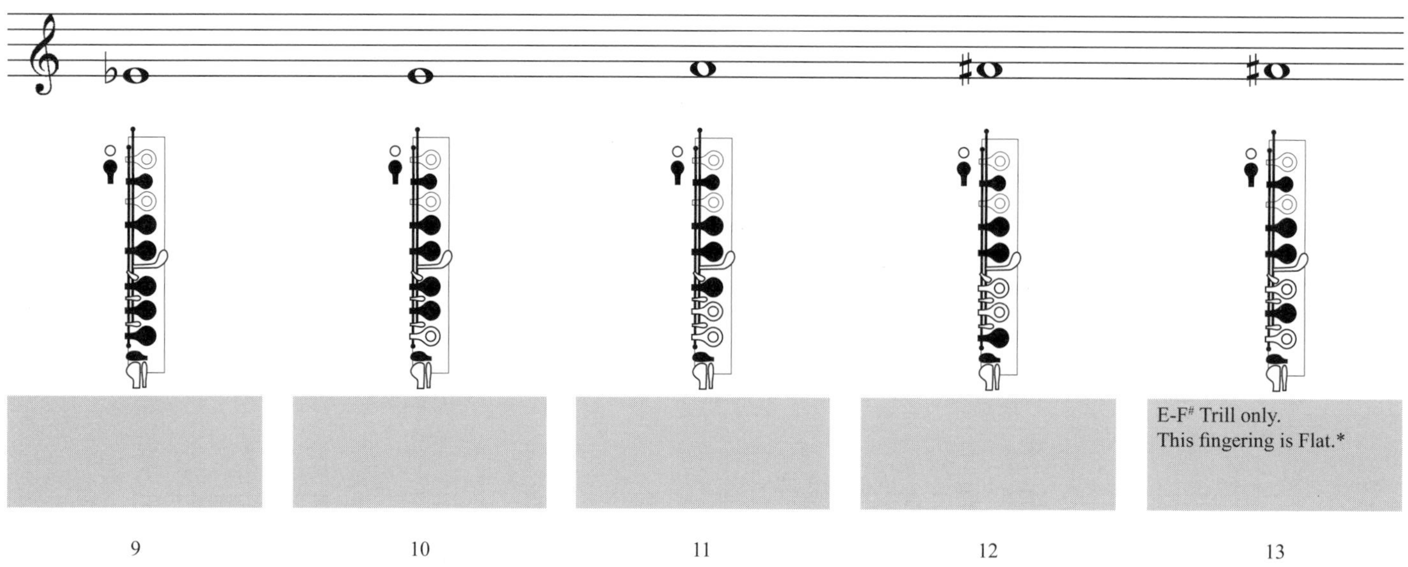

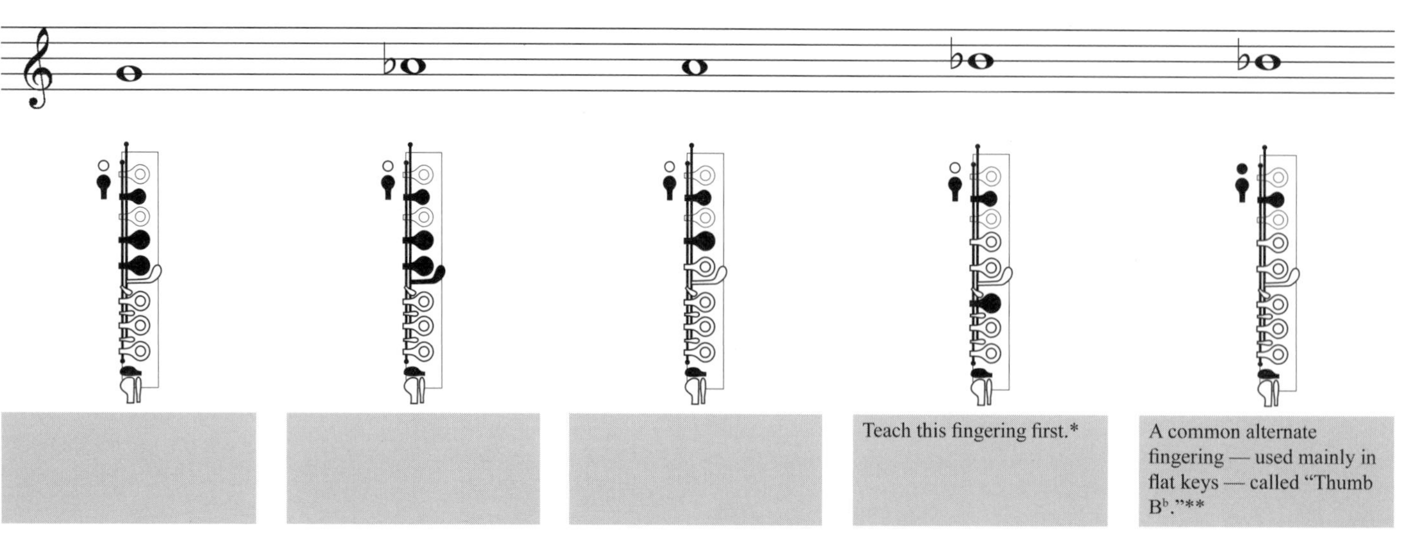

* — see "common problems"
** — the Thumb B-flat lever may be used with all notes involving the thumb except B-natural and high F♯

14

15

16
"Open."
Often sharp.

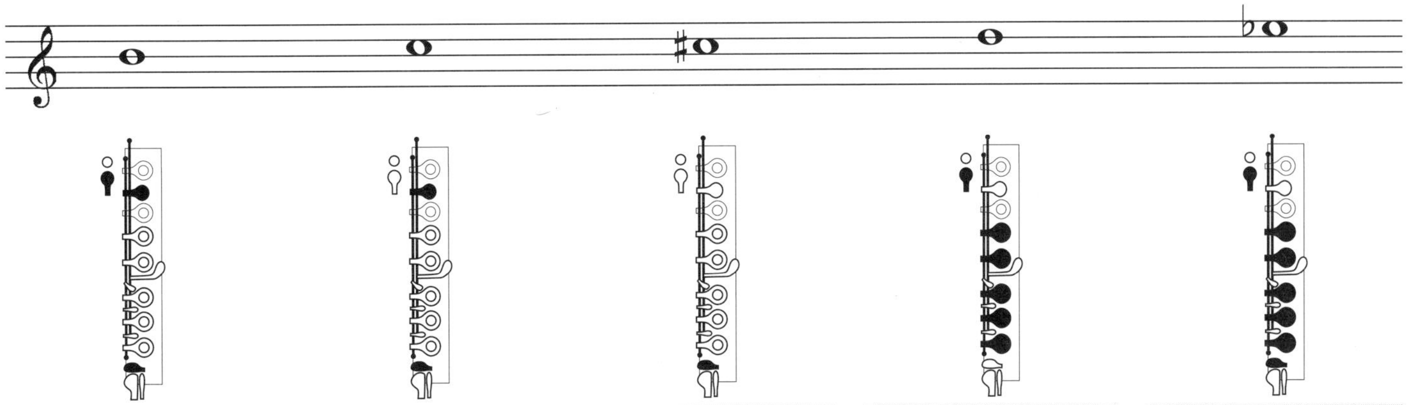

17
Notice: 1L is up. The first note above the "break."

1 8
Notice: 1L is still up.

19
Notice: 1L is down.

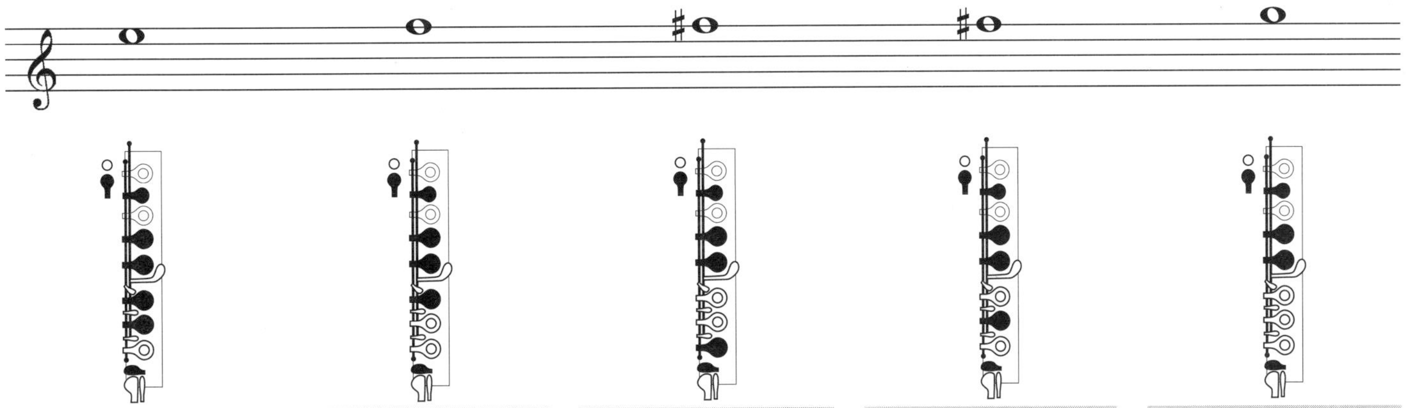

20

21

22
E-F# Trill only.
Like fingering 8, this is flat.

23

24

25

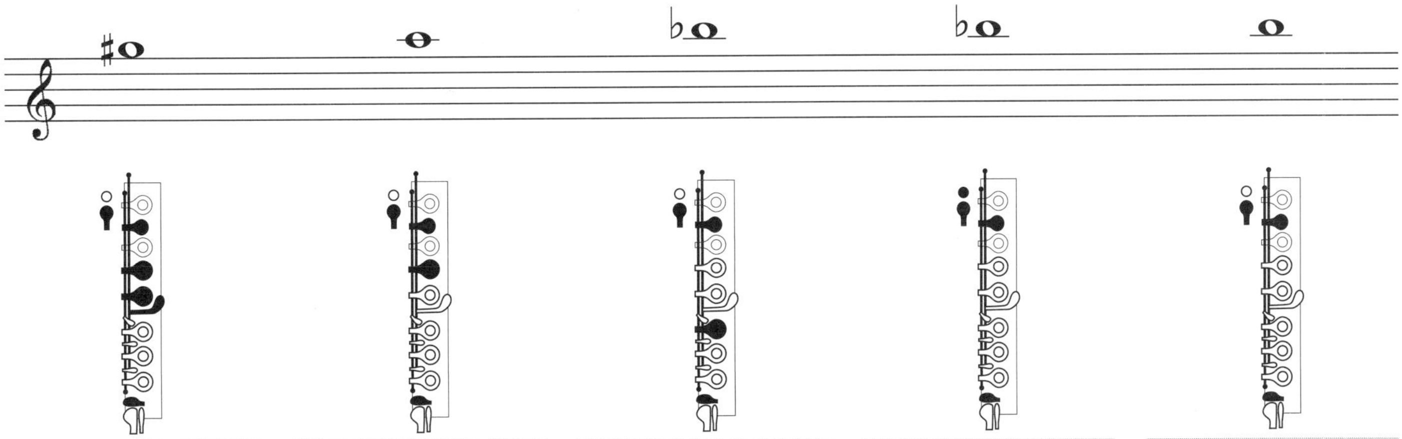

26

27
See comment on 13.

28

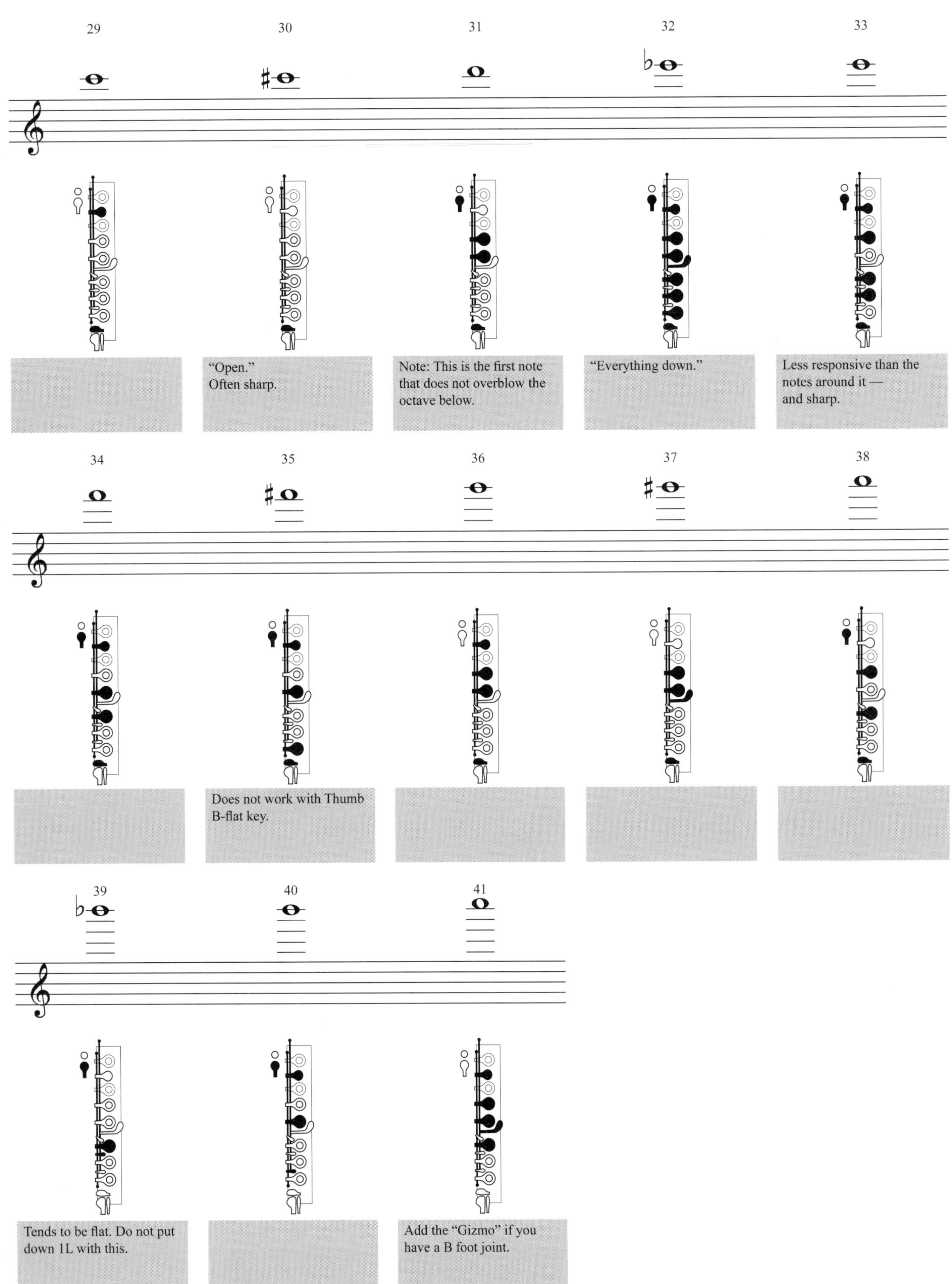
29
30
31
32
33
"Open."
Often sharp.
Note: This is the first note that does not overblow the octave below.
"Everything down."
Less responsive than the notes around it — and sharp.
34
35
36
37
38
Does not work with Thumb B-flat key.
39
40
41
Tends to be flat. Do not put down 1L with this.
Add the "Gizmo" if you have a B foot joint.

Flute Trill Chart

1

2

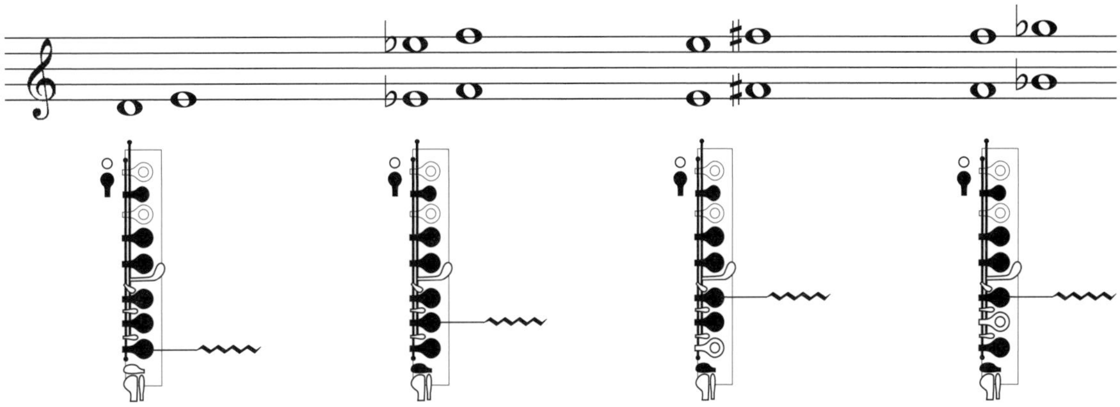

Upper register may be helped by slightly opening 1L.

3

4

5

6

7

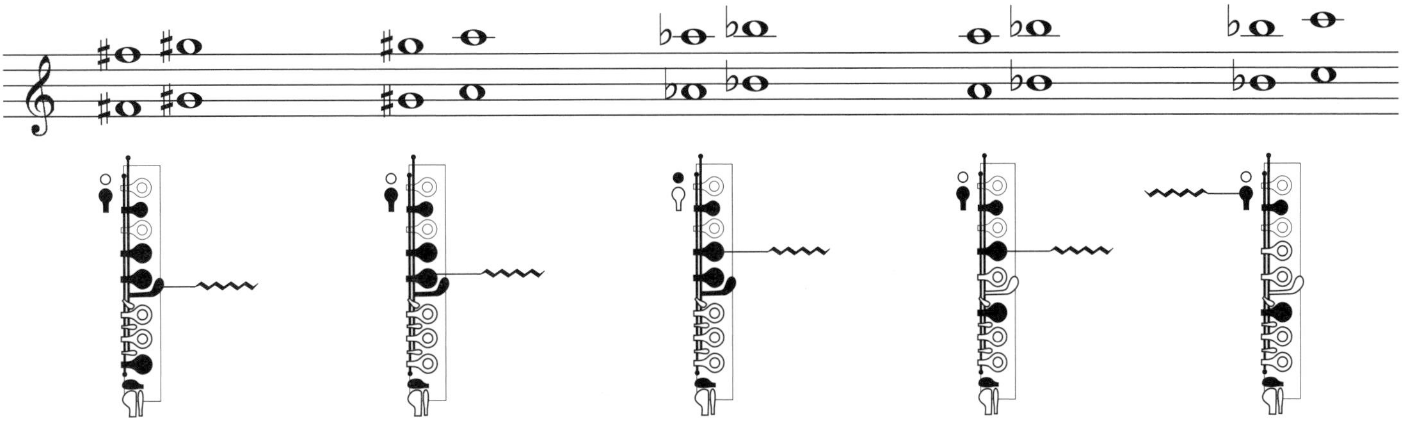

Trilling with both 2L and 3L improves the intonation but increases the technical difficulty.

8

1R is unnecessary if Thumb B-flat is used.

9

1R is unnecessary if Thumb B-flat is used.

10

11

12

13

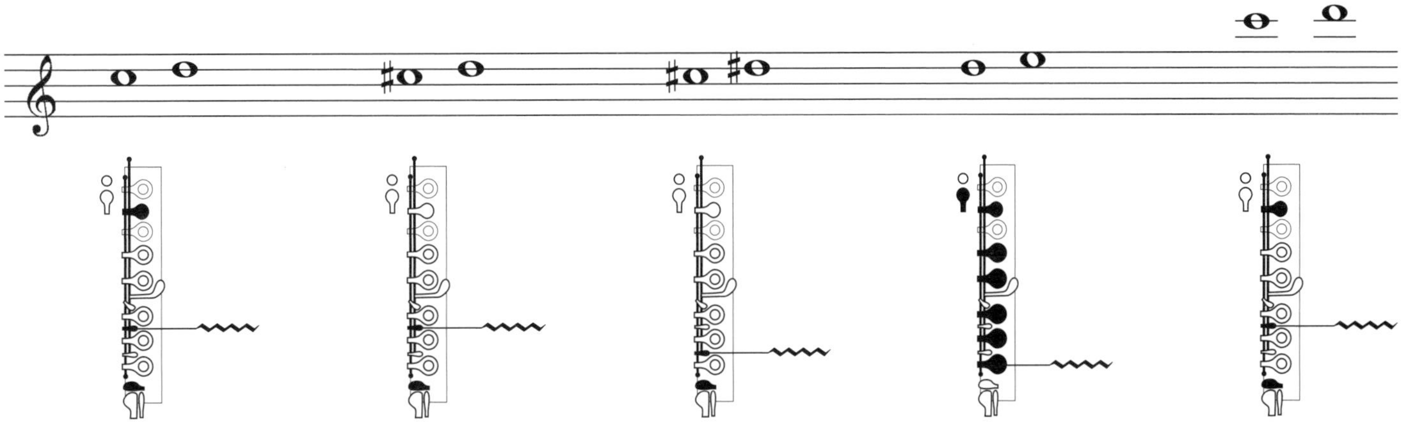

If convenient, lift 1L just slightly.

14

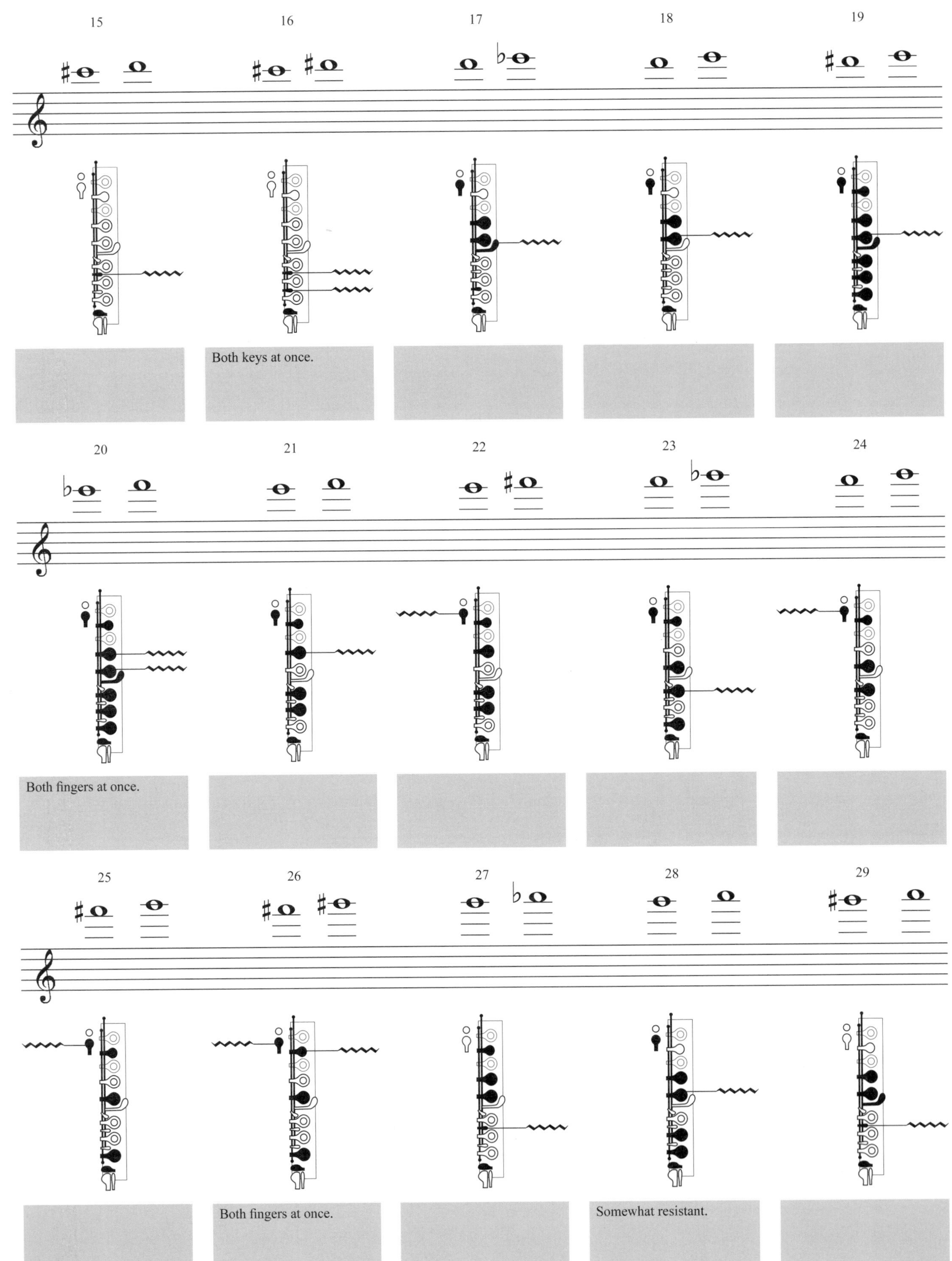
15
16
17
18
19
Both keys at once.
20
21
22
23
24
Both fingers at once.
25
26
27
28
29
Both fingers at once.
Somewhat resistant.

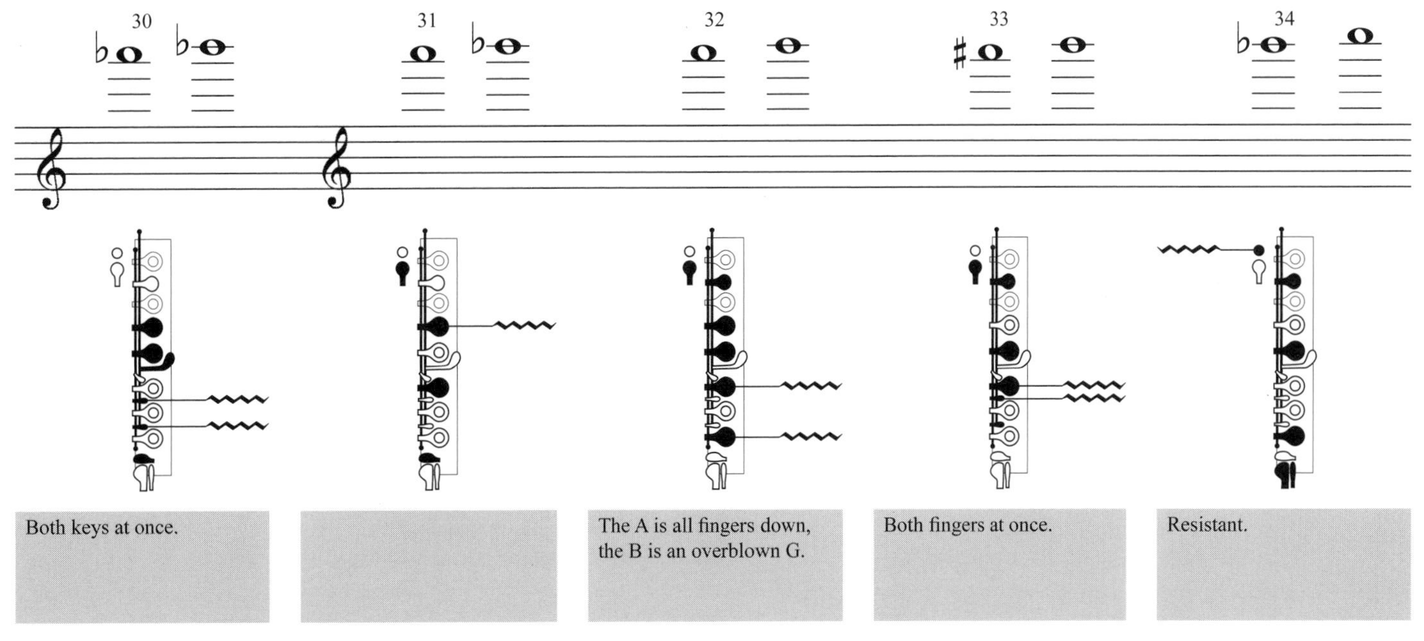

Both keys at once.

The A is all fingers down, the B is an overblown G.

Both fingers at once.

Resistant.

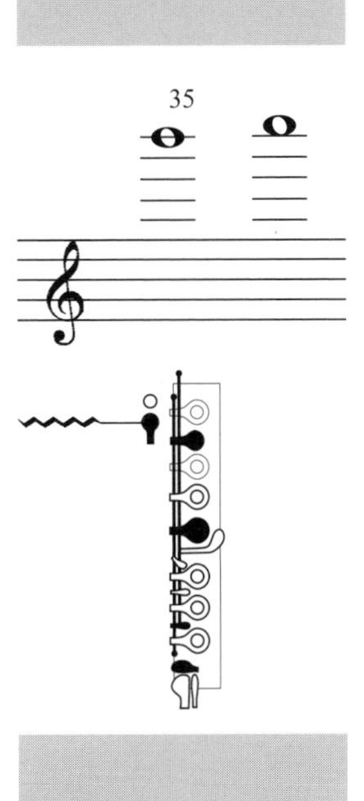

OBOE

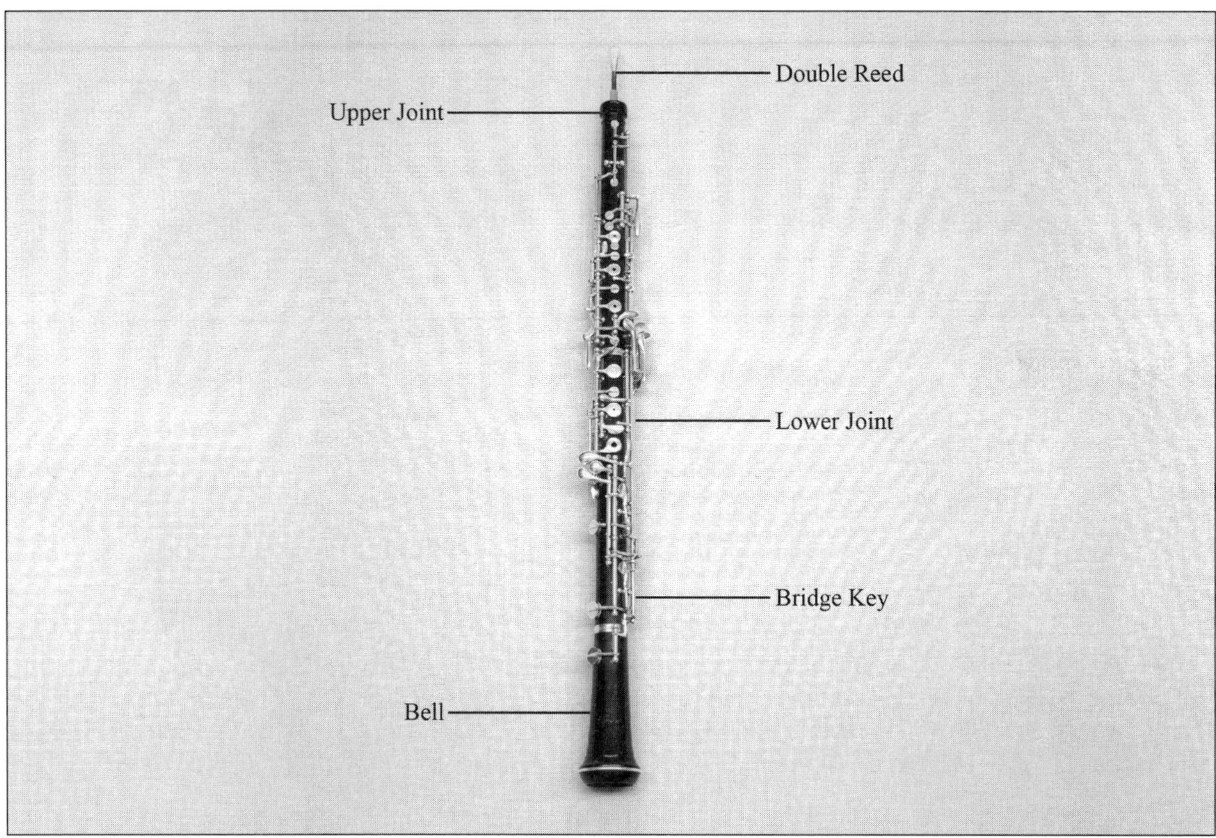

Before You Begin

- Be sure all tenon corks are lightly lubricated with cork grease.
- Do not grab a joint in such a way that keys that are not designed to be depressed directly by the fingers are being depressed or torqued in the twisting process.
- Begin assembling from the bottom of the instrument and disassemble in reverse order from assembly. Generally the less side-to-side pressure one puts on the pads, rods and key cups, the longer the instrument will stay in adjustment.
- The oboe has "bridge keys," which transfer motion from one part of the instrument to another. These are delicate and are easily thrown out of adjustment—be careful not to twist too far and remember to raise them when pushing the parts together.
- All woodwind instruments should be cleaned (swabbed) with the appropriate swab after playing. An oboe swab with some of the cord trailing behind the cloth is recommended so that a stuck swab may be "backed out" of the larger end of the upper joint.

Assembly

1. Place the oboe reed, blades down, into a small container of water, submerging the blades and a small amount of the wrapping completely.
2. Grasp the bell in one hand. If a key exists on the bell, raise the bridge key by gently closing the pad with your thumb.
3. Grasping the lower joint at the point which is designed for pressure from the hand (*not* over the mechanism at the lower end of the joint), gently twist the bell onto the lower joint, carefully aligning the bridge key mechanism.

Soaking the oboe reed

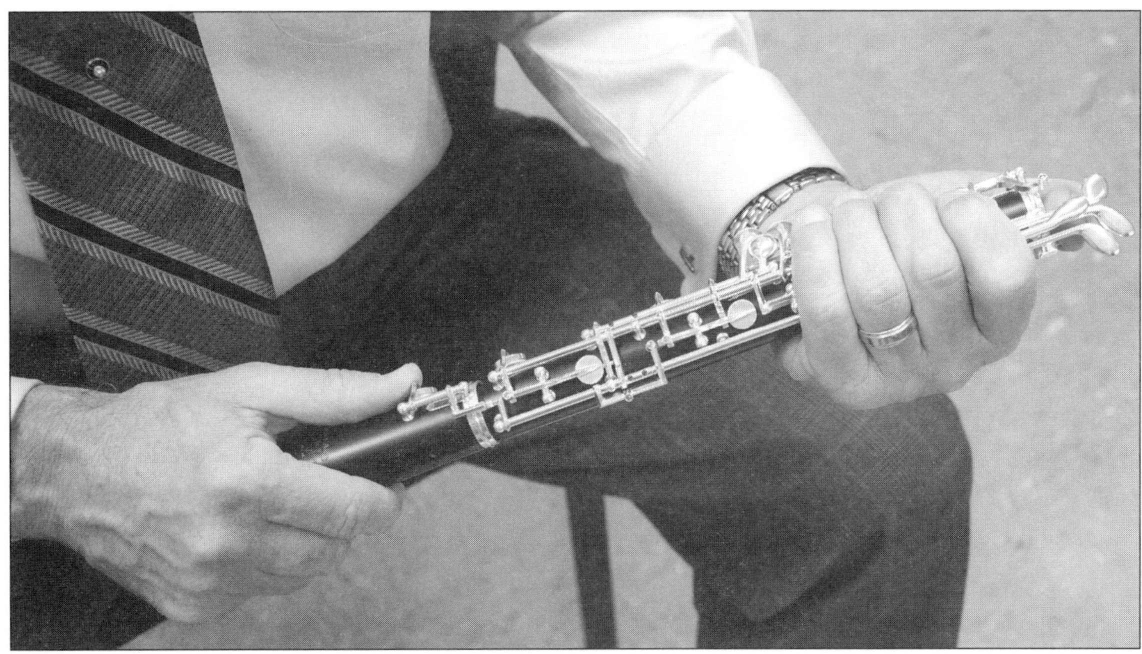

Raising the bridge key on the bell and aligning

4. Grasp the upper joint, again by the area which is designed for direct finger pressure. With the back side of the oboe facing you, carefully slide the tenon of the upper joint *directly into the lower joint*, raising the bridge keys to protect the small pieces of cork on the bridge keys themselves.

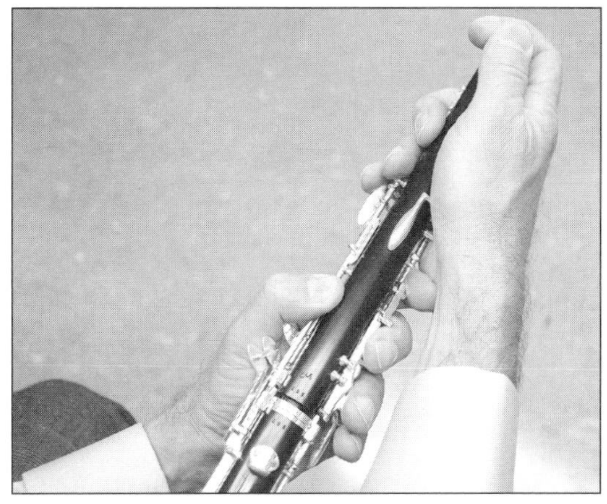

Raising bridge keys on the upper joint

5. Holding the reed by the cork and wound part—not the blades—slide the reed *all the way down into the reed receiver.* If the fit is too tight, compress the cork by rolling it between a hard, flat surface and a butter knife. Do not use cork grease on the oboe reed.

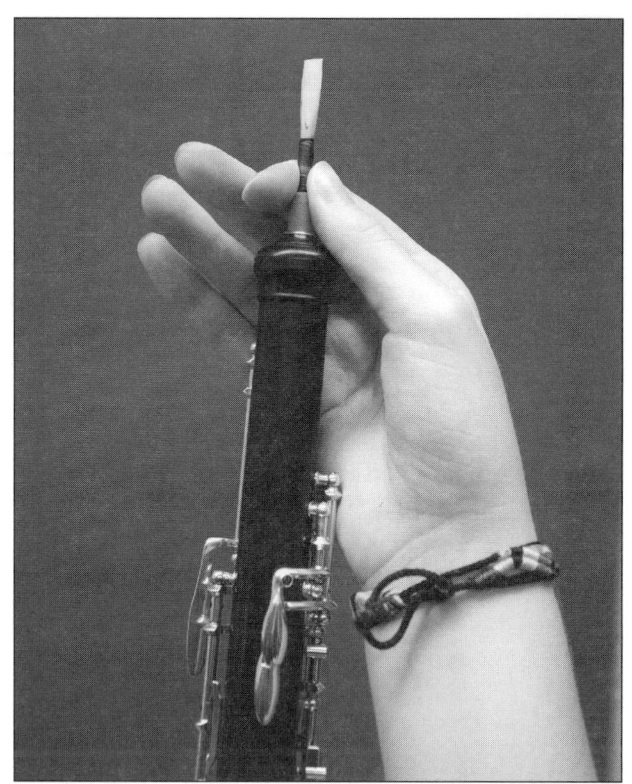

Inserting the reed into the reed receiver, avoiding the blades of the reed

Teaching and Learning the First Sounds—Suggested Beginning Steps for Oboe

1. Be sure the reed "crows," with at least two discernable pitches heard when the reed is inserted into the mouth all the way to the strings without touching the blades of cane with the lips. If it does not, see the Troubleshooting section.
2. Insert the reed all the way into the reed receiver.
3. Show the student the first fingering—remember that the oboe is the only woodwind with no "open" note. This text begins with low A and works downward rather than upward so that the habit of playing on the end of the reed is established.
4. Place the tip of the reed on the lower lip, just to the inside of the junction between the two types of skin. Push the lip in with the reed and close the upper lip over the upper reed as though to pronounce "P," and blow. The lower lip "muffles" the lower reed and adds some resistance.

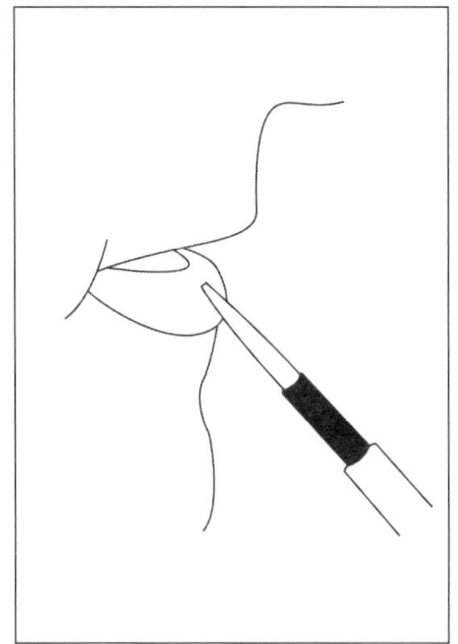

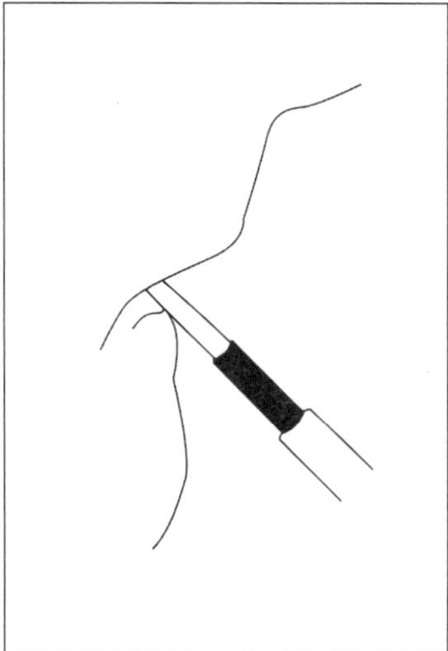

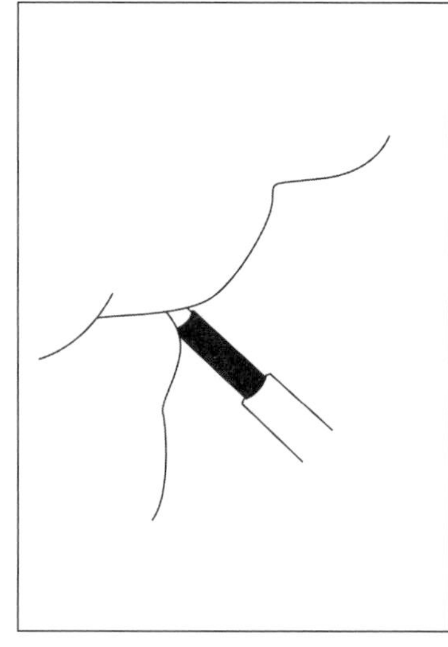

The oboe will require considerably more air pressure than any other woodwind. The facial muscles are firm and dynamic in an oboe embouchure—not merely used as a cushion over the teeth. So the lips are more like a "spring" and less like a "mattress."

Placing the tip of the reed on the lower lip

Bringing the corners of the lips to the center

5. Check the pitch against a stable pitch source such as a piano or electronic tuner. If the pitch is too low, blow harder rather than either bite or push the reed too far into the mouth. If the first pitch is too high and the tone is bright, most likely there is too much of the reed inside the mouth. It may be helpful to have the student drop the pitch by creating more room between the teeth, and then increasing the air pressure to push the pitch back up where it belongs. The tone will invariably improve.

6. Learn to articulate by placing the tip of the tongue on the lower reed and then drawing it back in an "eh" syllable. The syllable (and thus the tongue position) will become more "ee" on higher notes and more "ah" on lower notes.

Correct playing position

Articulation

The articulation process on the oboe and bassoon are highly similar to each other. Only the size of the instrument and reed create the few differences that exist rather naturally.

Begin with the tip of the tongue on the reed, drawing back quickly as though to spit a piece of paper off of the lip. The back of the tongue changes position on the double reeds from a higher, more "eeee" syllable in the upper register to a lower, more "ahhh" syllable in the lower register, but the tip always articulates on the tip of the reed. The player's ear governs all decisions about the appropriate tongue position in any given register.

On both double reeds, embouchure pressure on the reed will vary to control the ends of notes. Increase pressure on the reed to keep the pitch from dropping. For this reason, you will see embouchure movement while articulating, which will be more pronounced with bassoonists on the larger reed than with oboists on the smaller one.

Multiple tonguing on the oboe is virtually non-existent.

Common Problems

1. Taking too much reed into the mouth. The overall pitch will be sharp, and C-natural in the staff will be extremely bright and out of control. Taking too much is far more common than taking too little reed. (Remember to "muffle" the lower reed).

2. Incorrect exit angle from mouth. The oboe must be held up and blown more directly into than clarinet—more like a brass instrument, saxophone or bassoon. Holding the instrument more up allows the lower lip to participate in the control of the lower reed and thus the sound will be markedly better than if the instrument exits in a clarinet-like angle

3. Wrong fingerings. One of the great challenges of teaching double reeds is that wrong fingerings almost produce the right notes, though often with a sound that does not match that of the notes around it. Unless one knows *how each fingering should look*, the instructor can easily assume that the tone or pitch is not ideal because of student inexperience or reed. Using the wrong octave keys or half hole to overblow is especially prevalent. If a student has switched from clarinet or saxophone, their habit may well be to use only one octave key for the entire register—which almost works on oboe. *Remember: Oboe and Bassoon have three half-hole notes each—the first three in the second register, and the oboe is the only woodwind that has no open note!*

4. Poor reed. The reed needs to "double crow" when inserted all the way into the mouth to the strings. Lower register notes will not work if there are no "lows" in the crow. Splits in a reed probably mean that the reed is ruined—especially if the split is toward the center of the blade. A split closer to the side of the reed may not be completely debilitating. See Troubleshooting.

   - Wire on the reed. While wires on English horn reeds and bassoon reeds are necessary, they are generally a hindrance on an oboe reed. Carefully removing the wire often improves the reed.

- Poorly cut reed. A reed needs to have a well-defined tip, a heart and a spine. If the design of the reed does not include these three features, a different brand of reed should be sought.

5. Not understanding the various fingerings for F. "Regular" F (fingerings 9 and 24) gives the best sound and pitch, but must be avoided if the result requires 3R to slide laterally. In the absence of a left-hand F key, "Forked" F provides a solution for this problem, but the sound is inferior and the pitch is not as reliable. If flat, it may be brought up by opening the E-flat key with 4R, though this is likely to overcorrect the problem. However it may also be sharp, depending on the presence or absence of an "F Resonance" key which opens automatically when Forked F is being played. On more expensive oboes, there is a third option, which is a left-hand F key, played by 4L, with the touchpiece sitting just above and beyond the B and B-flat keys. Anyone who has such an oboe should learn this fingering instead of Forked F and use it in virtually all circumstances where "regular" F is technically not favored due to lateral motion.
6. Biting. Remember that the lips hold the reed and thus they stand up by their own strength. The lips are not pads into which the teeth bite. They are strong and dynamic, not listless and static.
7. Instrument out of adjustment. See Troubleshooting.
8. Upper octave notes from E-natural upwards sound "split" between the lower and upper registers. The upper register note is not completely in that register—there is residue of the lower octave: There is water in the octave key. If E-A-flat has this problem there is water in the back octave key hole (which is on top of the oboe). If A-C have the residue, the water is in the second octave key. Remove the upper joint and swab it dry. Then, place a sheet of cigarette paper or a tissue between the octave key pad and the tone hole. Close all of the holes on the upper joint and plug the open end. Blow into the reed receiver on the top end and open and close the octave key with the paper under it. You should see a very small drop of water on the paper that has been blown out of the needle-size vent hole.

English Horn

C-natural in the staff drops in pitch in softer dynamics. Most likely this is an issue with the bocal. Try another bocal.

Tuning

Sharpness—Ideally, the oboe should be played with the reed inserted all the way into the reed receiver. Pulling the reed out slightly creates a significant interruption in the flare of the conical bore of the instrument, often creating more intonation challenges than it solves. Remember also that, since the most common error young students make is taking too much reed into the mouth, an oboe student may sound sharp for this reason. In this case, pulling out would only allow the student to continue with a bad habit, preventing the tone from developing into the beautiful solo sound that one expects of an oboist. Assuming the reed crows sufficiently, have the student do the octave exercises given on the "20b Oboe tone development" page of this book while watching an electronic tuner to develop a proper "grip" on the reed.

Flatness—The student may not be blowing hard enough. Or, the staple is the metal tube upon which the two blades of an oboe or English horn reed are tied. The standard oboe reed is 70mm long, and the standard staple length 47mm, though staples may be bought that are shorter. If flatness is a consistent problem with 47mm staples, one might seek reeds tied on 45mm staples. Because it is critical that the string be wrapped only to the end of the staple and not beyond, simply measuring the distance from the far end of the cork to the top of the strings should be an accurate measurement of the staple. Shortening the reed from the tip end is not practical for the non-oboist, because it would require that the tip itself be re-made, and because the amount of wood left to vibrate would not be sufficient for a fully satisfactory oboe reed.

The way the oboe reed is scraped also affects the pitch. A shorter scrape (leaving bark some distance up onto the blade of the reed above the strings) may play sharp. In this case, scraping between the center and the sides in the back third to lengthen the "W" design in the back of the reed will allow the reed to play lower while making the lower register respond more easily. If the spine of a reed has been scraped through however, the upper register will play flat, rendering the reed unusable. This may be determined by looking at the profile of the reed from the side against a dark background (for visual contrast), or by looking through the reed with a bright light.

No wind instrument "plays in tune" by itself—it must be played in tune. This is particularly true of the double reeds, and it's why a teacher is wise to pre-screen oboists and bassoonists for a particularly good sense of pitch. The angle of the tongue inside the mouth (the vowel sound being made while playing), the amount of reed in the mouth, and the tightness with which the reed is held and the intensity of air pressure being used all have an effect. In the end, an oboe student must match pitches correctly, either by ear or with the visual aid of an electronic tuner.

English Horn

The English horn bocal presents a few unique options and potential problems. As with bassoon, the no. 2 bocal is the standard length. Given the same manufacturer, a lower number is a shorter bocal and a higher number is longer.

A very common pitch problem on English horn is that fourth-space "C" (concert F) may drop in pitch as the player plays more softly. This happens with some bocals and not with others.

In the very highest (altissimo) register of English horn, players often develop a set of fingerings that speaks and tunes better than standard oboe fingerings.

Choosing Double Reed Students

Selecting oboe and bassoon students requires some thought, because you are providing solo voices for a complete instrumentation of your ensembles for years, until the student graduates from your program. Double reed players are often recruited from the ranks of the clarinet or another woodwind section *for the privilege of being an oboist or bassoonist*. Factors to be carefully considered:

- A strong musical background—perhaps some earlier piano training
- A good sense of pitch
- Discernable intelligence

- Persistence—not inclined to quit
- Parental support, including willingness to buy reeds and to provide private lessons
- For bassoonists, large hands with long, nimble thumbs, though this problem can be mitigated somewhat if a short reach bassoon is available, especially in the first few years. Look at the students' biological parents for an indication of how the student might develop physically.
- Someone who seems to like to play as a soloist
- Someone who likes uniqueness

Oboe Fingering Chart Introduction

The oboe has the narrowest convenient range of all of the woodwinds, and thus has the fewest fingerings. The complications that come into play are (1) there are three mechanisms of overblowing—the half-hole and two (sometimes three) octave keys—which must be used in the correct ranges and, (2) the oboist absolutely must learn to use both regular and forked F from the outset. Because most oboists' early years are spent in a band class playing in flat keys, without vigilant teaching, it is not uncommon to find a young player using forked F in every situation, and depriving himself or herself of the best-sounding F on the instrument.

The oboe is designed for more lateral motion than the clarinet, and thus the keys for the right and left little (4th) fingers are designed for sliding. Some of the logic behind this design is that the added weight and mechanical complication of additional keywork is not justified by the very small amount of technical passage work involving the lowest five notes of the range. Only the C# and D# fingerings repeat in the second octave, so only D# is provided with an alternate (on the left) to remove the necessity of sliding laterally from C# to D#, most often in the second octave. In the lowest range where lateral motion is absolutely necessary, oboists learn to use a little facial grease from beside the nose or forehead to facilitate the lateral motion.

Oboe Fingering Chart Commentary

1. This note does not exist on the very least expensive student oboes.

1&2. These keys are designed to accommodate lateral motion between B-flat and B-natural. It is the only option in a chromatic context.

3&4. These keys are designed to accommodate lateral motion between C and C#. A common practice is to use a tiny amount of facial grease (as from one's nose or forehead) on the tip of the finger to facilitate this movement. As with fingerings 1 and 2, passages requiring facile technique on these low notes are rare.

6&7, 21&22. Fingerings 6 and 21 are used in the vast majority of cases, and fingerings 7 and 22 only exist to eliminate the need to move laterally with 4R. Such a case would be an E-flat adjacent to a D-flat, as in a D-flat major scale.

19. The oboe is the only woodwind instrument that does not have an open fingering as a principal fingering, so there is no "open C#." This is the first note of the second register.

23. This note (E-natural) is extremely sensitive to any obstruction or variation in the airspace around the bell, including the interior of the bell itself. To accomplish the proper reed position in the mouth, the oboist is much less likely to rest the bell on a knee that a clarinetist, but the note will be unmanageably flat if one does. If this E-natural is consistently sharp, some oboists have inserted a few thicknesses of tape inside the bell to flatten the pitch. Be careful before altering or switching bells though—since the reed can cause E-natural to be unstable also, it's possible that the problem is the reed and not the bell.

34. This is the only note where 1L is neither down nor on the half hole. Because the height of the pad greatly affects the pitch of high C#, an adjustment screw is mounted on the striker portion of the key (where the open key's motion is stopped by striking the body of the instrument) on higher-end oboes. Tightening the screw brings high C# down and loosening it makes the note sharper.

Oboe Fingering Chart

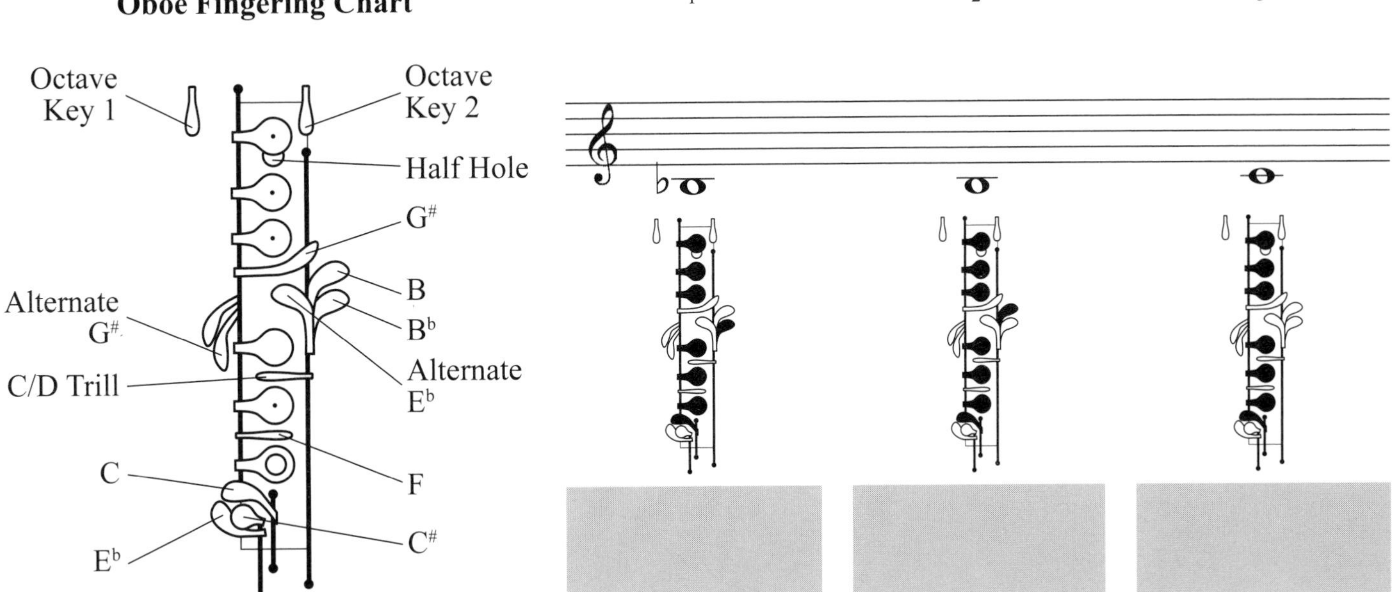

4 5 6 7 8

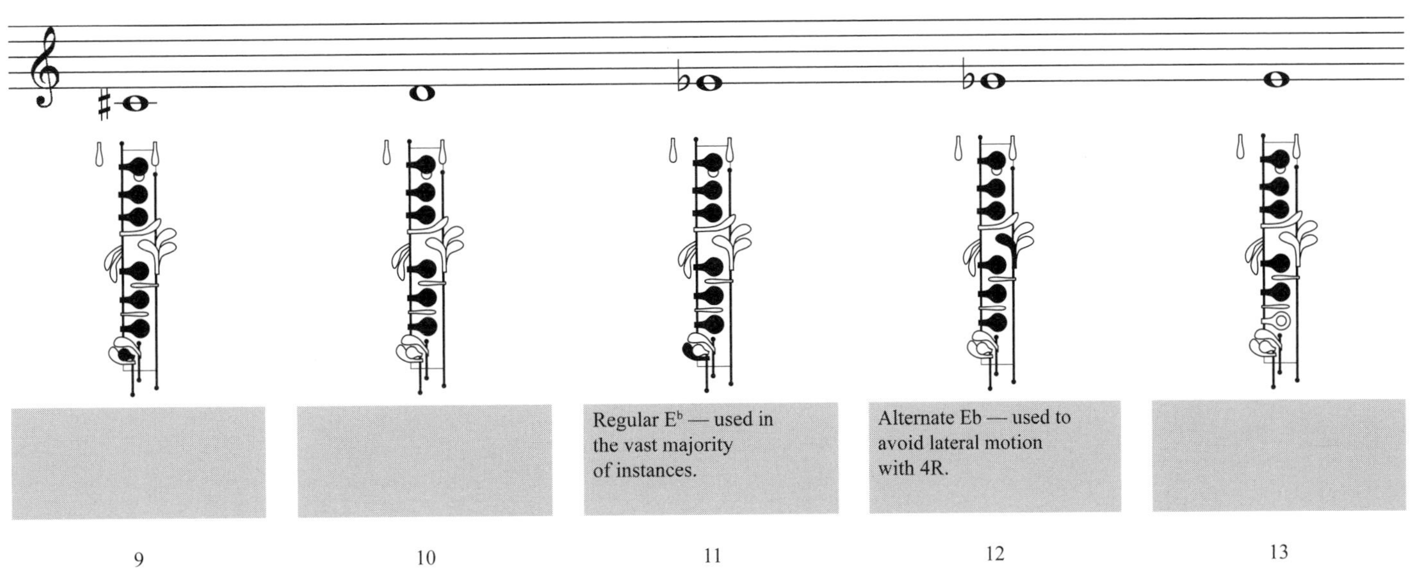

9 10 11 12 13

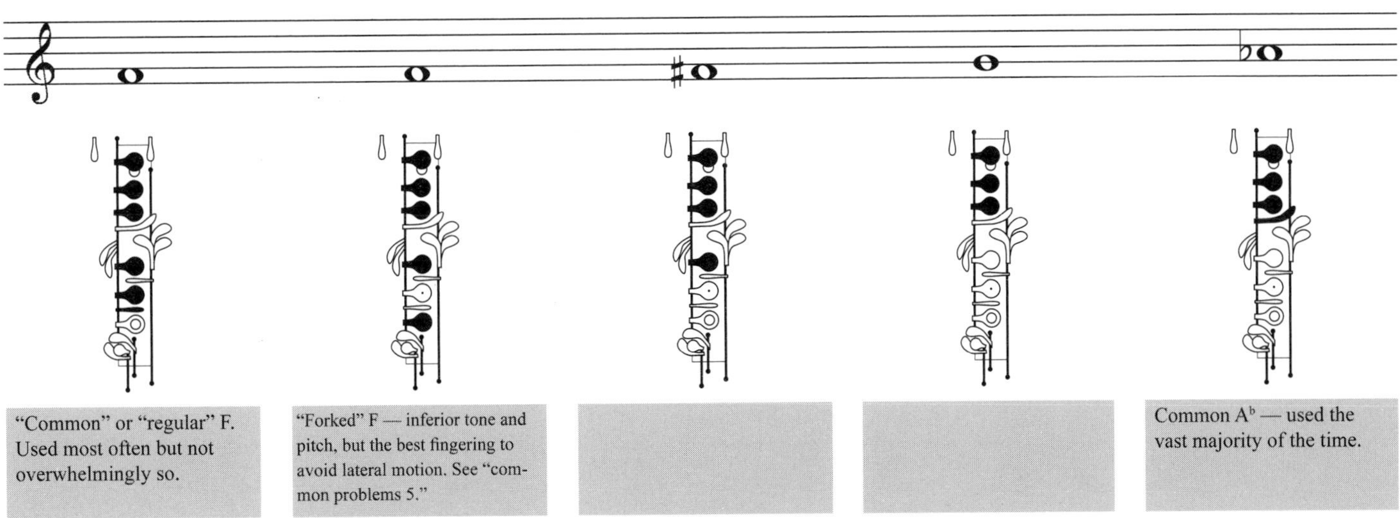

On more expensive oboes, a "side F key" exists for 4L. If present, "side F" replaces most but not all instances in either octave where "forked F" would be used.

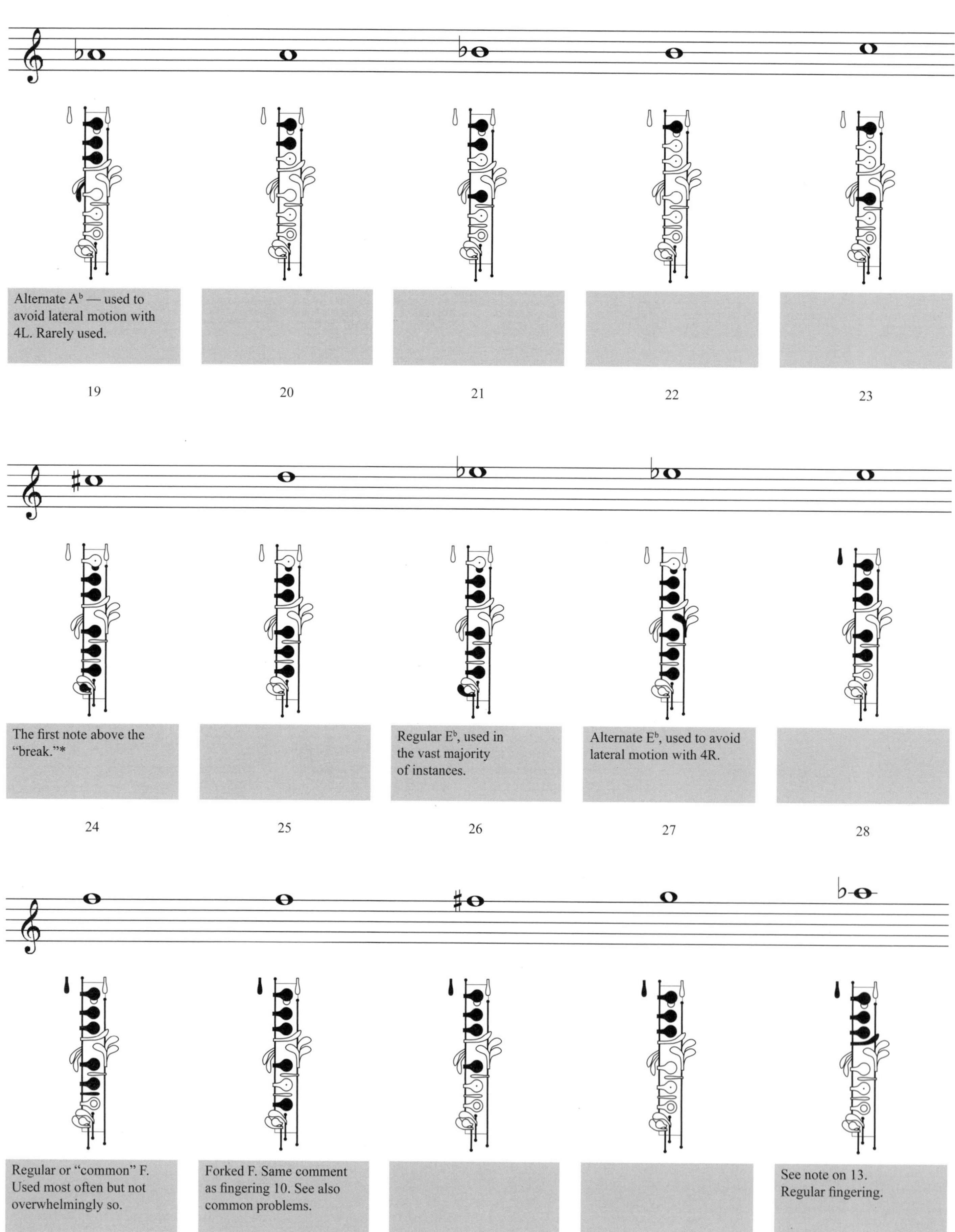

* – Notice: These are three half-hole notes on the oboe. (also true of bassoon)
Also notice: Half-hole and octave key are not used at the some time.

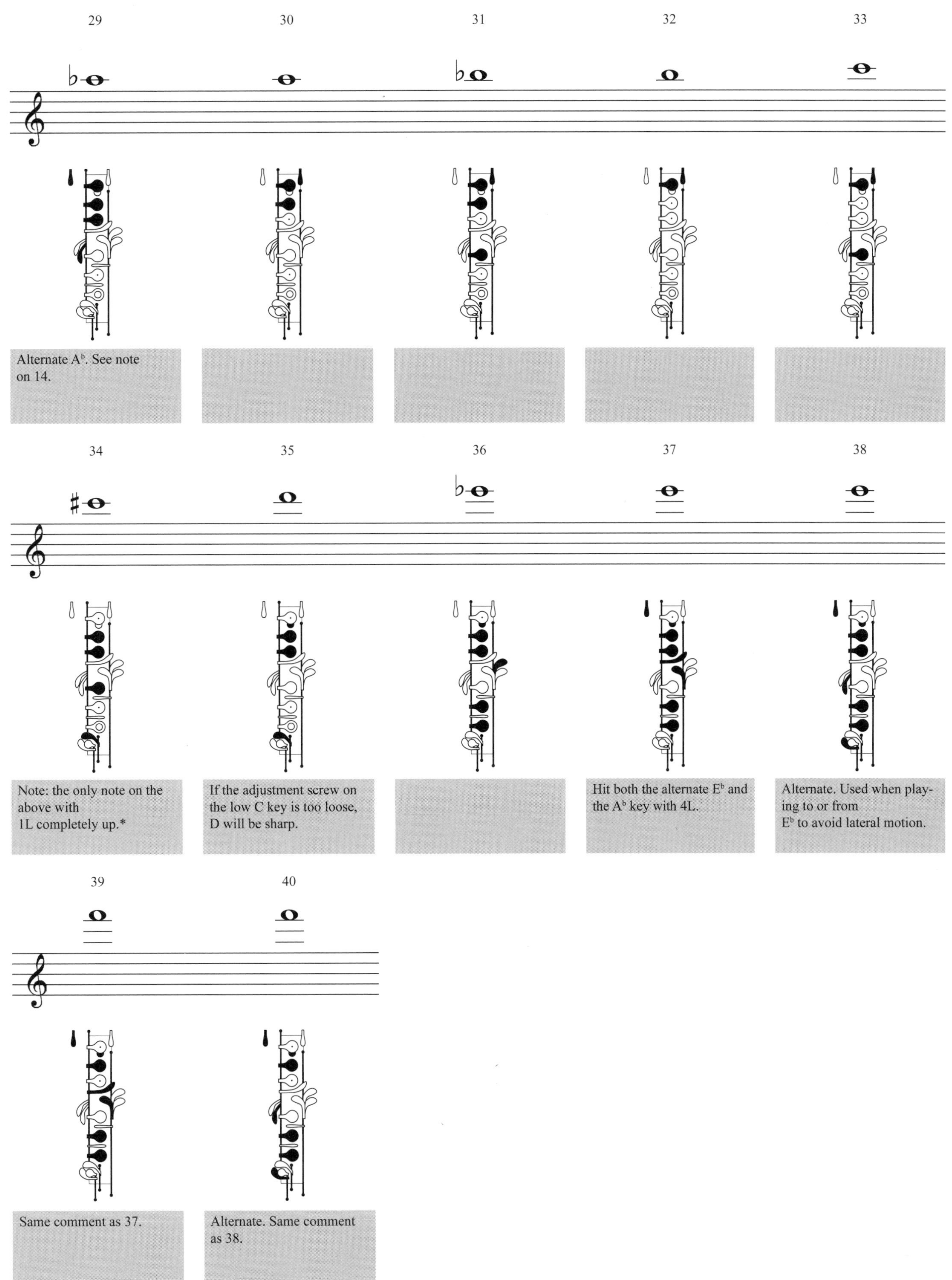

* — This high C# may be tuned by adjusting the screw on the 1L key.
Notes above Eb are considerably more resistant than D. (unlike flute)

Oboe Trill Chart

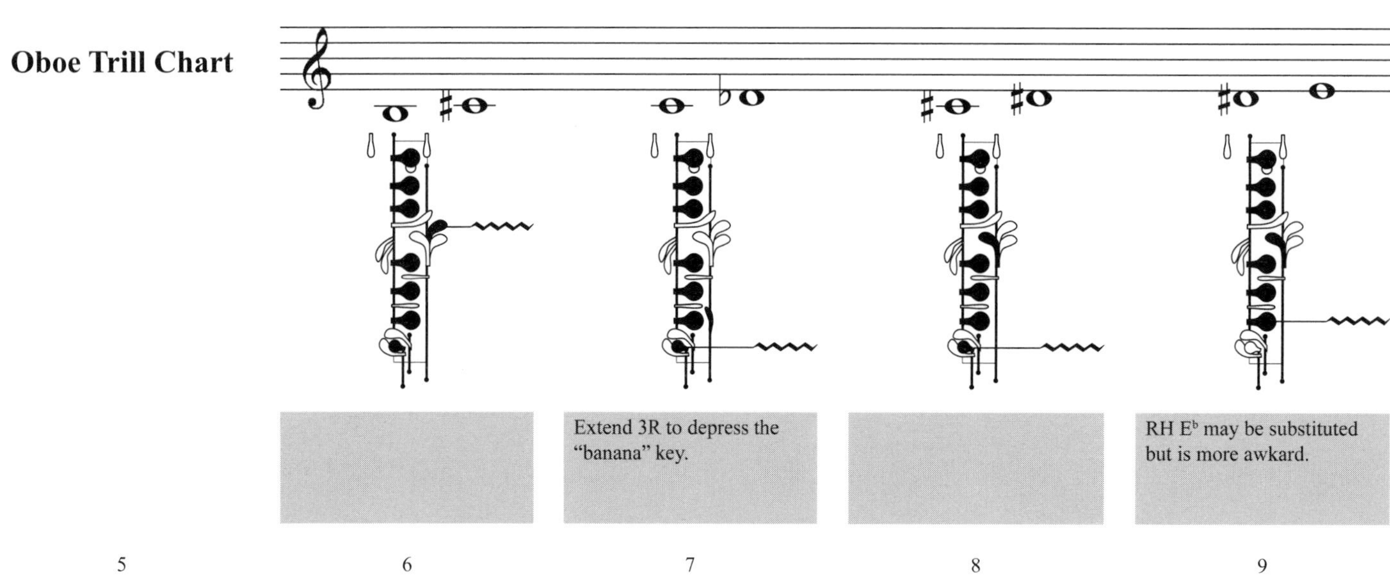

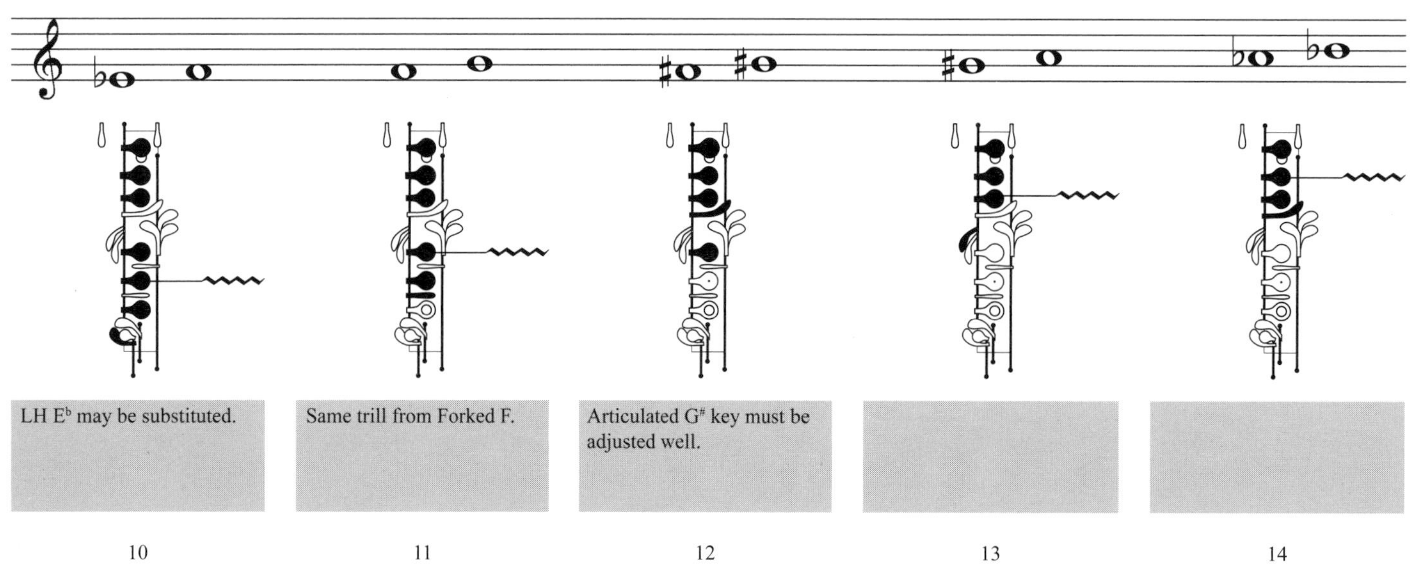

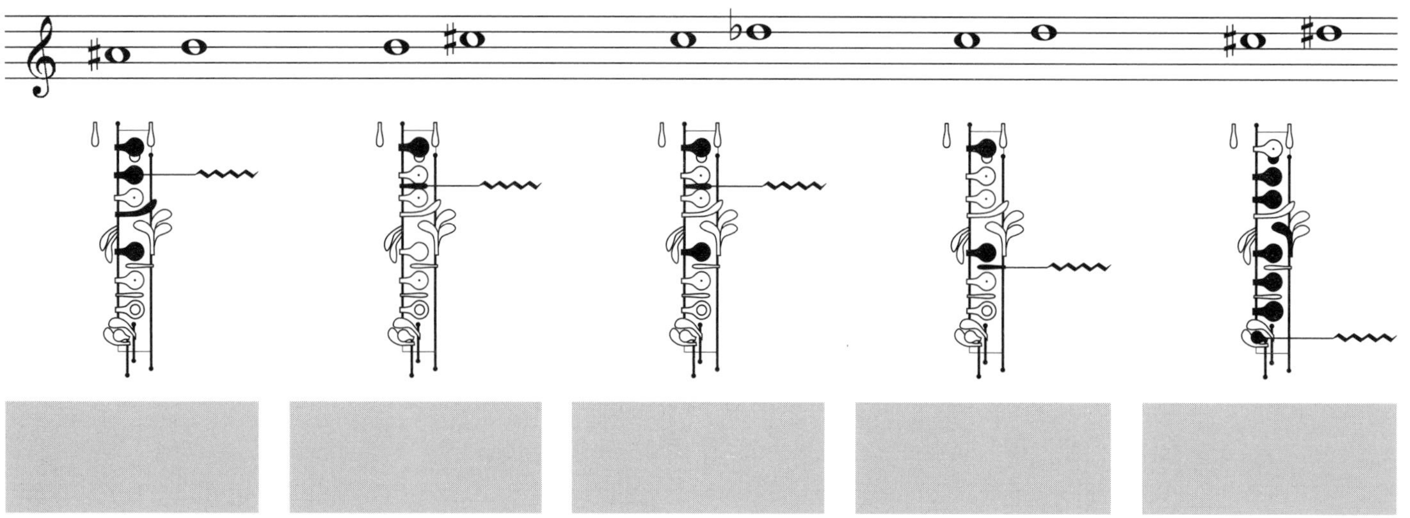

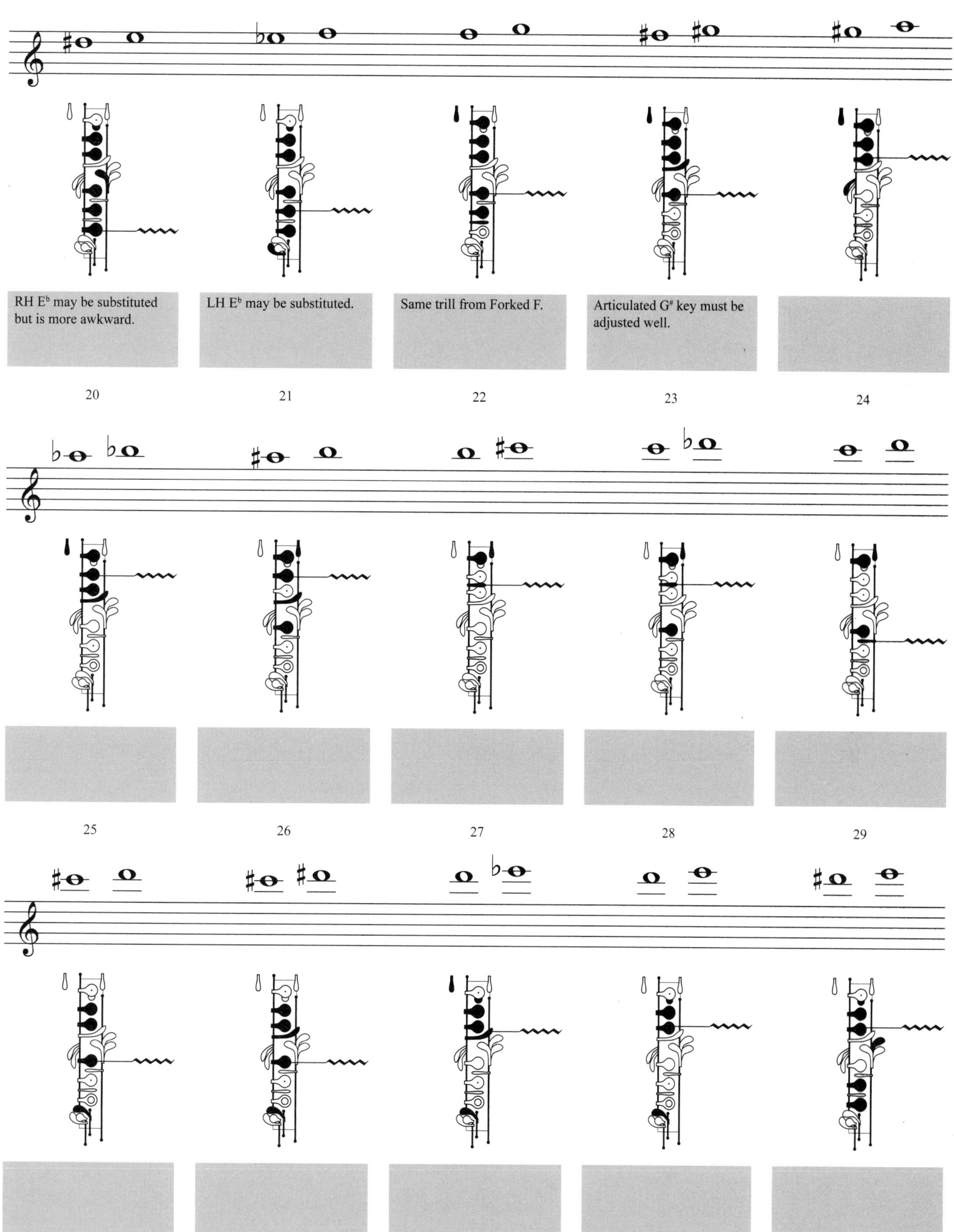
15
16
17
18
19
RH E♭ may be substituted but is more awkward.
LH E♭ may be substituted.
Same trill from Forked F.
Articulated G♯ key must be adjusted well.
20
21
22
23
24
25
26
27
28
29

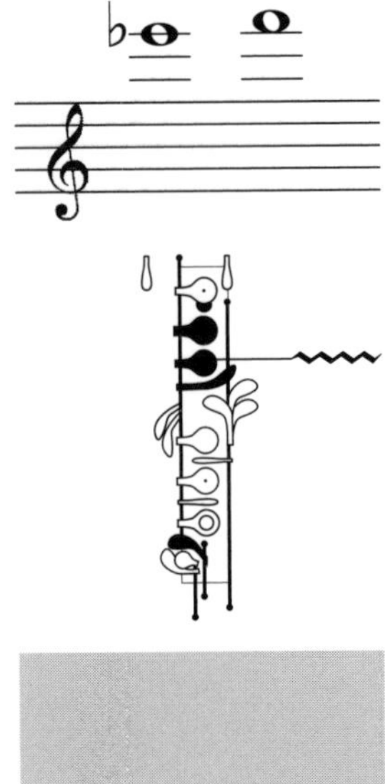
30

CLARINET

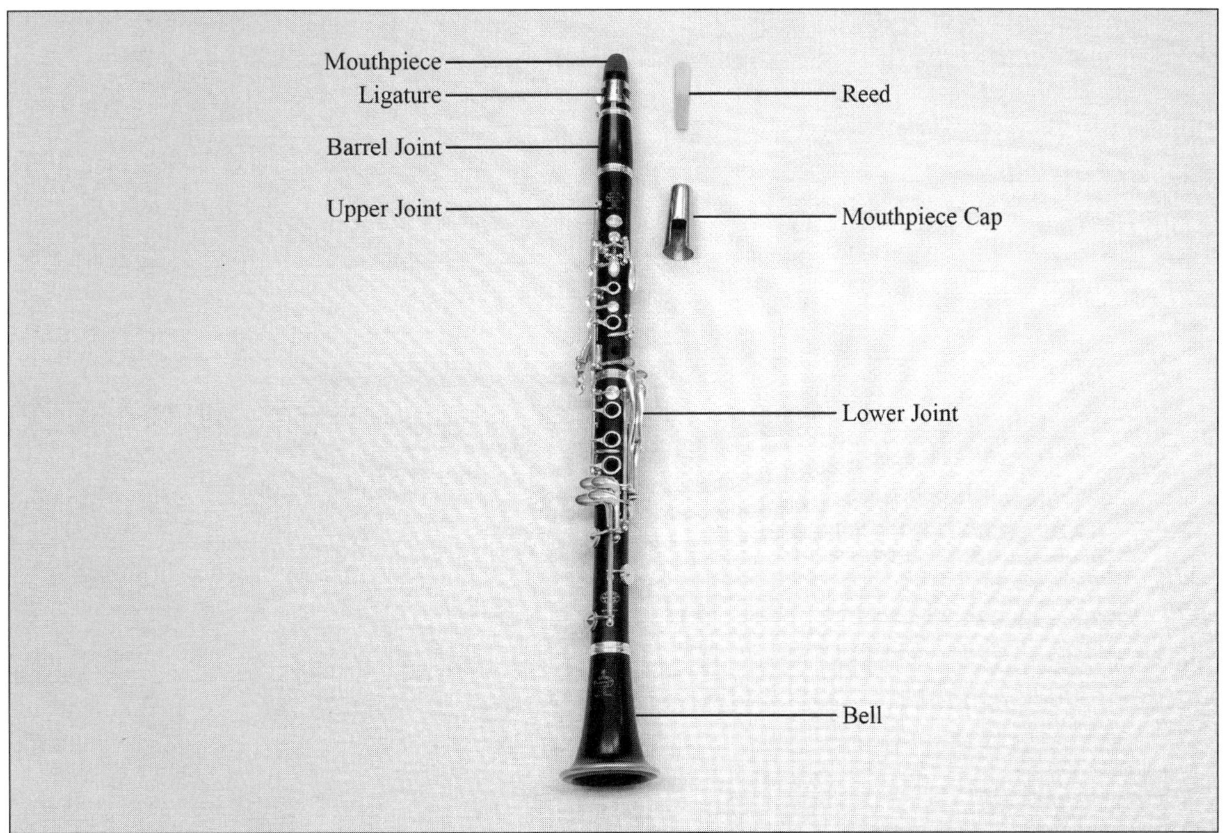

Before You Begin

- Be sure all tenon corks are lightly lubricated with cork grease.
- Do not grab a joint in such a way that keys that are not designed to be depressed directly by the fingers are being depressed or torqued in the twisting process.
- Begin assembling from the bottom of the instrument and disassemble in reverse order from assembly. Since the mouthpiece and reed are delicate and in the greatest danger of damage, putting them on last and taking them off first reduces the likelihood of damage.
- The clarinet has a "bridge key," which transfers motion from one part of the instrument to another. This is delicate and easily bent, throwing it out of adjustment. Be careful not to twist too far.
- For larger clarinets (bass or contra) it is advisable to work with the case in front or beside you on the floor, rather than in your lap.
- Always swab the clarinet with the appropriate swab after playing.
- Even when larger instruments (baritone saxophones, contrabass clarinets, etc.) are nested in the case, they can be thrown out of adjustment by simply jarring the case or setting it down with too much force. Carry and set cases down carefully.

- Do not run a swab through a mouthpiece. Gently clean it with a separate cloth.
- Do not over-tighten a ligature. A drop of oil on the threads of ligature screws considerably prolongs their useful lives.

■ *Assembly*

1. Soak the reed by placing it into your mouth or into a small container of water. It is best to soak the whole reed—not just the thin part.
2. Grasping the lower joint by the area which is designed for the hand (not by the lower end where there are rods and pads) and the wide end of the bell in the other, gently twist the bell onto the lower joint.
3. Grasping the assembled lower half over the tenon so that there is no pressure on pads or rods in one hand and the upper joint by the area designed for the hand so that the bridge key raises, carefully insert the upper joint into the lower. You cannot twist these joints fully around or you will bend keys—only twist enough to get the two joints to slide together. Line up the bridge key mechanism.

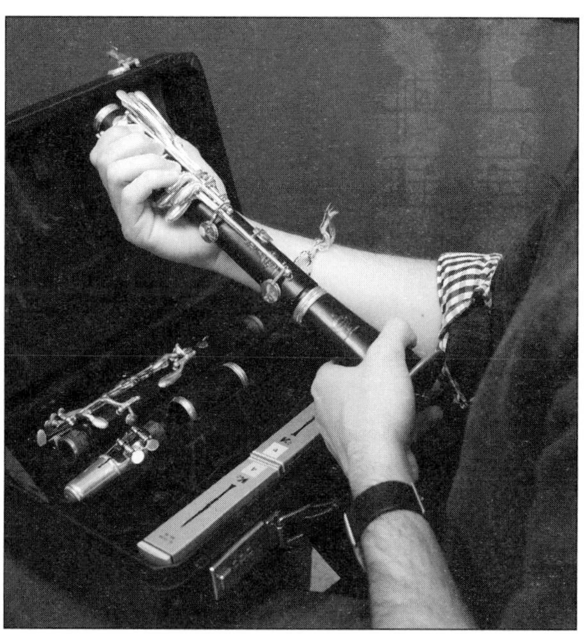

Putting bell and lower joint together

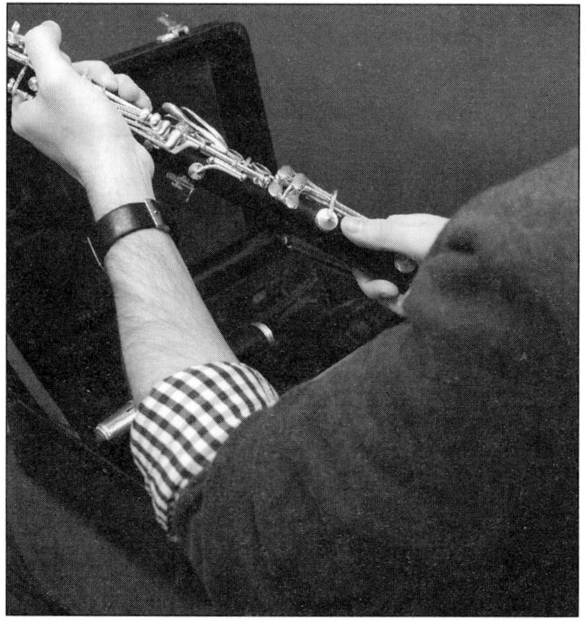

Putting upper and lower joints together

4. Grasping the upper joint by the area designed for the hand, twist the barrel joint onto the upper joint. Only one end of the barrel joint will fit.
5. Grasping the mouthpiece by the fattest area in the center of the mouthpiece, twist the mouthpiece onto the upper tenon of the barrel, lining up the flat part of the mouthpiece with the thumb hole and thumb rest on the upper and lower joints.

Putting barrel joint onto upper joint

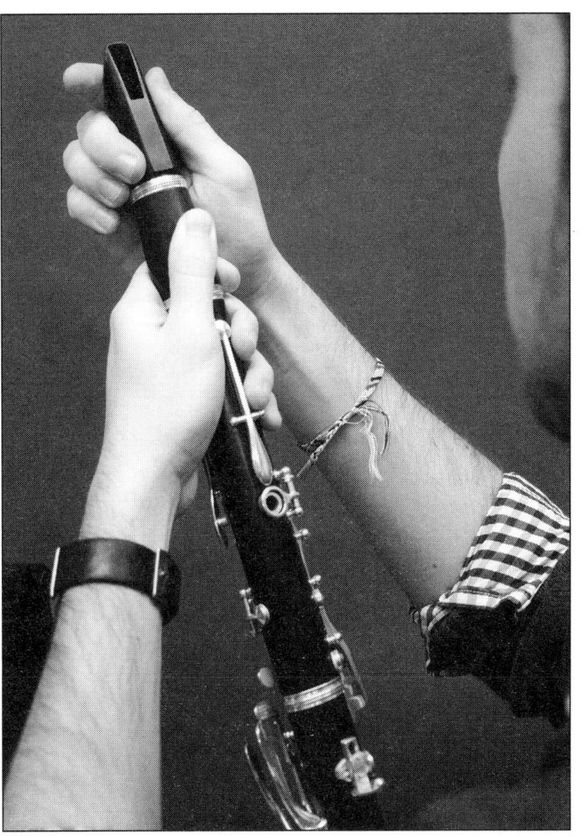

Adding the mouthpiece, carefully protecting the facing

6. Carefully slide the ligature over the beak of the mouthpiece, being careful not to scratch the mouthpiece. Notice that the ligature only fits one direction and not the other.
7. Pushing the ligature upwards to create a space between it and the flat side of the mouthpiece, slide the blunt end of the reed under the ligature, matching flat side of the reed to the flat side of the mouthpiece.
8. Maneuvering the reed by the sides and not by the tip, adjust the reed so that the tip of the reed is at exactly the same height as the tip of the mouthpiece. You can judge this by having your line of sight at a perpendicular angle to the clarinet. Gently tighten the ligature.

Assembling mouthpiece, ligature and reed

■ *Teaching and Learning the First Sounds—Suggested Beginning Steps for Clarinet*

1. Soak the reed, either in saliva or in a glass of water. Push the ligature slightly toward the tip of the mouthpiece to create some space on the flat side of the mouthpiece and slip the reed, thick end first, under the ligature, lining up the tip of the reed with the tip of the mouthpiece.
2. The first fingering in this text is "open" G. College students can usually hold a clarinet without accidentally pressing keys, but as a teaching procedure, consider having the student hold the clarinet with the right hand on the barrel joint to eliminate the possibility of opening the wrong key by accident. If starting with both hands in position, the right hand makes a "C" shape and side of the thumb goes beneath the thumb rest.
3. Placing the top teeth on the mouthpiece and curling the lower lip slightly over the bottom teeth, bring the lips toward the mouthpiece as though to say "oooo." Freeze the lips in this firm position just as a body builder "freezes" the muscles while flexing for the camera. Create a seal around the mouthpiece with the lips.

4. Place the tip of the tongue on the face of the reed and as you begin to blow, draw the tongue slightly away from the reed. The syllable you will use will be "tee" or "teh," with the tip of the tongue remaining very near the reed while playing.

Playing the first "open G"
with right hand on barrel
to avoid opening keys accidentally

Clarinet embouchure
with chin
pointed

5. Placing the side of the right thumb beneath the thumb rest and the left hand over the open holes and little finger keys with the feeling that both hands are holding a tennis ball, stabilize the clarinet by pushing the right thumb toward the mouth.

Correct embouchure, playing position and posture

Articulation

Ideally, the tip of the tongue touches the face of the reed right at the tip and retracts at a right angle to the face of the reed. This allows the player to use the back of the tongue to "voice" the tone, resulting in a focused sound. Thinking of the tongue in three parts, the front approaches the reed at a right angle, the middle is held downward as though to have a small weight in the center, and the back is up to focus the sound. Find the back of the tongue by pronouncing "key." Where the sound is being made is the part of the tongue which is kept high, such that the syllable being "voiced" while playing the clarinet is in the range of "ee" or "eh." The syllable "ah" is not recommended.

A second style of tonguing called "anchor tonguing" is advocated by a considerably smaller number of clarinetists. In this style, the tip of the tongue stays "anchored" to either the lip or the lower teeth and the middle of the tongue does the articulating. There are strongly negative feelings in the clarinet community about this, and the majority of clarinetists at the very highest level discourage it because it makes it virtually impossible for the tongue to be used to effectively focus the sound.

There should be no embouchure movement in the articulation process on clarinet.

Common Problems

1. Embouchure:
   - Chin not pointed. Often a student needs biofeedback (one's own hand on one's chin) or visual feedback (mirror) to learn the correct feel and sound.
   - Puffing cheeks. Making the "shhhhh" sound is often helpful to hold the cheeks against the teeth, showing the student how eliminating the puffing feels.
   - Biting, pinching, especially in the upper register. Remember—the jaw moves forward, not upward for higher notes. The pitch made on the soprano clarinet mouthpiece alone should be no higher than concert C, two octaves above the piano's middle C. Any higher indicates the reed is being bitten into the mouthpiece
   - Corners of the mouth not sufficiently firm.
   - Student is taking too little mouthpiece: The sound is muffled and the upper register is nearly impossible to produce. The student may have discovered that taking too little mouthpiece helps to avoid squeaking, but in doing so has made other sacrifices.
   - Student is taking too much mouthpiece: The sound is open, hollow and bright. Tone is unstable and squeaks are frequent.
2. Fingers not covering holes, especially 3R and 3L. Ask students to press their fingers into the holes so that the tips of the fingers retain the circular impression of the hole when lifted suddenly.
3. Not understanding "Principal" vs. "Alternate" fingerings. The principal fingering is the one that falls "under the hand." See the Introduction to the Clarinet Fingering Chart for a detailed discussion.

4. Bridge key bent, making it impossible to play below low C.
5. Poor mouthpiece. Injection-molded plastic mouthpieces that come with student instruments are rarely adequate. The first thing that should be upgraded is the mouthpiece. "Your (son/daughter) is doing really well and has outgrown the mouthpiece that came with the instrument."
6. Poor or inappropriate reed. Having a quantity of fresh reeds of good quality is the beginning of being able to play well.
7. Tonguing with some part of the tongue other than the tip.
8. Moving jaw while tonguing.
9. Dropping the back of the tongue down in an "ahhh" position. The back of the tongue needs to be arched, in an "eee" or "ehh" position. Tongue positions (i.e. vowel sounds) that work for brass and flute do not work on a reed instrument. *This problem is the great danger of suggesting that the student to "keep an open throat."*
10. Adding the E-flat key with 4R to high C#, which makes a note which is naturally slightly sharp into one which is extremely sharp and bright in tone.
11. Upper clarion (especially B-natural) "grunts" before the correct pitch comes out. The jaw is too far back or the tongue is in an "ah" position. Think of the reed as a ladder and the lower teeth as someone climbing the ladder. The higher notes are closer to the ligature than the lower notes. The note will also grunt if the register key opens too far or on an A clarinet, if the register tube is too long.
12. An individual note sounds with a stuffy "wheeze." If the note is also flat to the notes around it, the pad is either too close to the tone hole or there is dirt in the hole itself. Correct by adjusting the key so that the pad lifts higher. The C#/G# key and the register key for throat B-flat naturally "wheeze" slightly because of the way the clarinet is designed. Using a cork or other solid pad instead of a pad with skin over felt may minimize this problem.
13. Tonguing against the roof of the mouth. When a student does this, one hears a small explosion inside the mouth considerably before the note speaks. To solve the problem, have the student place the tongue directly on the reed and blow, and then release the tongue after the air stream has begun.

■ *Tuning*

The pitch on the clarinet is the least flexible of the woodwinds, with some potential to push ("lip") the pitch downward, but with very little flexibility upward. In contrast to the flute, the instrument's natural tendency is to be sharper at soft dynamics and flatter at loud ones, and the clarinet will generally be sharp at the very beginning of a breath because of the density of the fresh gas present at the beginning of a breath.

Sharpness overall—Third-space C-natural is called "tuning note C," but is not an ideal note to tune because it is naturally sharp to the notes around it. Ideally, tune "open G" to a pitch standard first, lowering the pitch by pulling between the barrel joint and the upper joint of the instrument. With open G matching the pitch standard, then check the written C-natural immediately above it and lower the pitch of that note by pulling out between the upper and lower joints. Never pull the mouthpiece out of the barrel, because this creates an irregularity in the bore very close to the source of vibration.

This creates much more dramatic problems than the gap created in the bore farther down the bore at the bottom of the barrel. If the instrument needs to be pulled out a long way, consider obtaining a longer barrel or getting some tuning rings. Tuning rings look like flat washers that are inserted in the tenon at the bottom of the barrel to fill the air gap created by pulling out. The advantage is that they are much less expensive than buying a longer barrel—the disadvantage is that they are very easy to lose.

Flatness overall—If the clarinet is flat overall, and if the student is using a reed with some resistance with a good embouchure and tongue position, then the problem is the equipment itself. Longer and shorter barrel joints are readily available. If, for example, a student is playing on a Buffet instrument and is very attached to the mouthpiece being used but the mouthpiece causes flatness, then obtaining a barrel shorter than the stock 66mm will solve the problem, at least until the student changes to a sharper mouthpiece when the opposite problem may be encountered. Some mouthpieces are made to play higher—others to play lower. This is why one should always take a tuner along when buying a mouthpiece so one does not "fall in love" with the sound of a mouthpiece that will not play in tune with the rest of the equipment being used.

Remember that mouthpieces are designed to work on all clarinets, but barrel joints may not be interchangeable. Some companies do this on purpose so that after-market equipment will not be used on their instrument.

Erratic scale—Mouthpieces and barrels vary in interior design and dimension. A barrel with a very narrow bore will cause the clarion register to be flatter to the lower register than one with a wider bore. A mouthpiece with a very large chamber can cause short fingerings—throat tones especially—to be very flat to the rest of the scale. So the best advice is, don't buy a mouthpiece or a barrel unless it tunes well on the instrument. Fortunately, most common student and professional clarinets found in American music stores come with reasonably-matched barrels. Just be sure that the mouthpiece works well on these instruments.

With one of the largest selections of fingerings, clarinetists have at their disposal a wealth of fingerings, some of which are flatter and some of which are sharper. In the altissimo especially, selecting the best fingering for a particular note in a passage removes or reduces the necessity to manipulate the note with the embouchure, and so these notes will sound better than if they were "lipped" a long distance to find the correct pitch. In the lower registers, a pitch problem that cannot be adjusted with the embouchure might be better addressed by altering a fingering—even putting an extra finger or key down some distance below the highest open hole, or by shading or slightly closing one of the open holes. These decisions are made in consideration of the technical obstacles that are present in a passage. For an extreme example, assuming an advanced level of playing, an exposed low B-natural (Concert A) played as the third of a concert F major chord at a soft dynamic and held for a long time, the forked fingering (14) will be lower and thus more satisfactory. If still sharp, closing a small percentage of the middle hole with the tip of R2 will more completely solve the problem.

E-flat Clarinet

Playing the e-flat sopranino clarinet in tune is particularly challenging. Beyond having good equipment with an appropriate mouthpiece and barrel, the player is left to use his or her ear to manipulate the pitch in the lower registers. The openings of the A and G# keys are particularly critical—A and G# do not need to be sharp compared to open G. These are keys whose openings are adjusted by adjusting the thickness of the striker corks.

The altissimo register on e-flat clarinet tends to be flat in general. In that register, E-flat clarinet players often develop a set of fingerings unlike those of the standard B-flat clarinet. While this can be an intellectual challenge for the player, ultimately just knowing fingerings that play in tune can be the best answer.

Remember that different mouthpieces can affect the scale of the sopranino clarinet dramatically.

Bass Clarinet

Professional model bass clarinets have an automatic double register key mechanism which compensates somewhat for the sharpness of the lowest notes in the *clarion* register. Student bass clarinets have a single register key, which not only renders middle-line B and some notes immediately above that note somewhat sharp, but they tend to speak with more resistance than on a professional instrument.

If one intends to use the same altissimo fingerings on bass (or alto) clarinet, all notes above high C# must be played with the half-hole (on the plateau extension similar to oboe) or the notes will be unreasonably sharp or will not speak at all. Virtually all professional bass clarinetists have a completely different set of altissimo fingerings that do not resemble those of the soprano clarinet, but these fingerings only work on professional model bass clarinets with the double register vent mechanism.

■ *Clarinet Fingering Chart Introduction*

Because the clarinet and the bassoon have such a large number of fingerings for any one note in comparison to the oboe, flute and especially saxophone, the following comments are provided to foster a clear understanding of exactly *why* we use a specific fingering in any one context. Some notes on the clarinet—especially in the *altissimo* range—have twenty or more fingerings. No attempt is made to provide a comprehensive list in this volume—only the principal fingerings and the indispensable alternates are listed here. For an exhaustive list, consult Thomas Ridenour's book, *"Clarinet Fingerings: A Guide for the Performer and Educator."*

The lowest octave is called the *chalumeau,* the notes from F(22) through B-flat(28) are the *throat tones.* These two groups of notes together are fundamentals (as opposed to harmonics) and together they make up the *lower register.* The octave plus one half step from B(29) through C(50) is the *clarion,* and the very highest register from C#(51) onward is the *altissimo* or sometimes called the *acute* register.

As with all woodwinds, *the Principal fingering is the one which falls under the hand* without shifting the hand's position, and the alternate is the one for which the hand shifts out of position. In the chalumeau register (and also a twelfth above in the clarion register) for example, the principal fingering for E is on the left, F is on the right, F# is on the right and G# is on the right. Obviously then, with so many principal fingerings on the right, the alternate F# is used frequently. To give an idea of how common the alternates are, an approximation of frequency of usage might be:

- E/B on the right (Fingering no. 3)—10%
- F/C on the left (Fingering no. 5)—5%
- F#/C# on the left (Fingering no. 7)—40%

Clearly, F#/C# on the right is the default or principal fingering, because it sits right under the hand, but the key on the left is absolutely essential, and is the standard chromatic fingering. Thus, it is built close to the E/B lever and requires the hand to shift out of position only slightly, as compared to the F/C lever on the left, for example. Both of these F# fingerings must be understood early in the learning process. To complicate matters, when F# is played adjacent to a G# (as in an E major scale), the left-hand F# is played without the F/C key in the right, so that 4R can go to the G# key without sliding laterally. While it is possible to play E/B and F#/C# without the F/C key for 4R, teaching the fingering with 4R down as the default prevents the development of an unwanted extra note between the these notes and the F or C adjacent to them.

Remember: Unless absolutely unavoidable, do not move the finger laterally between adjacent notes (as in left-left or right-right). Try to alternate between left and right, using the greatest number of principal fingerings possible to avoid shifting the hand out of position.

■ *Clarinet Fingering Chart Commentary*

Notice that the technical issues in the clarion register are identical to those a twelfth lower, therefore the upper register fingering number is included in parentheses at the end of each comment. This section elaborates on the comments given in the fingering chart itself.

Lower Register

1. Principal, teach first. Teaching this with 4R on the F/C key prevents an unwanted extra note between E and F. Low E and B a twelfth above it will be flattened by burying the bell in the player's legs. (29)

2. Still the principal fingering, but used without 4R when 4R is needed for the adjacent note. (30)

3. The alternate, used when 4L is needed for an adjacent note. (31)

4 & 5. F is played on the right the vast majority of the time, so fingering 5 is used only when 4R is needed for the note before or after—usually a G#, as in an extended A harmonic minor scale in the lower register or an E harmonic minor scale in the clarion. (32, 33)

6. This is the principal F# but only slightly, since it usually is not used in a chromatic context. Estimated frequency of use, 60% of the time. (34)

7. The alternate F#, used perhaps 40% of the time, is the normal chromatic fingering if there are no mitigating circumstances. Such a circumstance is found in the final lines of the Debussy *Premiere Rhapsodie,* but these circumstances are rare. Students who learn E/B on the right and F#/C# on the left as their default fingerings consistently stumble over the break. (35)

8. Use this fingering (without the F/C key) when the sequence requires 4R on the adjacent note, as in an E major scale in both the chalumeau and the clarion registers. (36)

10. G# in the chalumeau and D# in the clarion are notes which govern fingering decisions for all other 4th finger notes adjacent or near. Any E, F or F# adjacent to G#(10) is played on the left because there is only one possibility for the G#. Work backward from the G# or from the D# in the clarion to determine whether the first note of the 4th finger sequence will be played on the left or on the right. (38)

13 & 14. In spite of its shortcomings, fingering 13 is the principal low B because it falls under the hand, and thus is easiest to "get to." However, 2nd finger B and clarion F# (the same fingering with the register key), are both sharp and somewhat shallow in tone. Fingering 14 is the acoustically correct fingering producing a richer sound and lower pitch, but to use it all the time would require that finger 3R move laterally to and from the sliver key between fingers 2R and 3R, which would never produce a clean, facile technique. If a lower pitch is needed on a long note, the technical inconvenience may be worth the effort. (41 & 42)

16. Low C# "wheezes" because the hole is drilled too high and is too small to be acoustically correct, but allows for the placement of the tenon. (44)

18–20. Fingering 18 is principal and will be used in the vast majority of cases. 19 is sharp and shallow, and is also dependent upon perfect alignment of the bridge key between the upper and lower joints. See the Troubleshooting section for a more thorough discussion of this mechanism. Fingering 20 is controversial—regarded by some as the chromatic fingering and completely ignored by others, and some even seal the hole with wax. For sure, ignoring fingering 20 entirely does not create any technical problems, whereas the lateral motion that may occur, even by accident, is a potential technical problem. (46-48)

24. This fingering is flat and it "wheezes." In an ascending chromatic scale, coming into it from F natural is seamless but coming out of it to G is difficult to play smoothly. By contrast, the principal fingering (23) is somewhat difficult to approach from the semitone below but moving out of it to G is very easy. The disadvantages outweigh the advantages and it is best to limit its use to trills from F natural.

26–28. These are the principal fingerings for these throat tone notes. See Supplemental Fingerings 62-65 for some better-sounding "resonance" fingerings that are not listed as basic clarinet technique. Fingering 28 has a "wheeze" naturally—resonance 64 helps this considerably and is accessible in many situations. Playing B-flat with the A key and the second R1 trill key from the top of the instrument makes a very clean B-flat, but it is bright and it forces the right hand to move a great distance away from its normal position. Overuse of this fingering causes a serious technical obstacle.

Upper Register

Fingering 29 begins the second, or *clarion* register of the clarinet. Fingerings 1-50 are all fundamentals or first partials, and beginning with no. 51 the tones are third partials of the overtone series. Between B (29) and C (50), the technical issues in the clarion register are identical to those a twelfth below, and the same rules and recommendations govern fingering choice all the way to C-natural, fingering 50. For ease of reference, the upper register fingering number is listed at the end of each lower register comment above, or may be easily determined by adding 28 to the number of the lower register fingering.

Altissimo Register

Fingering 51 begins the third or *altissimo* register of the clarinet. Notice that the sequence of principal fingerings from C# (51) through F# (59) is identical to that of the notes a major sixth lower, from E (39) through A (45), with the omission of 1L to accomplish the same "venting" that opening the register key facilitated earlier, and the addition of the 4R on the A-flat/E-flat key to bring these notes up to pitch. Learn every principal fingering from D (52) upwards with the A-flat/E-flat key, but remember not to add the E-flat key on C#—a very common problem, causing C# to be much too sharp and extremely bright.

Many of the notes in the altissimo register may be brought down by placing 1L beneath the hole and covering enough of the hole to bring the note down to the proper pitch. Clarinetists call this the "half hole," though at times covering half of the hole is too much and at times it is too little. For the flat notes in the range—F (57) and F#(58) the half hole is inappropriate. Moving the jaw somewhat forward greatly improves the control of these notes.

51. Slightly sharp—if the A-flat/E-flat key is added with 4R it becomes extremely sharp and bright. Can be brought down with the half hole.

52–61. From D upwards, the A-flat/E-flat key must be added to bring these notes up to pitch.

53–55. No single fingering is sufficient for all high E-flats. The most common one is 53, which moves to any note that does not require 3R to move laterally because the sound and pitch are good. Fingering 54 is always flat, but should be used next to C# (51), as in an E major scale, if the scale is moving at a fairly fast pace. The best tone and pitch of all is Fingering 55, but it is also the hardest one to manage in most technical passages.

57. This is the standard high F fingering, but is slightly flat. The pitch may be corrected by adding the sliver key with 3R, but be sure to hit the key close enough to the rod so that the rings do not go down—otherwise this will flatten instead of raise the note. Unfortunately, the sliver key raises the pitch too much, so one can add the half hole to adjust it downward. High F is very flexible, and can be adjusted upward or downward by adjusting the degree to which 1L covers the hole.

58. An important alternate F which is higher and brighter than 57. Not easy to get to in a scale passage, but if one jumps to it from one of the lower registers, it is ideal. Called "long F." All of the "long" high fingerings are extremely sensitive to the proximity of the bell to the player's legs, and are flattened considerably by partial blockage of the bell.

59. The standard F# fingering. It is very flat but may also be corrected by adding the 3R sliver key without depressing the lower joint rings. See "Supplemental fingering 66" for another suggestion.

60. An important alternate F# which is higher and brighter than 59. Like "long F," it is not easy to get to in a scale passage, but speaks very easily if jumped to from a lower register. Called "long F#."

61. The standard high G, but it is sharp. Be sure you teach this one first though because it fits in most technical passages. See "Supplemental fingerings" for another suggestion. (Ridenour lists more than fifteen fingerings for this note).

Supplemental Fingerings

62–64. These are the normal resonance fingerings for throat G#, A and B-flat. They make the tone richer and they bring the pitch down slightly. They are, however, more complicated to move to and from.

65. This B-flat is much clearer than the normal B-flat (28). It requires the right hand to move out of position a considerable amount and thus is not useful in most technical passages. Furthermore, it overcorrects the "wheeze" and produces a note which stands out much more brightly than the notes around it. For this reason many limit its use to trills from A-natural.

66. This high F# really is an overblown B-flat (46) with a little pitch help from the E-flat key, which is optional but recommended. It is more reliable in pitch than either the regular or long fingerings, and is more stable than the principal fingering. The only drawback is that it does not fit into many technical passages.

67. Corrects the sharpness problem with the principal fingering (61) and speaks easily when approached from intervals larger than a step. It is technically more awkward than 61 though, and for this reason it is not considered the principal fingering.

Clarinet Fingering Chart

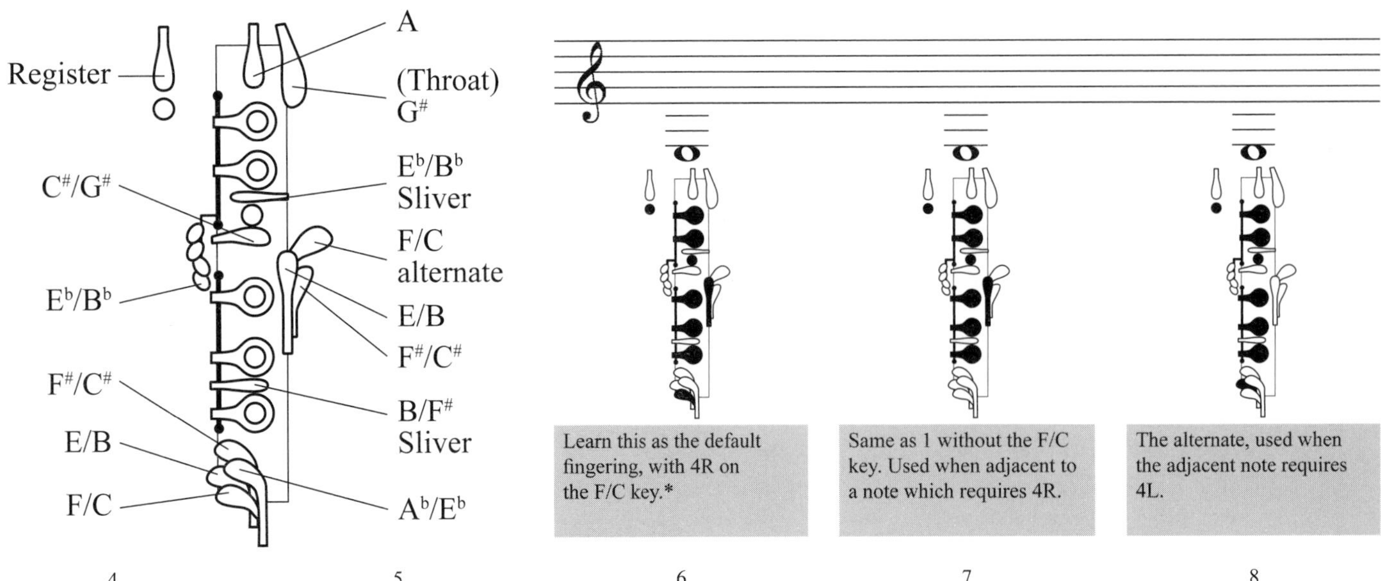

1. Learn this as the default fingering, with 4R on the F/C key.*

2. Same as 1 without the F/C key. Used when adjacent to a note which requires 4R.

3. The alternate, used when the adjacent note requires 4L.

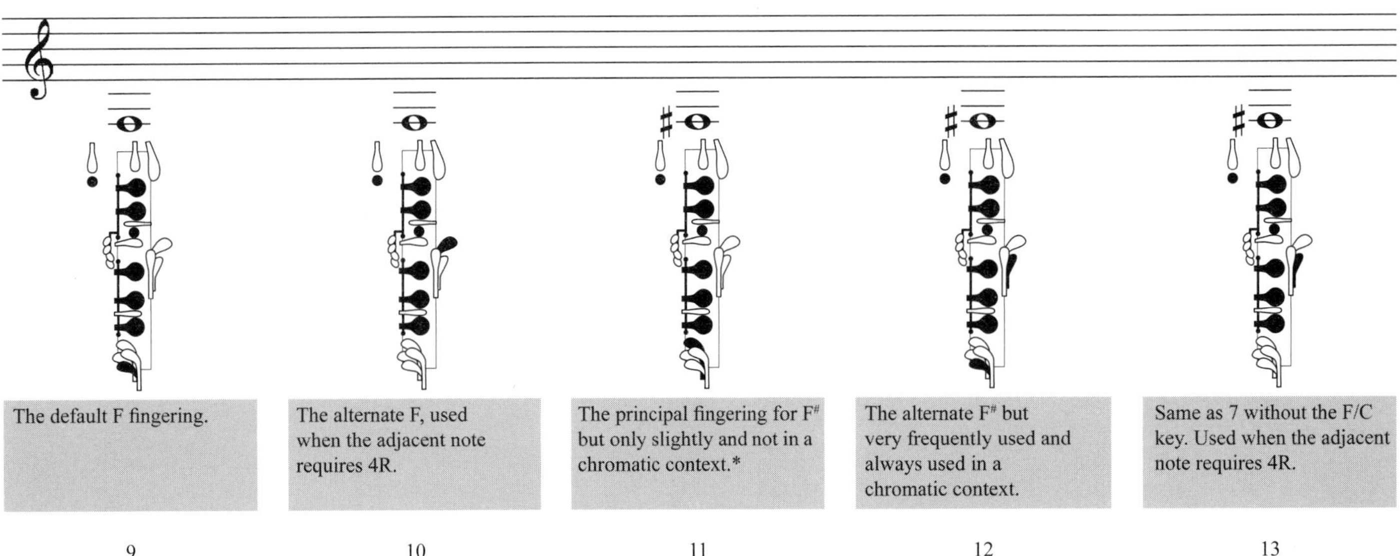

4. The default F fingering.

5. The alternate F, used when the adjacent note requires 4R.

6. The principal fingering for F# but only slightly and not in a chromatic context.*

7. The alternate F# but very frequently used and always used in a chromatic context.

8. Same as 7 without the F/C key. Used when the adjacent note requires 4R.

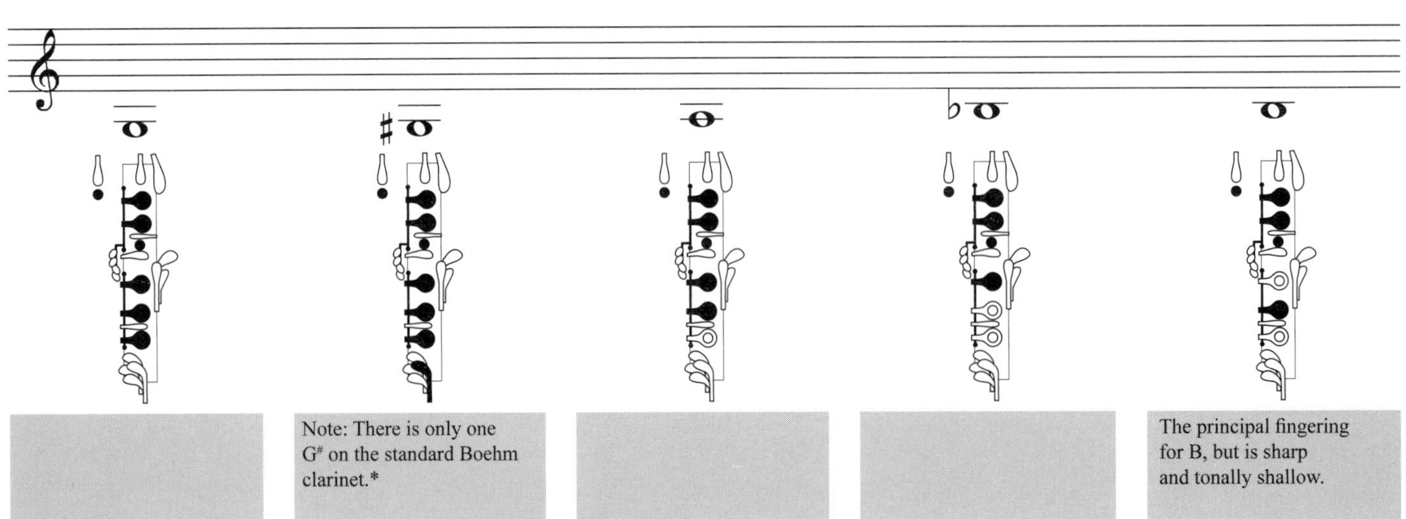

9.

10. Note: There is only one G# on the standard Boehm clarinet.*

11.

12.

13. The principal fingering for B, but is sharp and tonally shallow.

* — See Clarinet Fingering Chart Introduction for a discussion of principal and alternate fingerings.

14 15 16 17 18

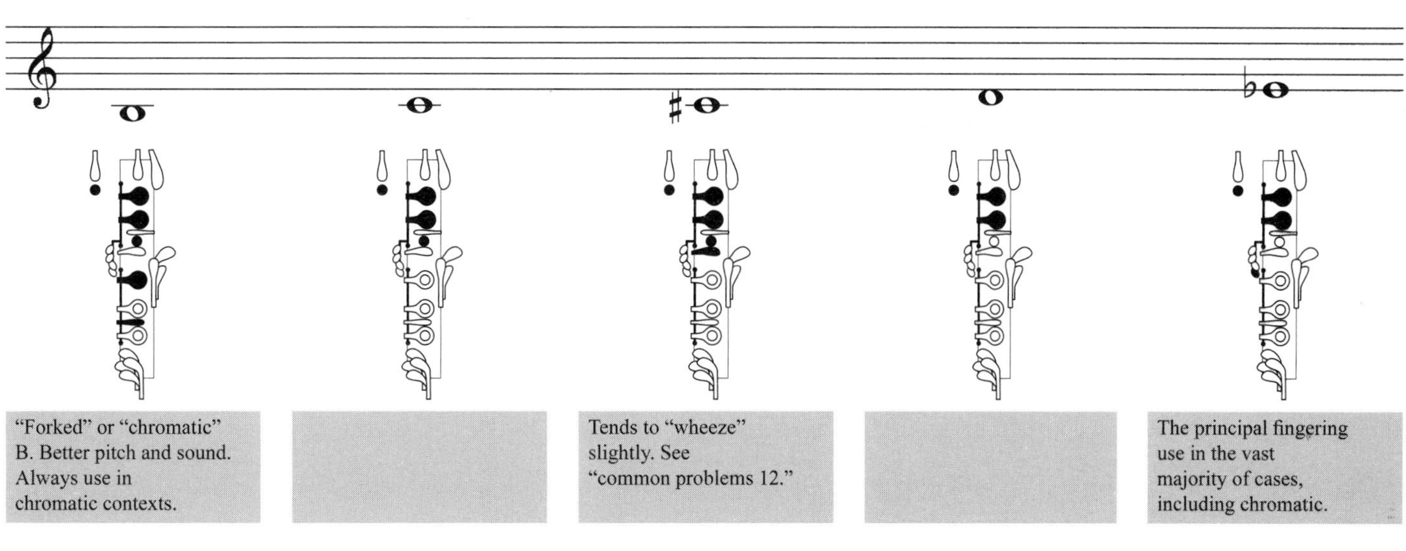

14 “Forked” or “chromatic” B. Better pitch and sound. Always use in chromatic contexts.

15

16 Tends to “wheeze” slightly. See “common problems 12.”

17

18 The principal fingering use in the vast majority of cases, including chromatic.

19 20 21 22 23

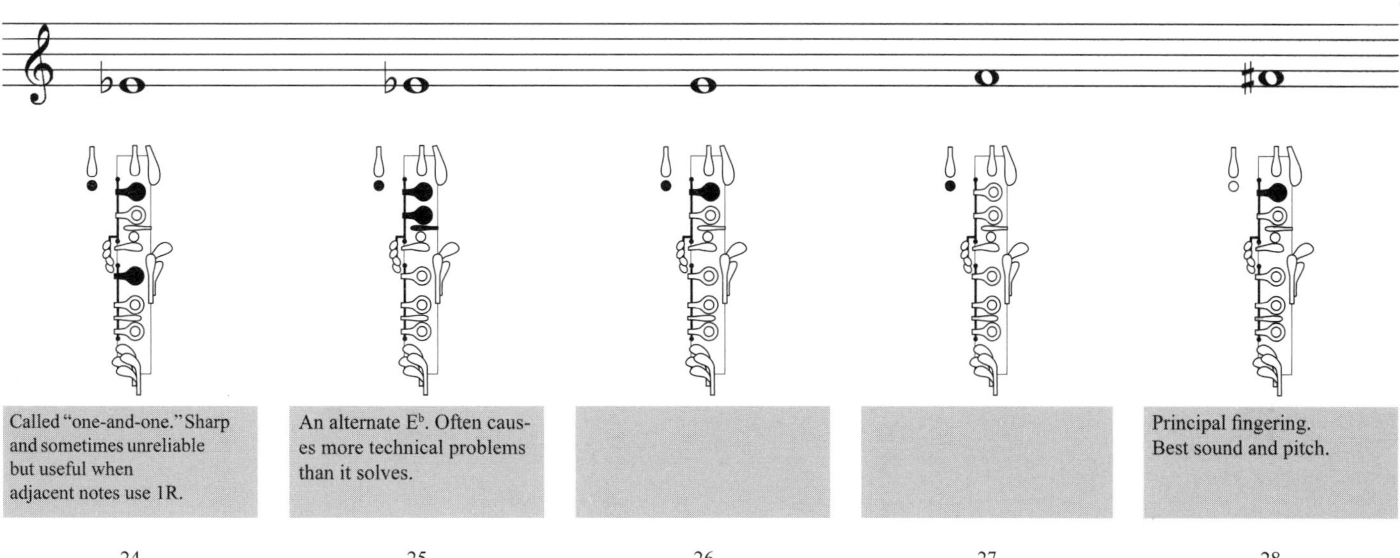

19 Called “one-and-one.” Sharp and sometimes unreliable but useful when adjacent notes use 1R.

20 An alternate E^{b}. Often causes more technical problems than it solves.

21

22

23 Principal fingering. Best sound and pitch.

24 25 26 27 28

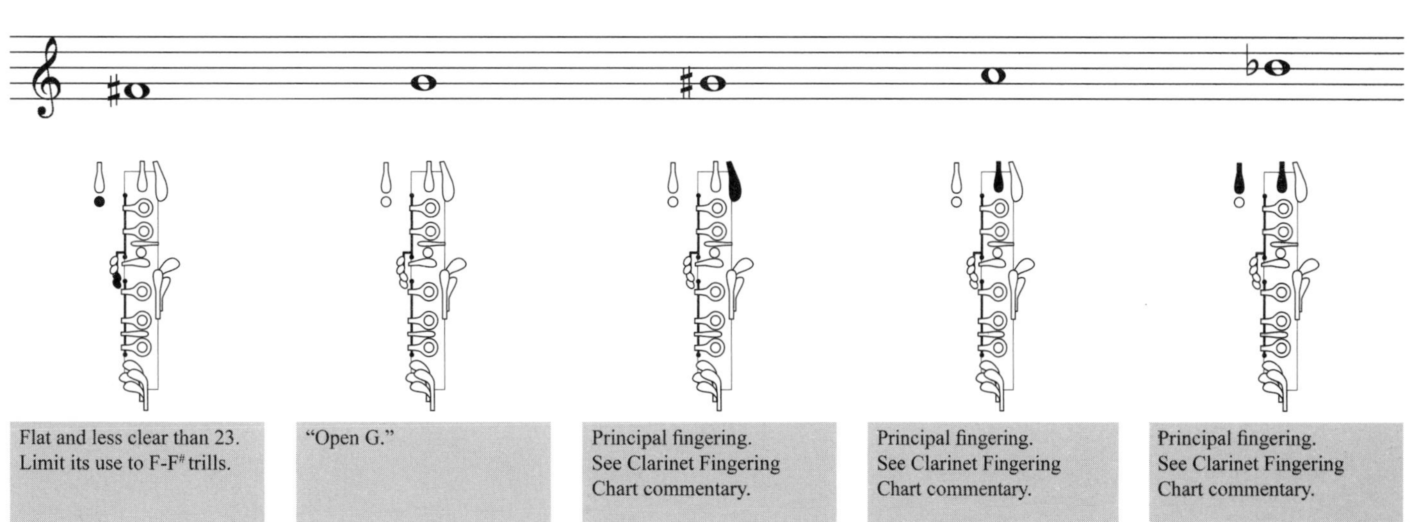

24 Flat and less clear than 23. Limit its use to F-F$^{\#}$ trills.

25 “Open G.”

26 Principal fingering. See Clarinet Fingering Chart commentary.

27 Principal fingering. See Clarinet Fingering Chart commentary.

28 Principal fingering. See Clarinet Fingering Chart commentary.

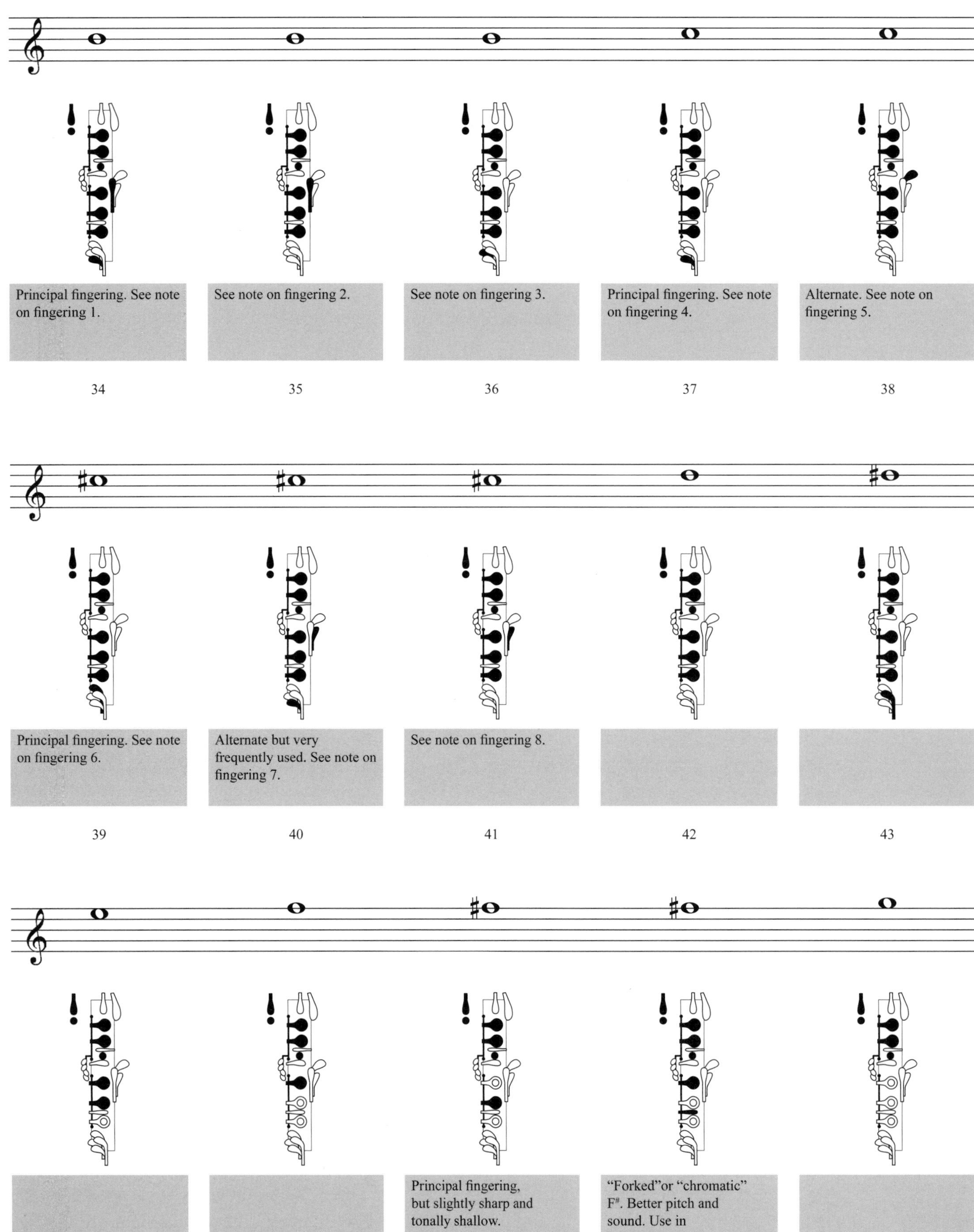
29
30
31
32
33
Principal fingering. See note on fingering 1.
See note on fingering 2.
See note on fingering 3.
Principal fingering. See note on fingering 4.
Alternate. See note on fingering 5.
34
35
36
37
38
Principal fingering. See note on fingering 6.
Alternate but very frequently used. See note on fingering 7.
See note on fingering 8.
39
40
41
42
43
Principal fingering, but slightly sharp and tonally shallow.
"Forked"or "chromatic" F#. Better pitch and sound. Use in chromatic contexts.

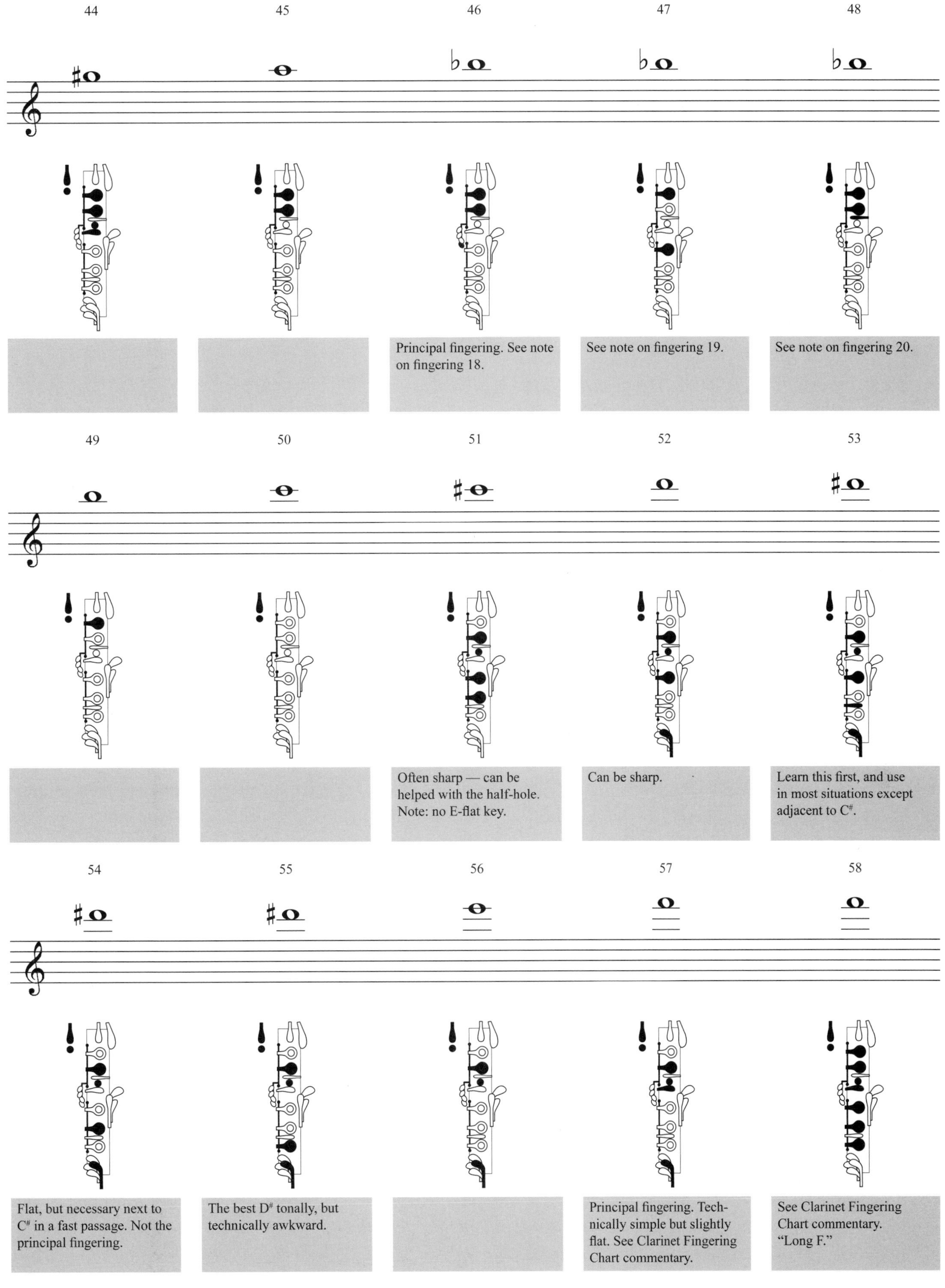
44
45
46
47
48
Principal fingering. See note on fingering 18.
See note on fingering 19.
See note on fingering 20.
49
50
51
52
53
Often sharp — can be helped with the half-hole. Note: no E-flat key.
Can be sharp.
Learn this first, and use in most situations except adjacent to C#.
54
55
56
57
58
Flat, but necessary next to C# in a fast passage. Not the principal fingering.
The best D# tonally, but technically awkward.
Principal fingering. Technically simple but slightly flat. See Clarinet Fingering Chart commentary.
See Clarinet Fingering Chart commentary. "Long F."

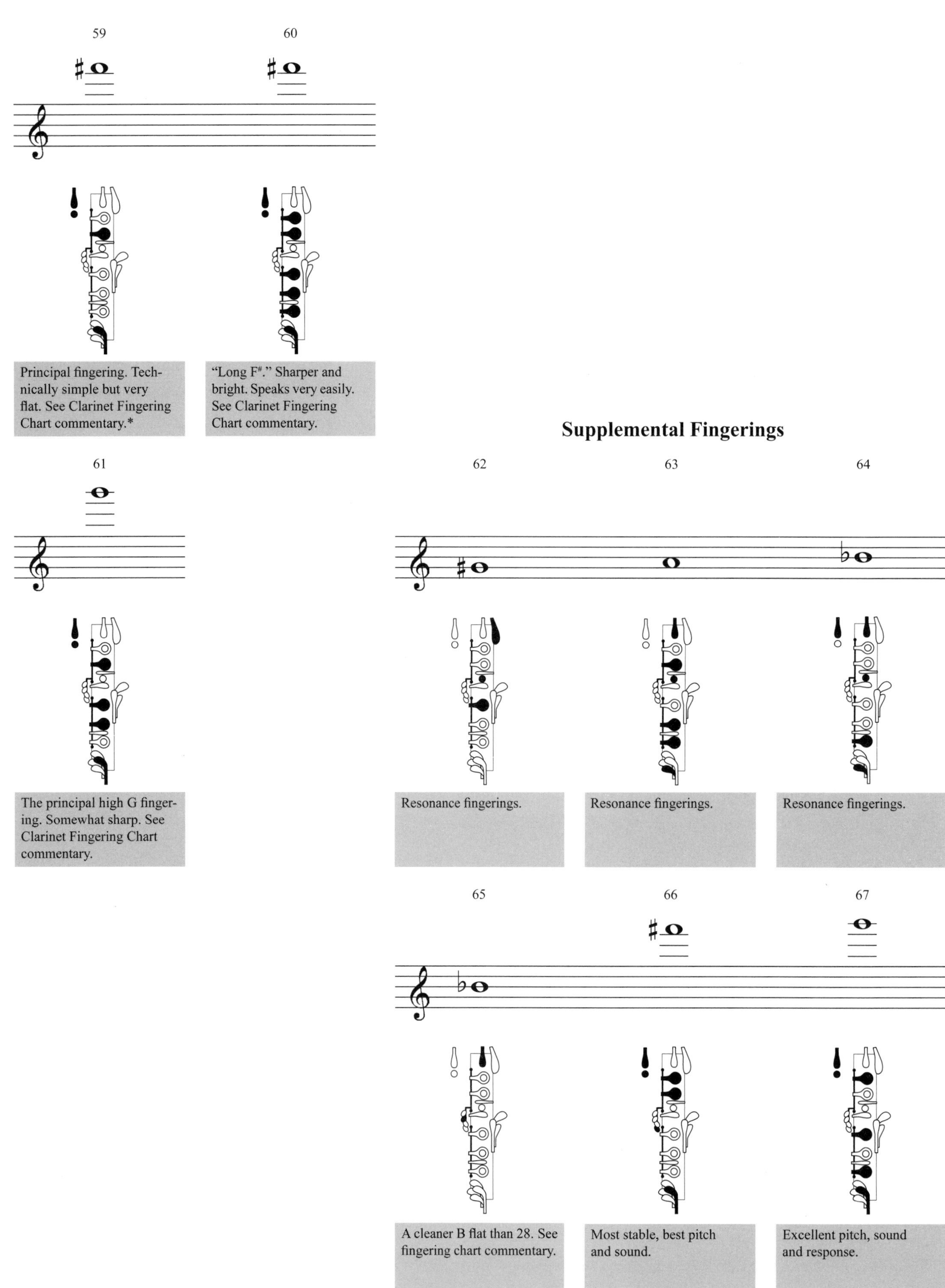

* — Pitch problem improved by adding the sliver key with 3R but not depressing the rings at the same time.

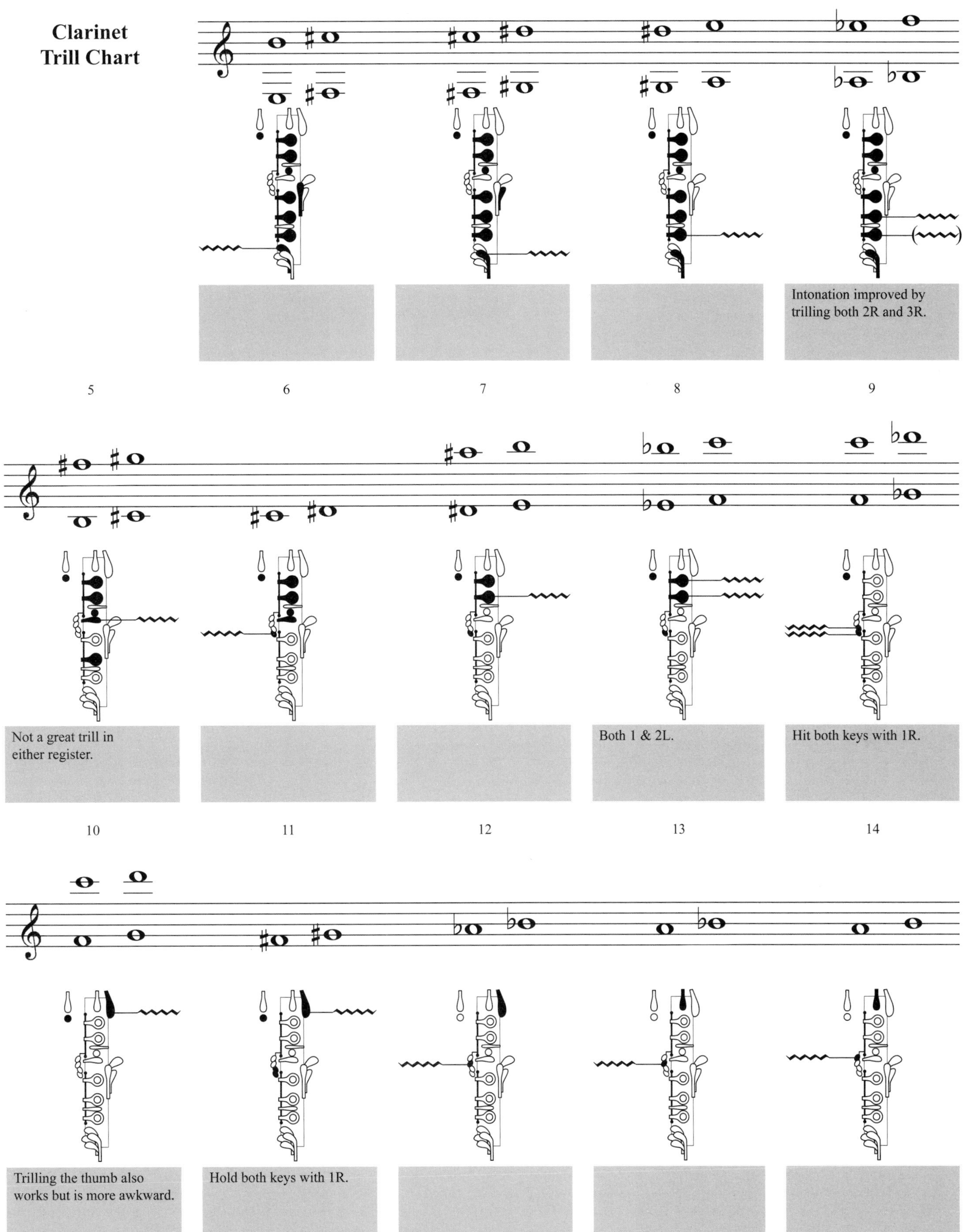

Note: Upper trill is the same fingering as the lower register with the register key added.

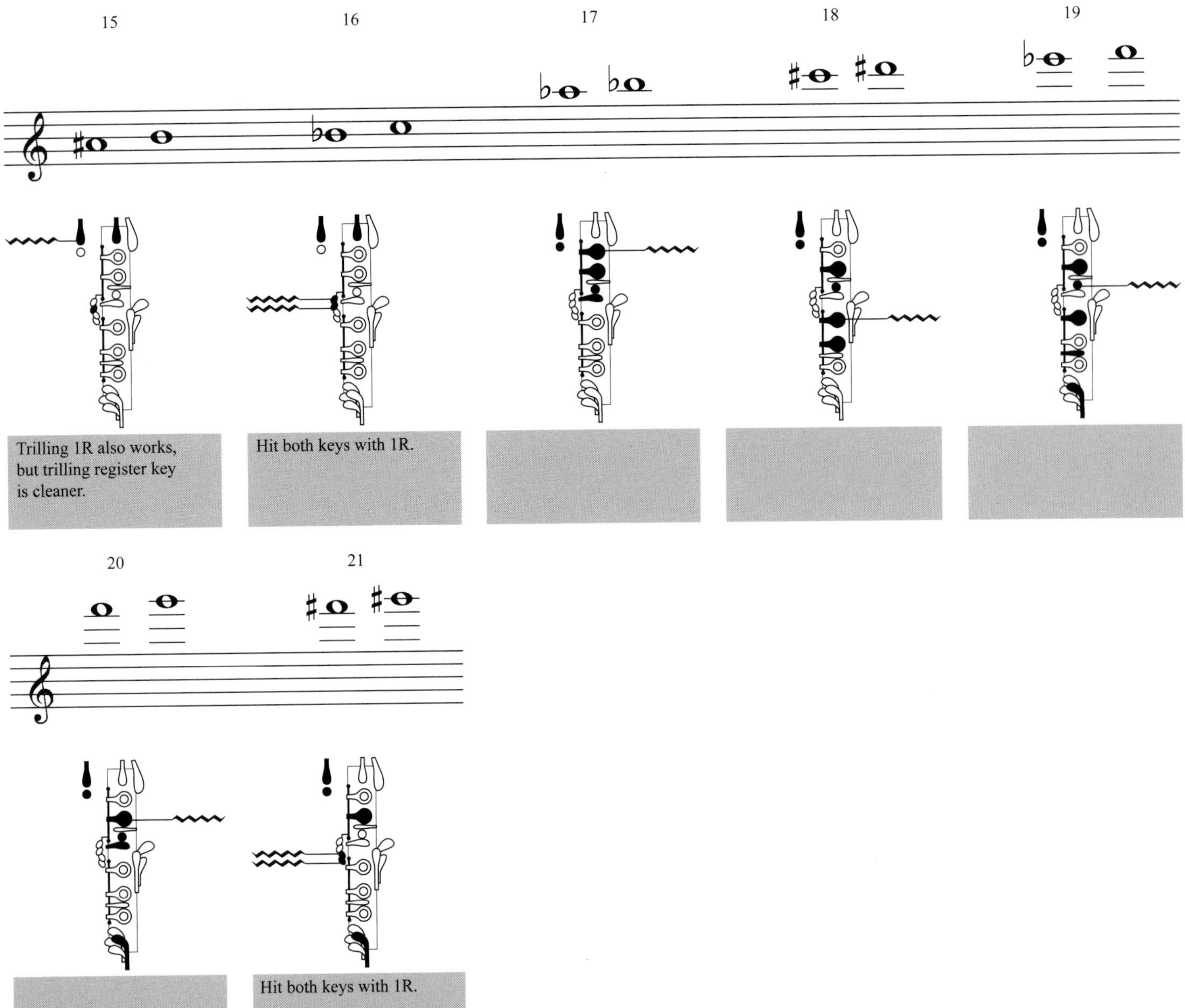
15
16
17
18
19
Trilling 1R also works, but trilling register key is cleaner.
Hit both keys with 1R.
20
21
Hit both keys with 1R.

BASSOON

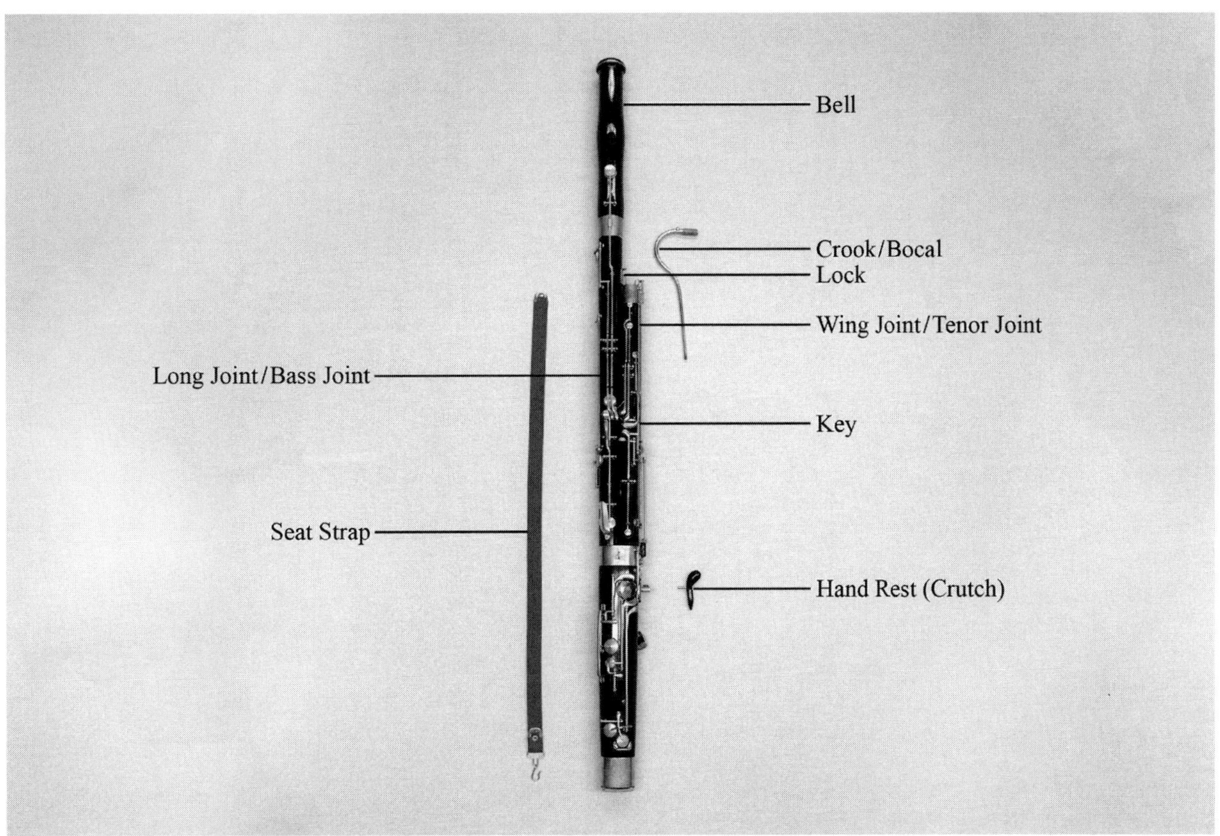

Before You Begin

- Do not use cork grease on string tenons (bassoon tenons are coated with paraffin).
- Do not grab a joint in such a way that keys that are not designed to be depressed directly by the fingers are being depressed or torqued in the twisting process.
- Generally the less side-to-side pressure one puts on the pads, rods and key cups, the longer the instrument will stay in adjustment.
- The bassoon has "bridge keys," which transfer motion from one part of the instrument to another. These are delicate and are easily thrown out of adjustment—be careful to raise them when assembling and do not twist too far.
- It is advisable to assemble with the case in front or beside you on the floor, rather than in your lap.
- The bassoon should be cleaned (swabbed) with the appropriate swab after playing. Get a swab that has some of the cord following the cloth on the end opposite the weight, so that a stuck swab may be "backed out" of the upper joint.
- Even when larger instruments (baritone saxophones, contrabass clarinets, etc.) are nested in the case, they can be thrown out of adjustment by simply jarring the case or setting it down with too much force. Carry and set cases down carefully.

Assembly

1. Place the seat strap across the seat of the chair with the attachment end on the right. It may be helpful to position the strap at a diagonal, with the right side closer to the front of the chair than the left. Sit on the strap.

Seat strap across chair

2. Holding the wing and long joints together with tenons even and raising the bridge key on the wing joint, insert both tenons at once into the butt joint sockets.

Inserting wing and long joints into butt

3. Align the locking mechanism and lock the two joints together. (If there is no locking mechanism, it is advisable to have one added by a repair technician).

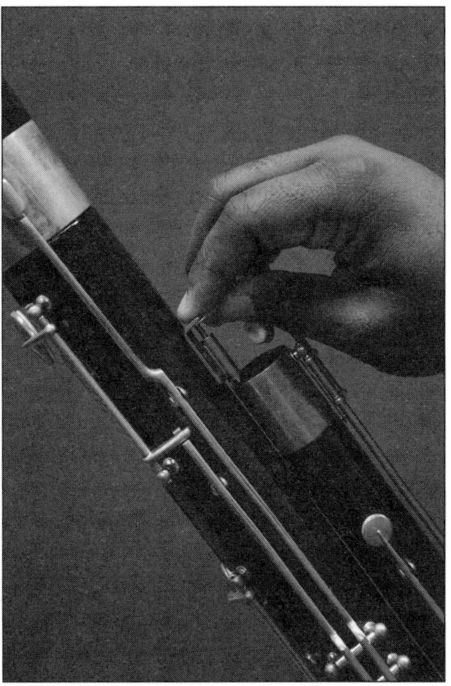

Securing the locking mechanism

4. Raise the bridge key on the bell by closing the pad and carefully twist the bell back and forth onto the long joint, aligning the bridge keys.

Raising bridge key to insert bell

5. Being very careful not to damage the pad on the whisper key, twist the bocal into the wing joint, pushing it down all the way. Position it so that the whisper key pad covers the small hole in the bocal.

Inserting the bocal
into the wing joint

6. Attach the crutch (hand rest) if you intend to use one.

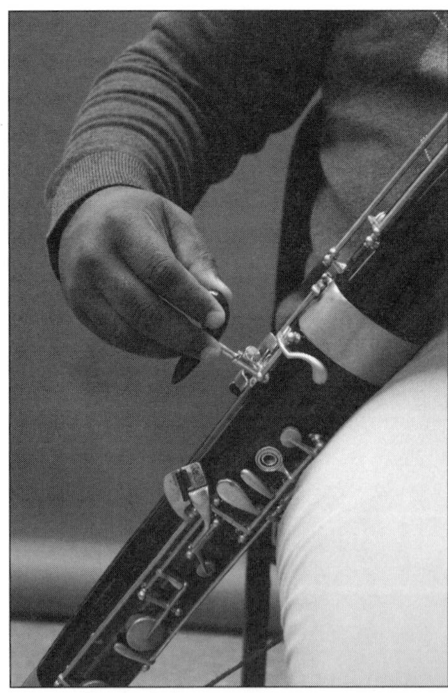

Attaching crutch

7. Attach the strap to the bottom of the butt joint.

Attaching the strap to the butt joint cap

8. Holding the reed in the center over the wires, twist the reed onto the bocal.

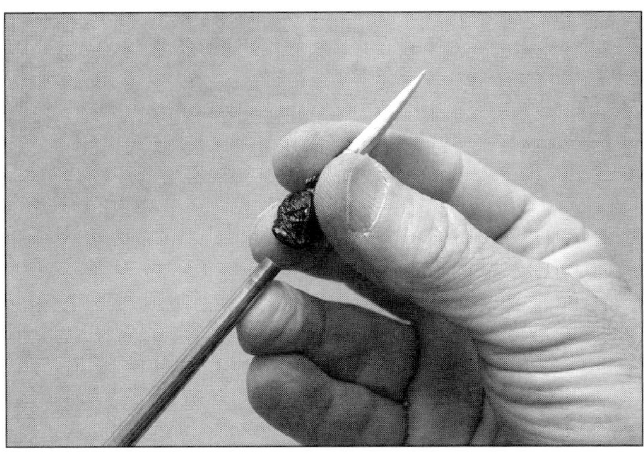

Attaching reed to bocal

■ *Teaching and Learning the First Sounds—Suggested Beginning Steps for Bassoon*

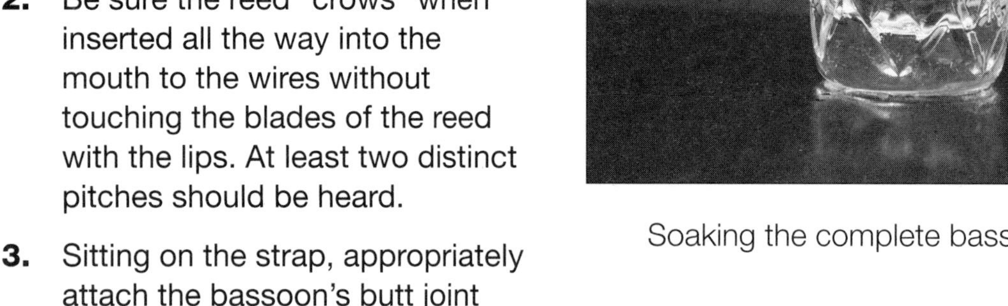

Soaking the complete bassoon reed

1. Soak the reed by submerging it completely in a glass of water. The bottom end needs to be wet and flexible in order to make a complete seal between reed and bocal.
2. Be sure the reed "crows" when inserted all the way into the mouth to the wires without touching the blades of the reed with the lips. At least two distinct pitches should be heard.
3. Sitting on the strap, appropriately attach the bassoon's butt joint to the strap and adjust the strap location so that the tip of the bocal comes to the player's mouth without needing to alter the player's posture.
4. Place the reed snugly on the end of the bocal.
5. Show the student the first fingering. This text begins with "open" F and works its way downward to establish a tone at the outset and retain it as one adds fingers.
6. Placing the tip of the reed on the lower lip just inside the junction between the two types of skin, push the lip in with the reed. Curl the upper lip slightly over the upper teeth and close the lips like a drawstring or a rubber band. The "overbite" should be more pronounced in a bassoon embouchure than in an oboe embouchure.

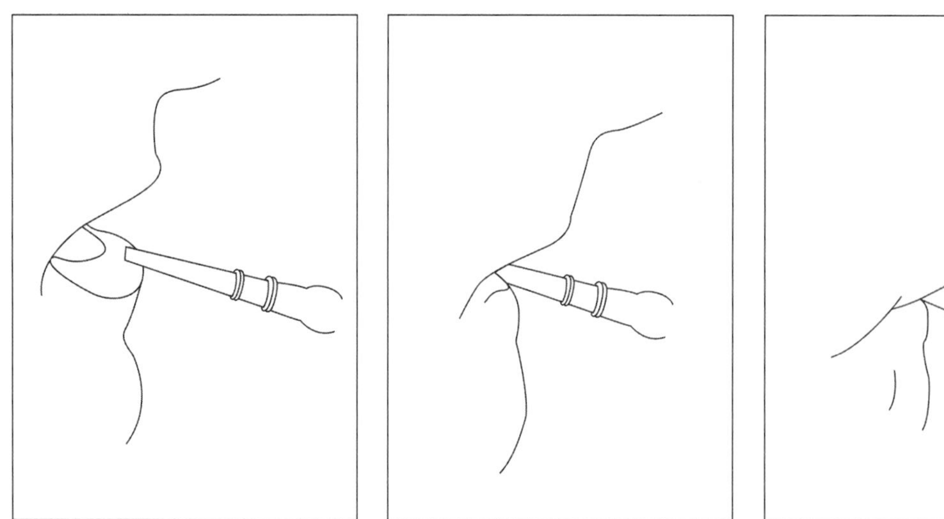

Formation of bassoon embouchure, step by step

Placing the reed on the lip and forming an embouchure

7. Blow. Remember that the lower reed will feel more muffled than the upper reed to produce a warm, characteristic sound. Try to exert equal pressure on both reeds.
8. Check the pitch against a stable pitch source such as a piano or electronic tuner. If the pitch is too low, blow harder rather than either bite or push the reed too far into the mouth. If the first pitch is too high, most likely there is too much of the reed inside the mouth. As with oboe, it may be helpful to have the student drop the pitch by creating more room between the teeth, and then increasing the air pressure to push the pitch back up where it belongs. The tone will invariably improve.
9. Learn to articulate by placing the tip of the tongue on the lower reed and then drawing it back in an "eh" syllable. The syllable (and thus the tongue position) will become more "ee" on higher notes and more "ah" on lower notes.
10. Be sure the bassoon is situated diagonally with the player's body so that the player reads over the top—i.e. with the bassoon to the left of the music—rather than under the bassoon with the instrument held vertically.

■ *Articulation*

The articulation process on the oboe and bassoon are highly similar to each other, making it convenient to think of them in the same way. Only the size of the instrument and reed create the few differences that exist rather naturally.

Begin with the tip of the tongue on the reed, drawing back quickly as though to spit a piece of paper off of the lip. The back of the tongue changes position on the double reeds from a higher, more "eeee" syllable in the upper register to a lower, more "ahhh" syllable in the lower register. As always, the player's ear must govern all decisions about the appropriate tongue position in any given register.

On both double reeds, embouchure pressure on the reed will vary to control the ends of notes. Increasing pressure on the reed will keep the pitch from dropping. For this reason, you will see embouchure movement while articulating, which will be more pronounced with bassoonists on the larger reed than with oboists on the smaller one.

Multiple tonguing on bassoon is possible.

Proper playing position

■ *Common Problems*

1. Too much reed in the mouth, making a very bright, hollow, and often sharp sound and with very poor lower register response.
2. Too little reed in the mouth, though this is less prevalent than no. 1 above. In this case, the upper register may be flat or unattainable.
3. Not forming an embouchure. Remember that the lips are dynamic—standing up by their own strength—and not static or relaxed.
4. Biting or pinching the reed
5. Balancing the instrument with the seat strap improperly adjusted and positioned. The left hand becomes tired or tight very quickly if the weight of the bassoon is held by the left hand rather than being counterbalanced.
6. Holding the instrument vertically and then reading the music under the bassoon, rather than diagonally and reading over the top side.
7. Reaching and covering the holes. If the hands are not large enough, reaching all of the holes will not be possible. A "Short Reach" bassoon may help—this is an instrument with an extended touchpiece over a hole that would otherwise be open, to allow a smaller hand to control the hole.
8. The reed does not fit on the end of the bocal, either causing leakage or not fitting securely.
    - Bocals are sometimes damaged at the reed end, causing them to not be absolutely round. To make matters worse, students (or their parents) might have jammed a pencil or another round object into the end to restore the roundness and the solder seam in the bocal may have been broken.
    - The opening at the bottom end of the reed may not be large enough for the bocal, in which case the opening may be enlarged with a reamer specially made for bassoon reeds.

9. Bent bocal. Usually the result of the student bending the bocal toward the mouth as one would bend a straw. This can cause a tiny leak where the tube crimps, rendering an expensive bocal useless.
10. Improper use of half hole
11. Using wrong fingerings, which "almost" work
12. Not tonguing
13. Whisper key pad not functioning or the pad is missing altogether. The whisper key pad is especially vulnerable since a careless twist of the bocal will shear the pad completely off of the key cup.
14. A "popping" sound when sustaining a note. There is water in the lowest part of the curve in the bocal. Remove the bocal and blow the water out from the large end. Do not "flick" or shake the bocal as the chance of hitting some object and bending the narrow end causing the reed to not fit is large.

■ *Tuning*

Aside from temperature, the two things that most affect the overall pitch of the bassoon are the bocal and the reed. The number on a bocal tells its length, and other letters indicate factors about the interior shape or dimension. Generally the no. 2 bocal is the standard bocal, but the specific length for a no. 2 will vary from one company to another. A lower number is shorter and a higher number is longer, so a no. 1 bocal will play sharper and a no. 3 will play flatter than a no. 2 *of the same maker.*

Bassoon reeds tend to be less standardized than oboe reeds, so one could find considerable variation in the length of a bassoon reed and in the distance that a bassoon reed slides onto the bocal. Reaming the bottom end of a bassoon reed to enlarge the hole into which the bocal slides can shorten the sounding length slightly, though the larger differences are found on the blade end of the reed. The scrape style of the reed can also affect the tuning of the instrument.

With one of the largest numbers of fingering options of all woodwind instruments, bassoonists often adapt their fingering vocabularies to their individual instruments. Certain problems are present on virtually all bassoons—especially fourth-line F# and fourth-space G-natural, for which the natural sharpness must be compensated. The degree to which 1L opens or closes the half-hole is an important variable, as is the possibility of adding additional keys or fingers to some notes. Most of these decisions are likely to be beyond the expertise of one who has not invested considerable time studying the instrument himself or herself.

■ *Bassoon Fingering Chart Introduction*

Fingerings for bassoon are the most numerous and the least standardized of all of the woodwinds. Even the number and locations of keys can vary from bassoon to bassoon, and often a fingering which works well on one bassoon does not work well on another—especially true on student bassoons. Thus to a certain extent, each bassoonist eventually develops his or her own fingering vocabulary.

With so many possible fingerings, in the following fingering charts, no attempt is made to provide a comprehensive list. These are standard fingerings that are most likely to work on most bassoons. The serious bassoonist should look elsewhere—on the internet or in Cooper and Toplansky's monumental *Essentials of Bassoon Technique* (Union, NJ: Howard Toplansky, 1968).

As with all woodwinds, *the Principal fingering is the one which falls under the hand* without shifting the hand's position, and the alternate is the one for which the hand shifts out of position. Most of these alternate fingerings fall within the right hand, or over the butt joint, with the principle of alternation between the front and back of the bassoon, similar to the that of alternation between the right and left on clarinet and oboe.

■ *Bassoon Fingering Chart Commentary*

5, 6, 7. The Whisper Key is optional because the E key (Pancake key) holds the whisper key closed. However, unless the passage descends to notes lower than D, leave the thumb on the whisper key.

In instances where the Whisper Key needs to stay down but the left thumb is actively involved in complicated lower register passage work, bassoons are provided with a Whisper Key lock, which holds the key in the closed position, allowing the left thumb to move freely. Whisper Key locks are found in various locations on different bassoons.

7. The low D-flat key is optional—it lowers the pitch and broadens the tone.

9–16. The principal fingerings for F# (9), G# (12) and A# (15) are designed so that no lateral motion of any finger is necessary. So in an F# major scale, the sequence of fingerings is back-front-back: low F# with the thumb, G# with 4R, and A# with the thumb again above the pancake key. Just as on clarinet and oboe*, the principal fingering is the one which lies under the hand.*

The alternate fingerings 10 and 13 exist so that the player may avoid moving laterally from one key to another. So if one skips from F# to A#, one uses F# (10) rather than 9, making a sequence from back to front with no lateral motion. (Using the other alternates would not avoid lateral motion in this case). The bassoon mechanism is provided with roller keys for both F and G#, so in this case unavoidable lateral motion is facilitated by the mechanism.

F# in the staff is a sharp note on bassoon—more so with the back fingering (24) than on the front (25). On the other hand, the best lower register F# is the thumb fingering.

18, 32. The left thumb hits the low D key near the palm of the hand, while the tip of the thumb depresses the C# key and (on fingering 18) the whisper key. In the upper register, adding the F# key may enhance the tone.

23-27. Like oboe, there are three notes just above the "break" on bassoon that require the index finger of the left hand (L1) to move down the bassoon and expose part of the open hole. As with oboe and clarinet, this is referred to as the "half hole," though the ideal situation is that perhaps 2/3 of the hole would be exposed for F#, 1/2 for G and perhaps only 1/3 for A-flat. Regardless of the amount of the hole exposed, the whisper key is always down, only opening on A-natural (28) and above, when the first finger hole is covered completely.

Fingerings 28-32 may need the high a or high c key, depending on the bassoon. (See "Flicking," page 114). On some student bassoons, it is very common to use one or the other of these keys all the time—not merely as a "flick."

36&37. Finger 1R may be left off of these fingerings for larger slurs to this E-flat and E.

40&41. Whisper key may be omitted if these notes precede high A and B-flat. Both of these notes are helped by adding the R thumb B-flat key and either 2R or 1R.

The higher one plays on the bassoon, the more options there are for fingerings and in fact, Cooper and Toplansky's *Essentials of Bassoon Technique* provides a complete page of blank fingering schematics after each multi-page discussion of each individual note.

Bassoon Fingering Chart

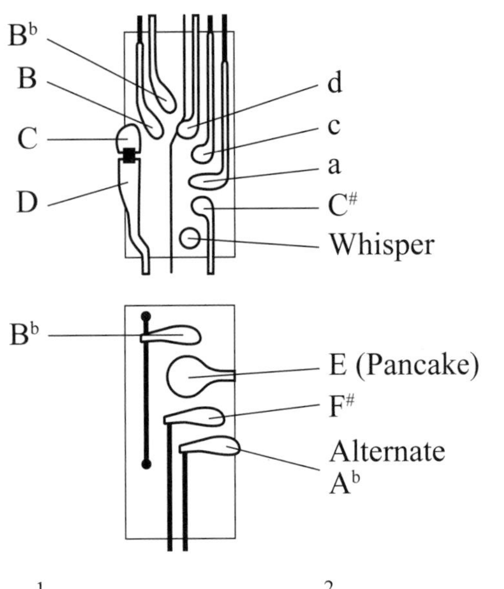

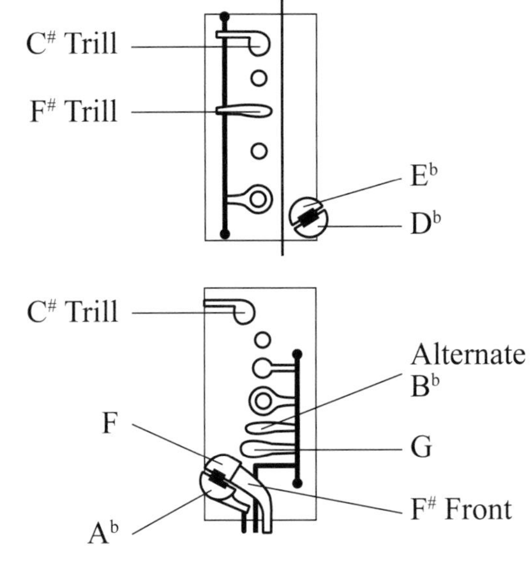

1 2 3 4 5

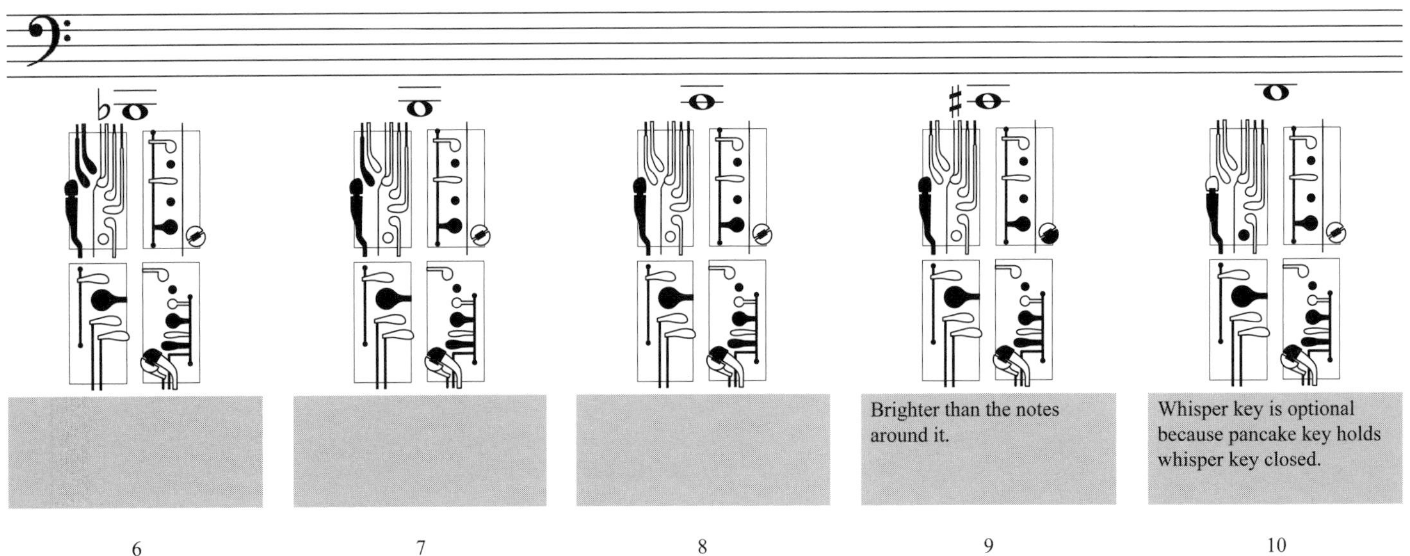

6 7 8 9 10

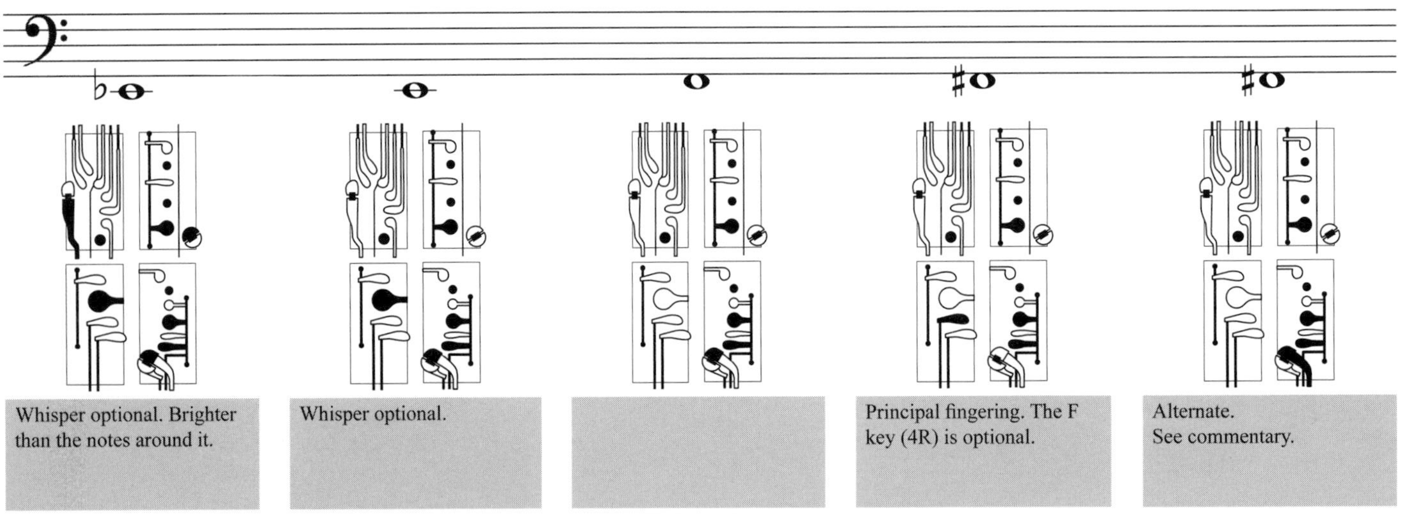

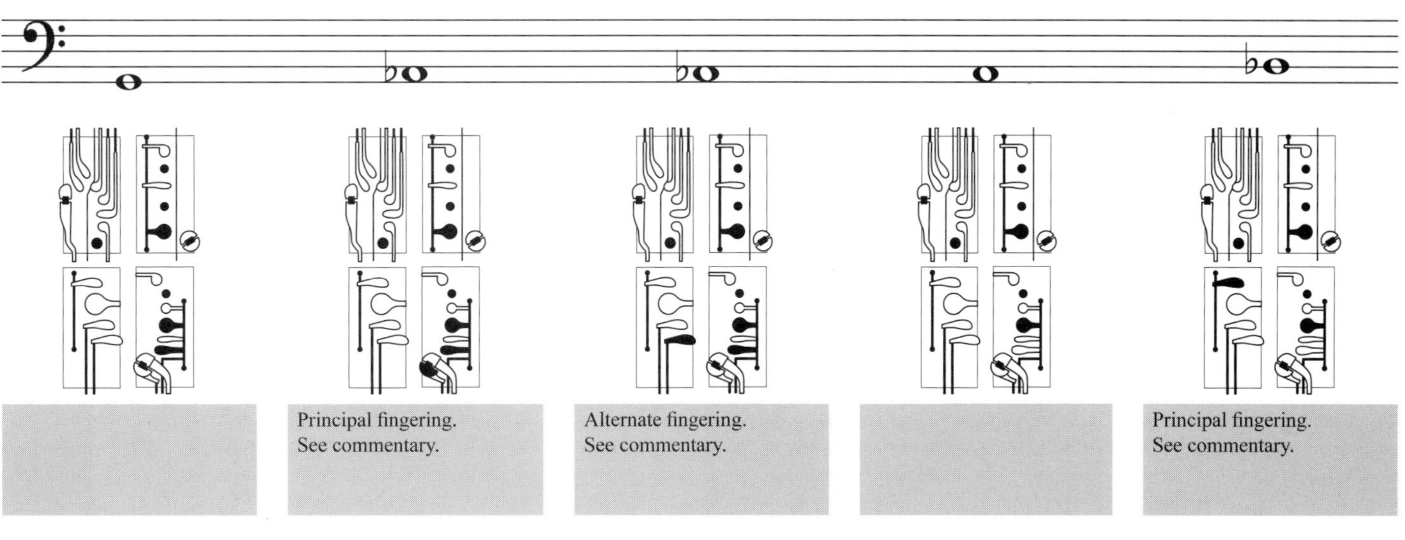

11	12	13	14	15
	Principal fingering. See commentary.	Alternate fingering. See commentary.		Principal fingering. See commentary.

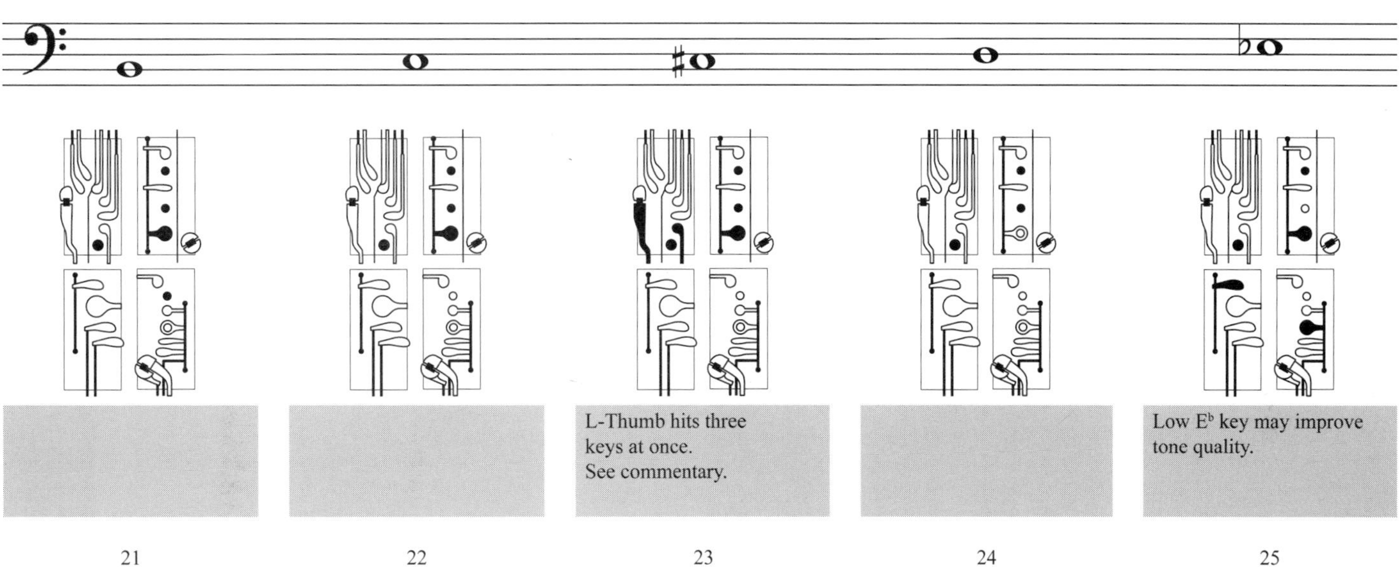

16	17	18	19	20
		L-Thumb hits three keys at once. See commentary.		Low E^{b} key may improve tone quality.

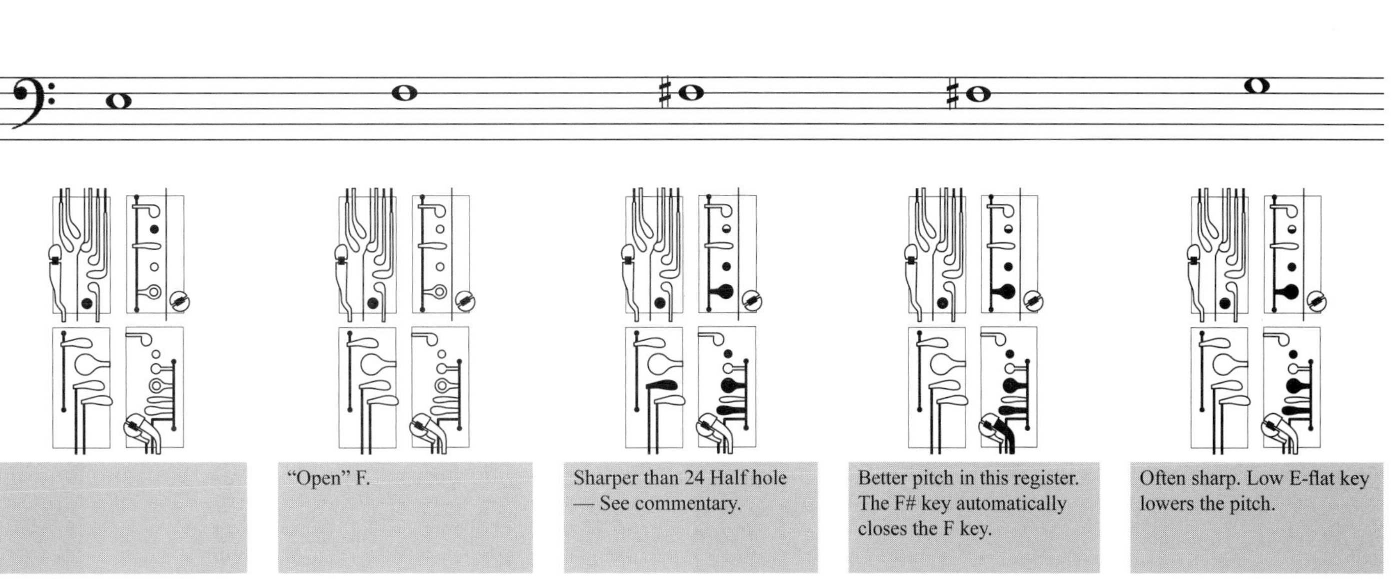

21	22	23	24	25
	"Open" F.	Sharper than 24 Half hole — See commentary.	Better pitch in this register. The F# key automatically closes the F key.	Often sharp. Low E-flat key lowers the pitch.

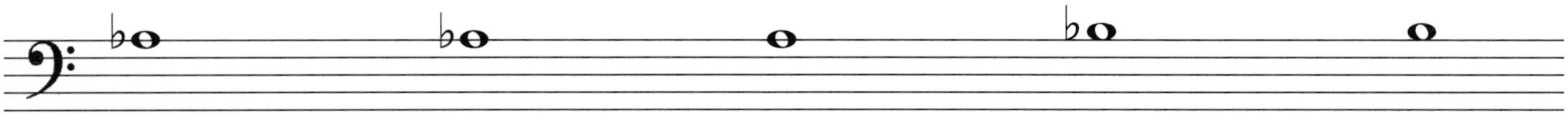

26

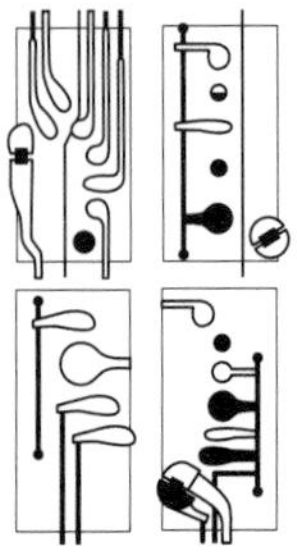

Principal fingering.

27

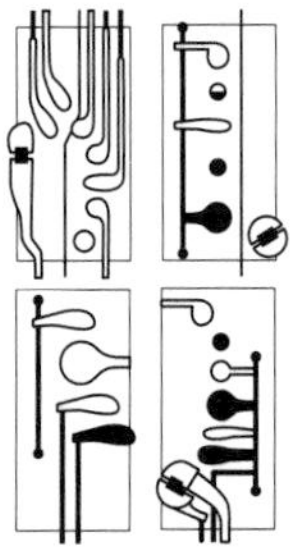

Alternate fingering.

28

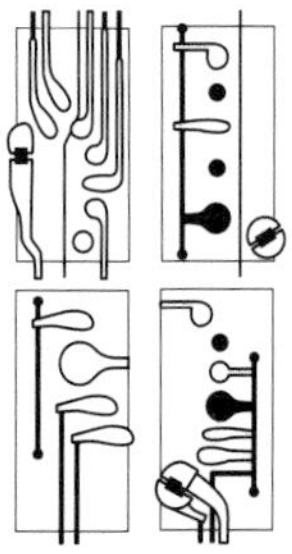

29

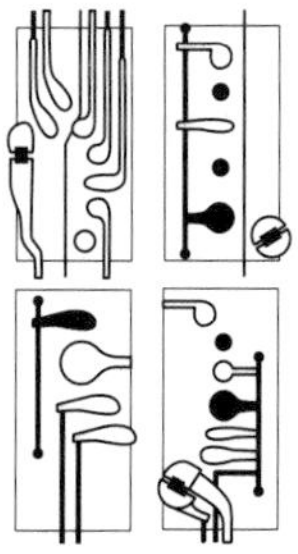

30

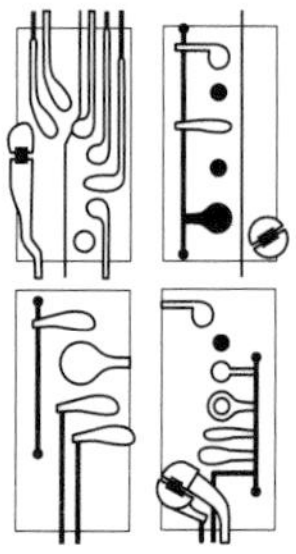

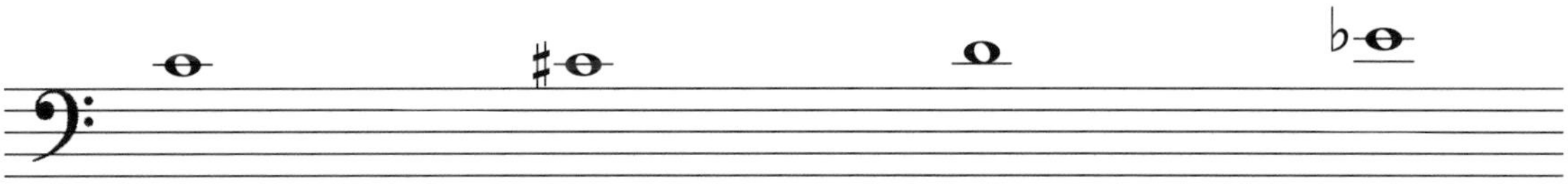

31

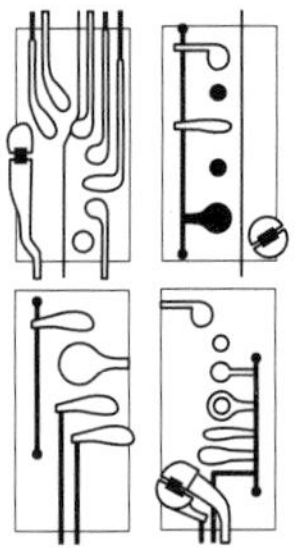

32

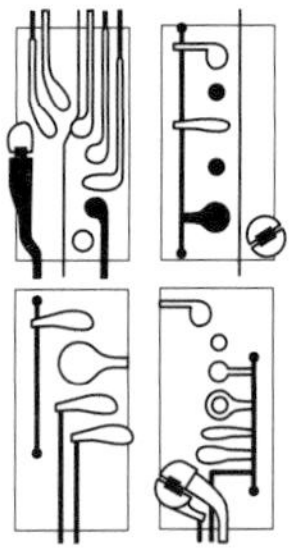

L Thumb hits two keys at once. See commentary.

33

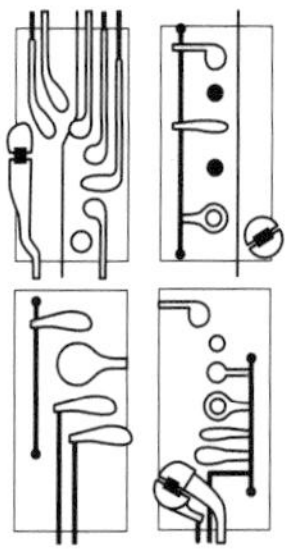

34

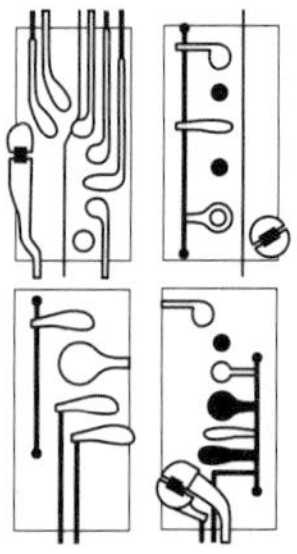

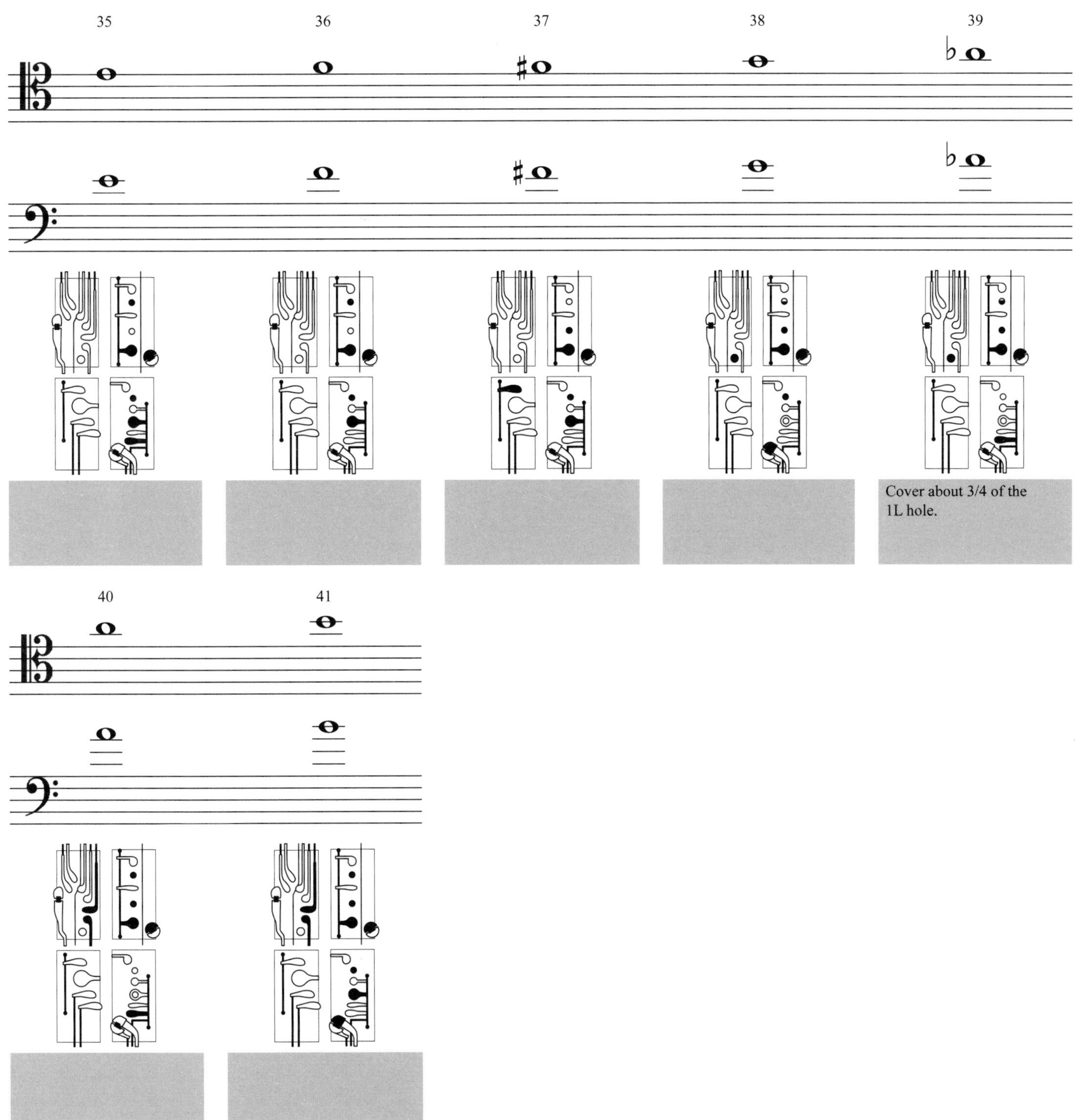
35
36
37
38
39
Cover about 3/4 of the 1L hole.
40
41

Bassoon Trill Chart

1 2 3 4

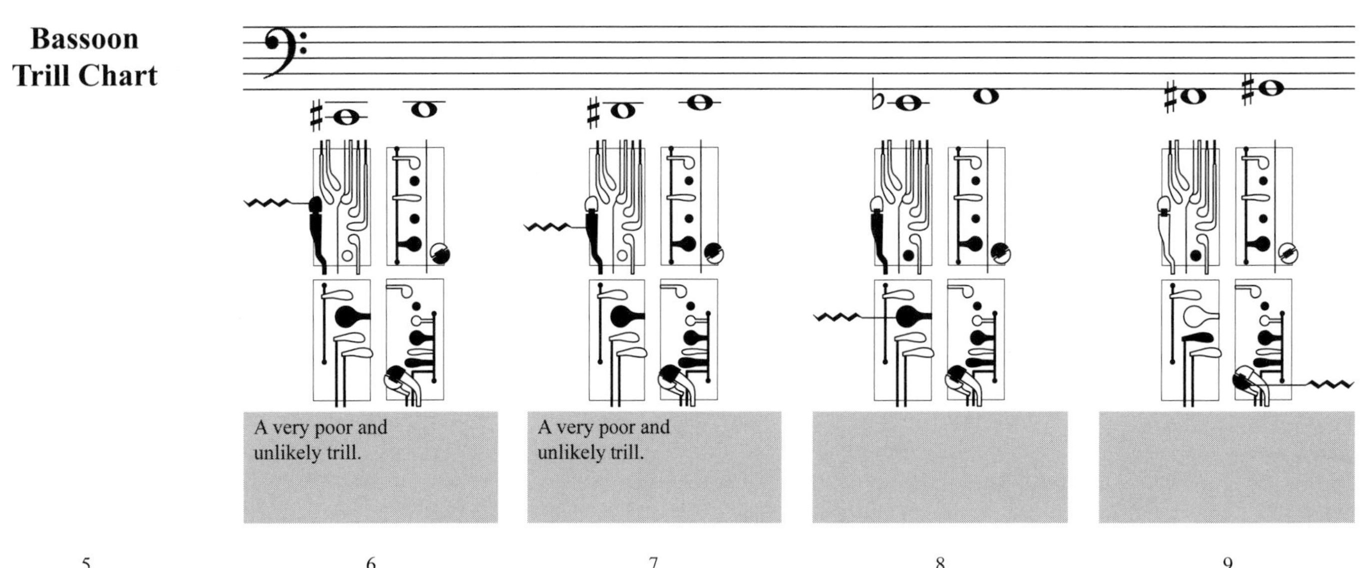

5 6 7 8 9

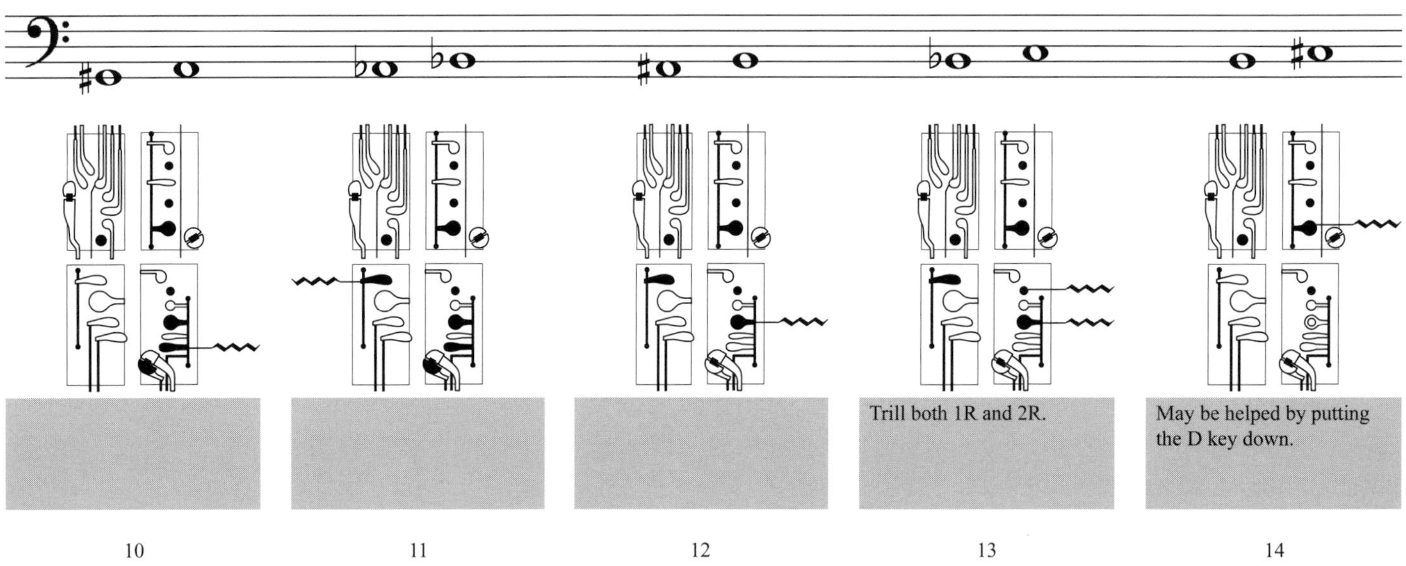

10 11 12 13 14

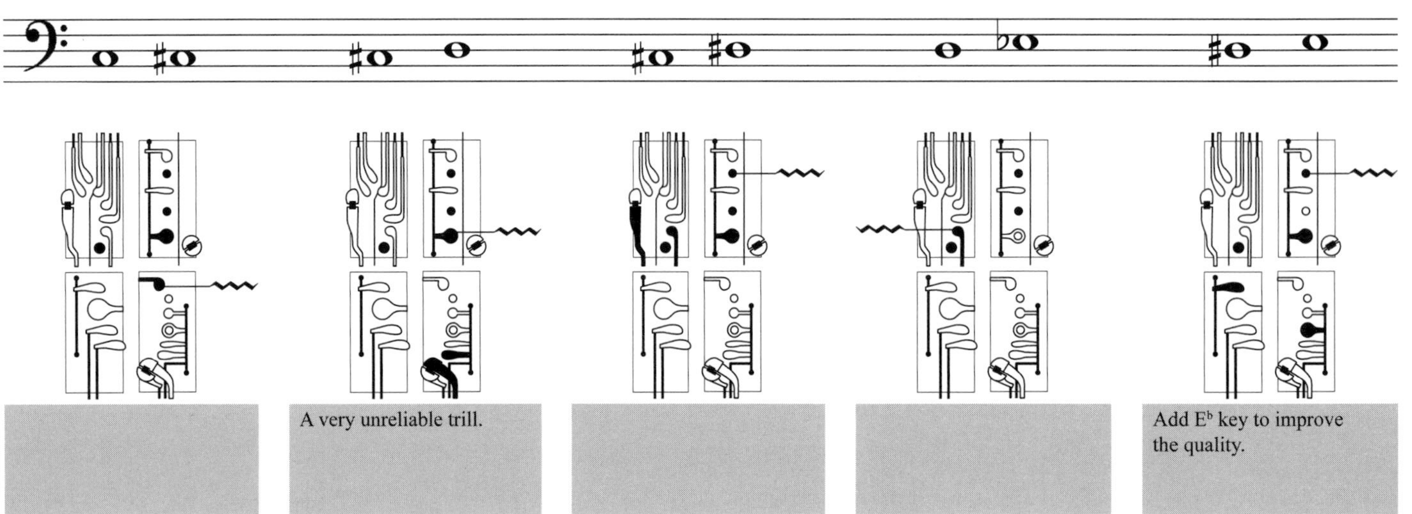

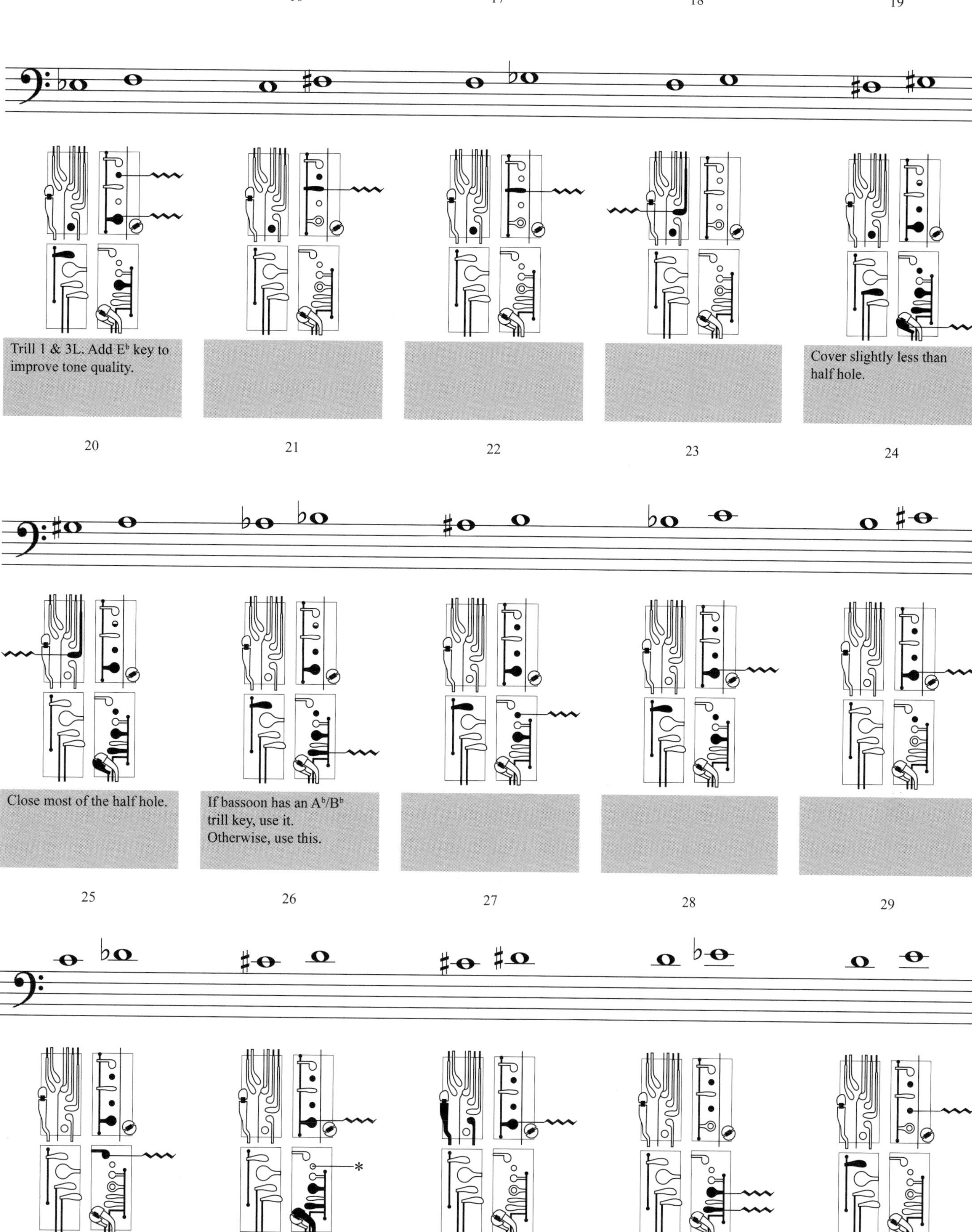
15
16
17
18
19
Trill 1 & 3L. Add E♭ key to improve tone quality.
Cover slightly less than half hole.
20
21
22
23
24
Close most of the half hole.
If bassoon has an A♭/B♭ trill key, use it. Otherwise, use this.
25
26
27
28
29
Start with 1R open and close it after the trill begins.
Trill either 2R or 2 and 3R.
*

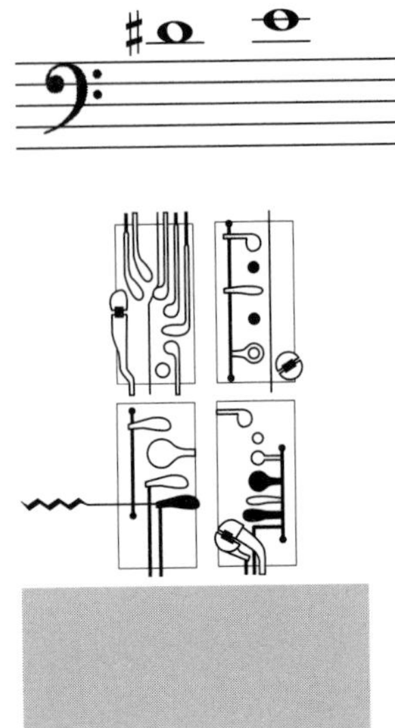

Saxophone

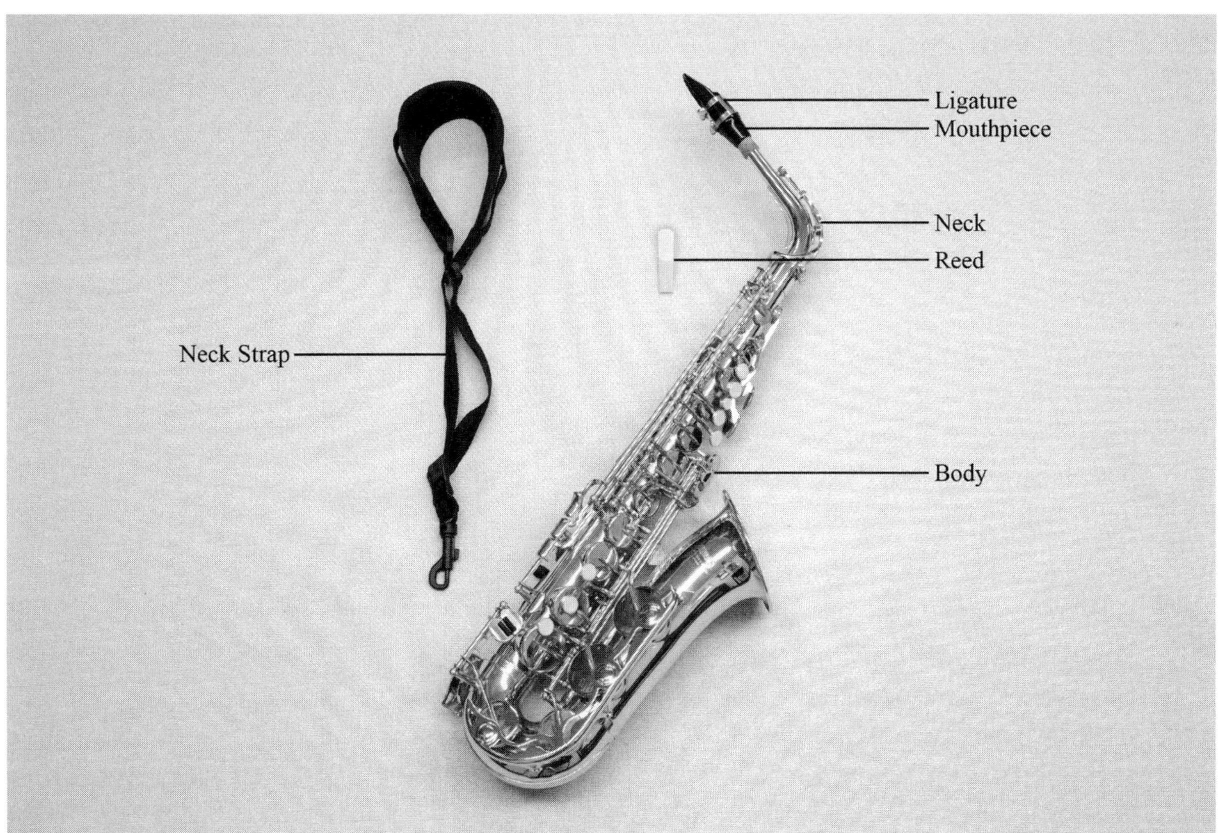

Before You Begin

- Be sure the neck cork is lightly lubricated with cork grease.
- Do not use cork grease on the metal tenon on the bottom of the neck.
- Lift the saxophone by the bell and not by the narrow upper end of the instrument over the keys.
- Do not grab a joint in such a way that keys that are not designed to be depressed directly by the fingers are being depressed or torqued.
- Generally the less side-to-side pressure one puts on the pads, rods and keys, the longer the instrument will stay in adjustment.
- It is advisable to work with the case in front or beside you on the floor, rather than in your lap.
- Saxophones should be cleaned (swabbed) with a saxophone swab after playing.
- Even when larger instruments are nested in their cases, they can be thrown out of adjustment by simply jarring the case or setting it down with too much force. Carry and set cases down carefully.
- Do not run a swab through a hard rubber mouthpiece. Gently clean it with a separate cloth.
- Do not over-tighten a ligature. A drop of oil on the threads of ligature screws considerably prolongs their useful lives.

Assembly

1. Soak the reed by placing it into your mouth or into a small container of water. It is best to soak the whole reed—not just the thin part.
2. Place the neck strap over your head so that it is in position to support the saxophone.
3. Grasping the body of the saxophone by the bell, remove the instrument from the case. Attach the neck strap to the saxophone.
4. Grasping the neck in such a way as to lift the bridge mechanism, gently twist it all the way onto the body of the instrument and tighten the thumb screw that secures the neck in its place. (Baritone saxophone does not have a bridge key on the neck.)

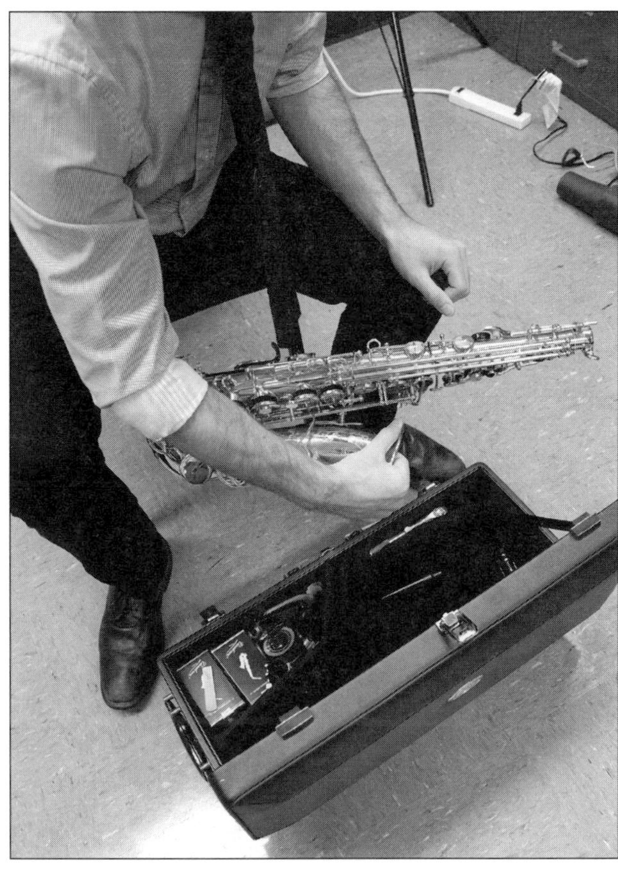

Removing saxophone from case by grasping bell

Raising bridge key to insert neck

5. Grasping the mouthpiece by the fat, lower part, gently twist the mouthpiece *directly onto* the neck, supporting the neck with the other hand so that the neck does not bend downward. Leave the flat side so that the bottom lip will be in contact with it.

6. Carefully slide the ligature over the beak of the mouthpiece, being careful not to scratch the mouthpiece. Notice that the ligature only fits one direction and not the other. Do not pull the neck toward you.

7. Pushing the ligature upwards to create a space between it and the flat side of the mouthpiece, slide the blunt end of the reed under the ligature, matching flat side of the reed to the flat side of the mouthpiece.

8. Maneuvering the reed by the sides and not by the tip, adjust the reed so that the tip of the reed is at exactly the same height as the tip of the mouthpiece. You can judge this by having your line of sight at a perpendicular to the saxophone. Gently tighten the ligature.

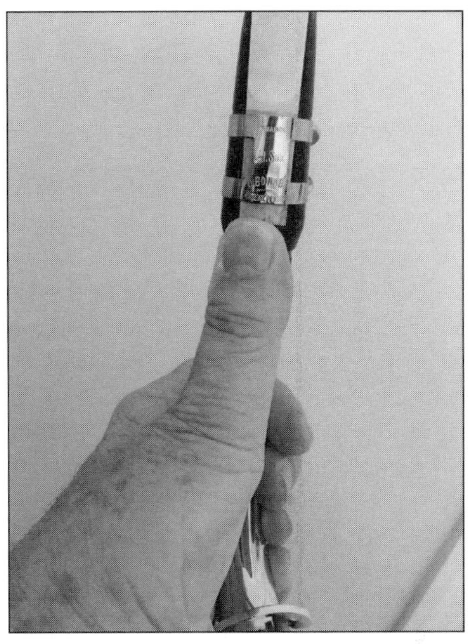

Supporting the neck while adjusting reed and mouthpiece

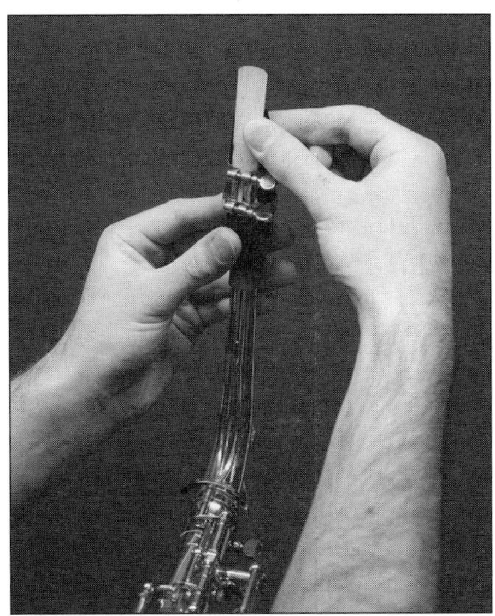

Inserting the reed by the heel, and adjusting the reed on the mouthpiece

Teaching and Learning the First Sounds—Suggested Beginning Steps for Saxophone

The saxophone produces a sound (or a noise) without a correct embouchure so easily that both teacher and student are at times tempted to accept the first thing that comes out of the instrument as success while the other instruments are struggling. If this is the case, the saxophonist will have an uncontrolled sound and will "honk" in the lowest register especially. Thus it is vital to teach an embouchure which correctly uses the consistent tension of the lower lip and the stability of the facial muscles.

1. Attach the neck strap to the instrument. Adjust the strap so that the mouthpiece comes comfortably into the mouth without causing the player's head position to be altered.
2. Show the student the first fingering. In this text the first note is low "A."
3. Place the top teeth on the mouthpiece, fold the lower lip over the lower teeth. Firm the lower lip as though to say "FFFFooooo." Close the lips on the mouthpiece like a drawstring. Touch the tip of the reed with the area just above the tip of the tongue. As you begin to blow, draw the tongue away from the reed as though to say "taaa." Remember that the facial muscles themselves stay firm, as a body builder would freeze in a flexed position for the camera.

Embouchure and playing position views

Articulation

The angle of the tongue's approach to the reed on saxophone is different from the clarinet because of the more horizontal angle at which the saxophone approaches the mouth. Most saxophonists touch the tip of the reed with the tongue somewhere above the tip—on the top flesh of the tongue. Because the ideal sound of a saxophone is less "pointed" than that of clarinet, the back of the tongue's function in focusing the sound is of somewhat less concern.

Common Problems

1. Complete lack of embouchure. Since it is so easy to make a noise on the saxophone by simply blowing, students may accept the sound that they are making as "success." This forces the student to accept not only any sound that emits, but also any pitch that comes out, and without the lower lip being actively engaged, eventually developing a vibrato is out of the question.
   - The lower lip must stand up by itself. Not doing so is the most common embouchure mistake.
   - "Blasting" lower notes is a strong indicator of this problem.
2. Low notes do not "speak." Low notes on conical woodwinds are naturally more difficult to control than those higher in the range. If the embouchure is actively engaged, there may a leak somewhere above the highest open hole. Especially suspect is the articulated G#, which is easily adjusted with a set screw located immediately on top of the pad that moves when the G# key is manipulated. Both pads must contact the instrument at the same time.

   Also helpful—especially on alto—dropping a small obstruction such as a cork grease box or a small cork into the bell often makes lowest notes speak more easily.
3. Strap not adjusted incorrectly, so that the student needs to "duck" downward or stretch upward to reach the mouthpiece. The weight of the instrument should be on the strap.
4. Keys caught in clothing.
5. Poor mouthpiece or an old instrument (often a hand-me-down) which is badly out of adjustment. The stock plastic mouthpiece that comes with a new instrument generally falls into this category.
6. Not having a classical saxophone sound in the "mind's ear."
7. Tonguing against the roof of the mouth. When a student does this, one hears a small explosion inside the mouth considerably before the note speaks. To solve the problem, have the student place the tongue directly on the reed and blow, and then release the tongue after the air stream has begun.

Tuning

Dynamic differences affect saxophone pitch similarly to clarinet—softer is sharper and louder is flatter. The saxophone is tuned by adjusting the location of the mouthpiece on the neck. Teachers sometimes draw a line on a neck cork made with a ball-point pen, which approximately locates the position where the instrument plays in tune most conveniently. Such a line should only be considered to be a starting point or its presence can give the student a false sense of security. It does, however, assure that the instrument will not be assembled in a way that would make it extremely flat or sharp.

Different saxophone mouthpieces will affect intonation differently—some playing generally higher or lower, and others rendering the short fingerings (ones with few fingers down) flat to the long fingerings (ones with more fingers down). Thus, if one has the option of trying several mouthpieces before buying, taking a tuner along is enormously helpful. There are only a few mouthpieces that dominate the classical saxophone market and pitch peculiarities on these top-line mouthpieces are rare. There is much more variety in the jazz mouthpiece market, and so there is greater variability of intonation tendencies one from another.

Certain notes—fourth-line D and D# especially—are naturally sharp on saxophones. See the Fingering Chart and Commentary sections that follow in this text. "Dropping the jaw" is the common advice to adjust for this. Remember also that key opening is critical, especially on the high notes played with palm keys and the lowest notes. On many saxophones, the felt bumpers that control the opening distance of the very lowest pads are adjustable by simply turning the screw upon which they are mounted clockwise or counterclockwise, and if striker corks have fallen off, the pitch of those notes is affected.

Soprano saxophones are available in curved and straight models. In general, the challenges of playing a straight model in tune, while formidable, are less than those of playing the curved instrument.

■ *Saxophone Fingering Chart Introduction*

The basic range of the saxophone is almost identical to that of the oboe, and the fingering patterns are the least complicated of all the woodwinds. Thus, a glance at the fingering chart reveals that there tends to be only one fingering for most notes from low B-flat to high F (or F# if an F# key is present). This can lead to the mindset that there only needs to be one fingering for *all* notes, resulting in some annoying technical handicaps. The most limiting common mistake is the use of only one fingering for the middle and upper B-flats, where the student uses "one-and-one" (fingering 15) or the "bis" key (fingering 16) to the exclusion of others. Otherwise, there are very few complications in comparison to the other woodwinds until one crosses into the altissimo register (above high F or F#).

■ *Saxophone Fingering Chart Commentary*

The following explains the few bits of technical confusion that do exist. Both upper and lower register fingerings are discussed in the same entry:

9&10, 24&25. Fingerings 9 and 24 are the principal F# fingerings but in a chromatic context they are not as smooth as 10 and 25—called the "forked" fingerings.

12, 27. While the G# key is the highest 4L key and is the standard fingering for G# in both octaves, any of the four keys for 4L will produce a G# when substituted for the key illustrated in 12 and 27. This coupling allows easy passage—especially slurring—between low B-flat, B or C# and G#. Otherwise, the illustrated key is the best option because the additional spring tension of the coupled keys considerably increases the resistance met by the finger.

14-16, 29-31. Fingerings 14 and 29 should be the first ones taught as the principal B-flat in both octaves. Fingering 15 (30) is useful if one or both of the adjacent notes require 1R to be down, as in a B-flat major arpeggio. However, 15 (30) is often overused. Fingering 16 (31), called "Bis" B-flat, is played with the left index finger (1L) on both buttons at the same time. It should be limited to situations where there are no B-naturals near, because to move to B-nautral from Bis B-flat requires an awkward lateral motion of 1L. This principle, unfortunately, is not universally adhered to, and many players struggle with a stumbling-block unnecessarily.

39&40. These two fingerings for high E and F are called "front" fingerings, as opposed to "palm key" fingerings. They slur particularly well from the C immediately below them, and they are the "doorway" to the *altissimo*— the next octave above fingerings 38 and 40. Because the altissimo is not basic technique they are not discussed here, though many good introductions to the high harmonics (Rousseau, Rascher, Sinta, etc.) are available.

On many modern saxophones above the intermediate level, a high F# key also exists as a fifth key added to the palm high F fingering. The touchpiece is located near the forked F# key beneath the right hand, and is played with 3R.

■ *Low A on Baritone Saxophone*

All saxophones finger the same in the basic range, from low B-flat to F above the staff. Many modern baritone saxophones have a low A-natural, the key for which is below the thumb rest for the left thumb, and is added to the low B-flat fingering (1) to produce low A (Concert C).

Saxophone Fingering Chart

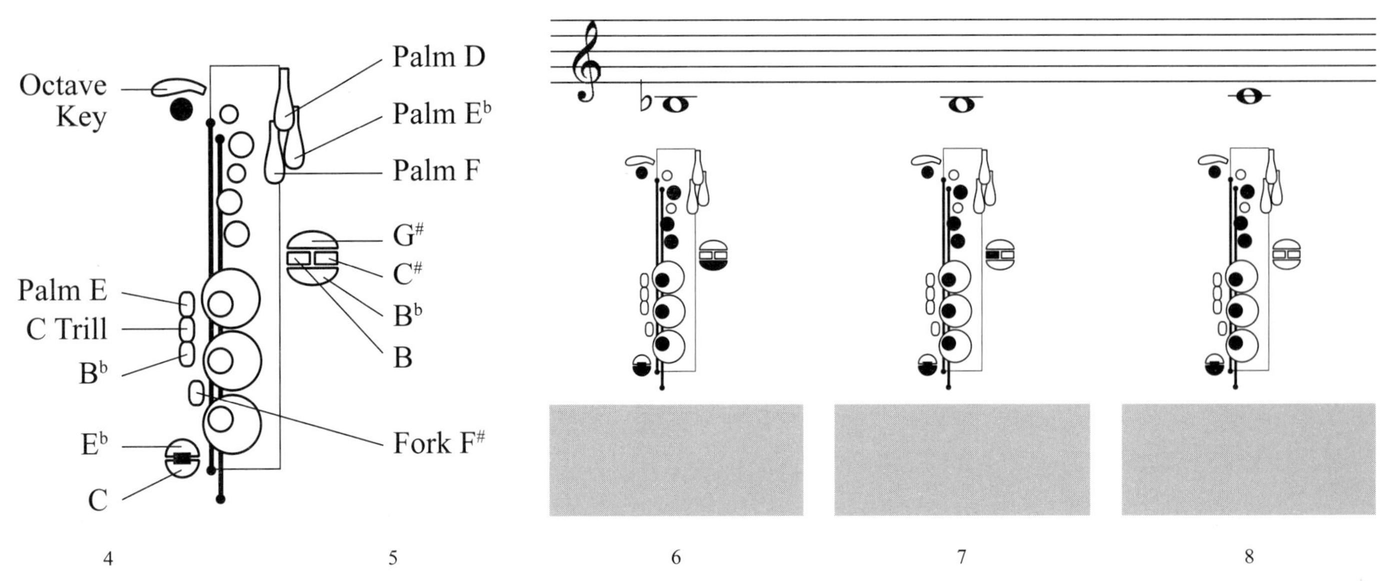

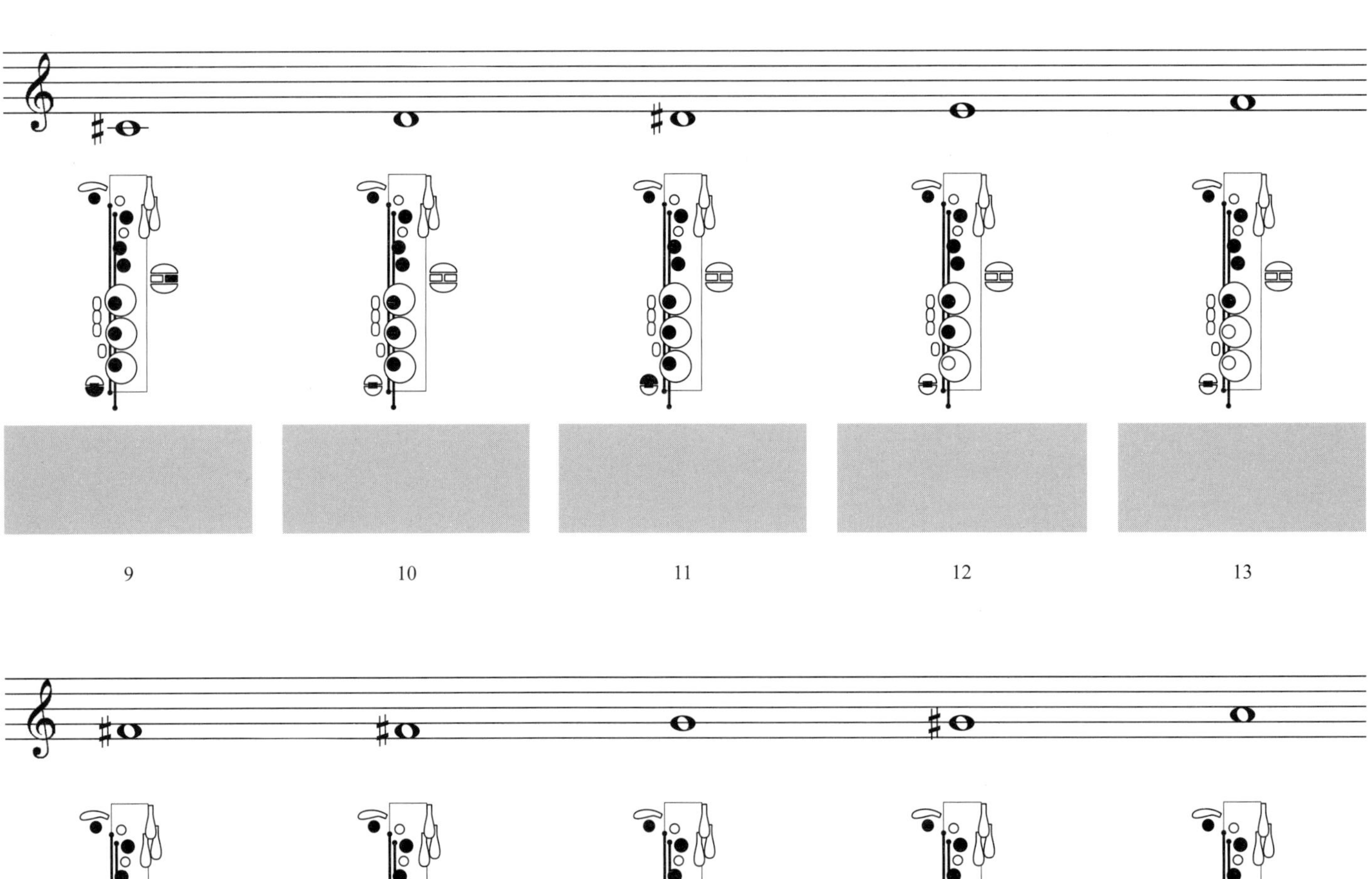

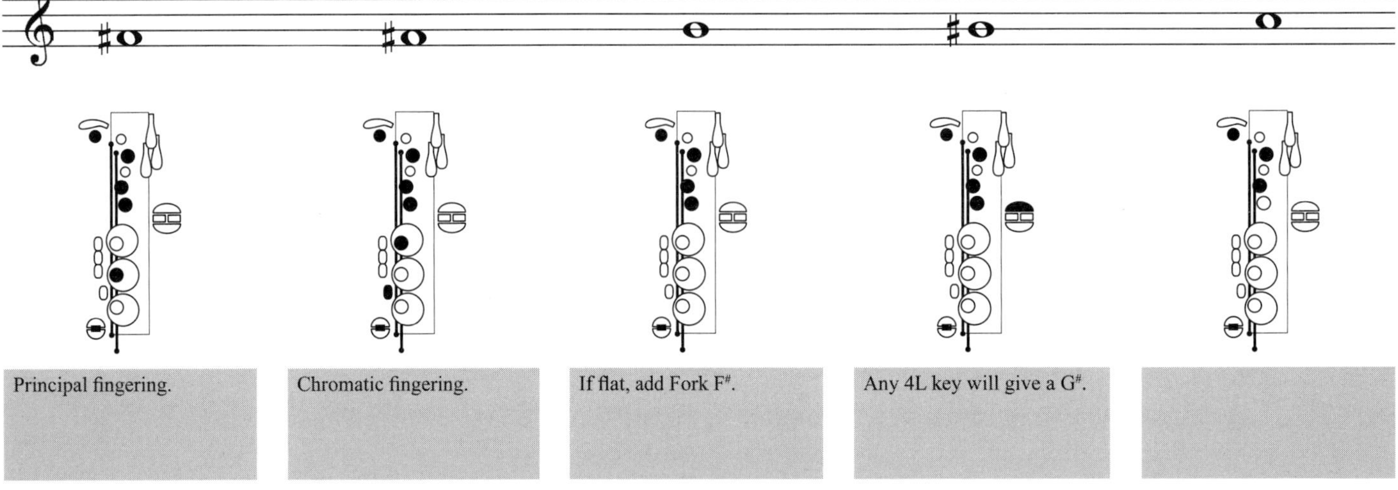

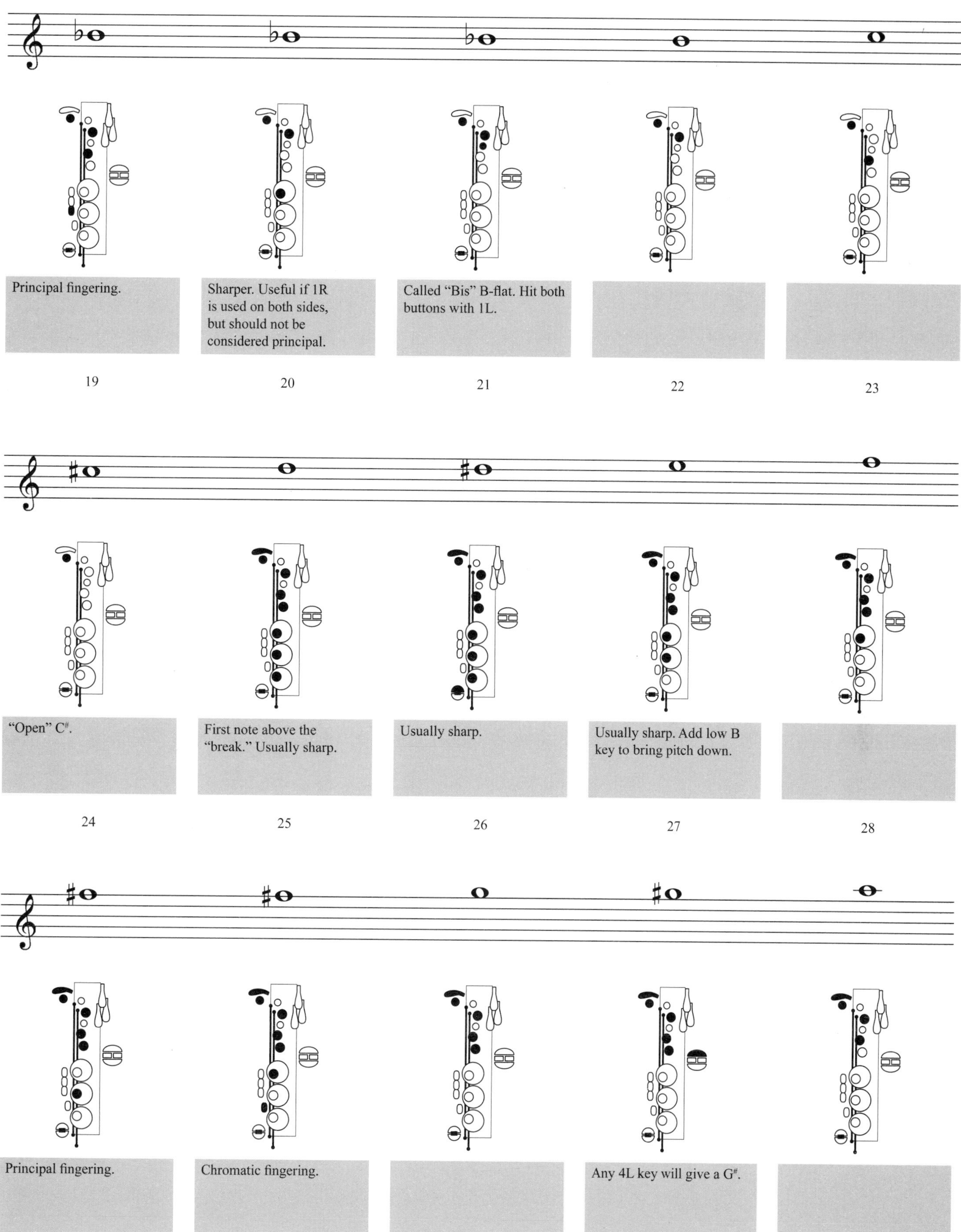
14
15
16
17
18
Principal fingering.
Sharper. Useful if 1R is used on both sides, but should not be considered principal.
Called "Bis" B-flat. Hit both buttons with 1L.
19
20
21
22
23
"Open" C#.
First note above the "break." Usually sharp.
Usually sharp.
Usually sharp. Add low B key to bring pitch down.
24
25
26
27
28
Principal fingering.
Chromatic fingering.
Any 4L key will give a G#.

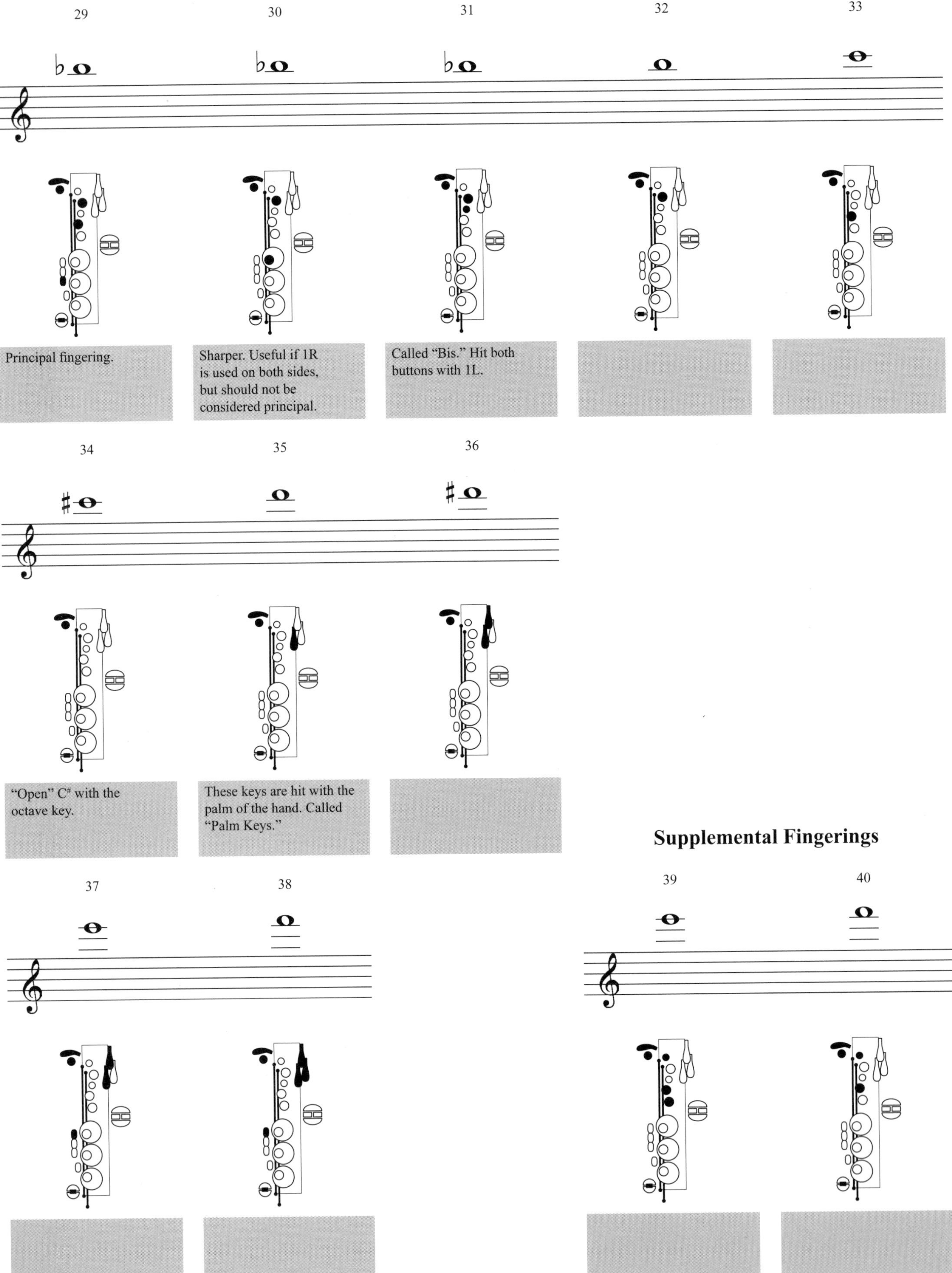

Supplemental Fingerings

Saxophone Trill Chart

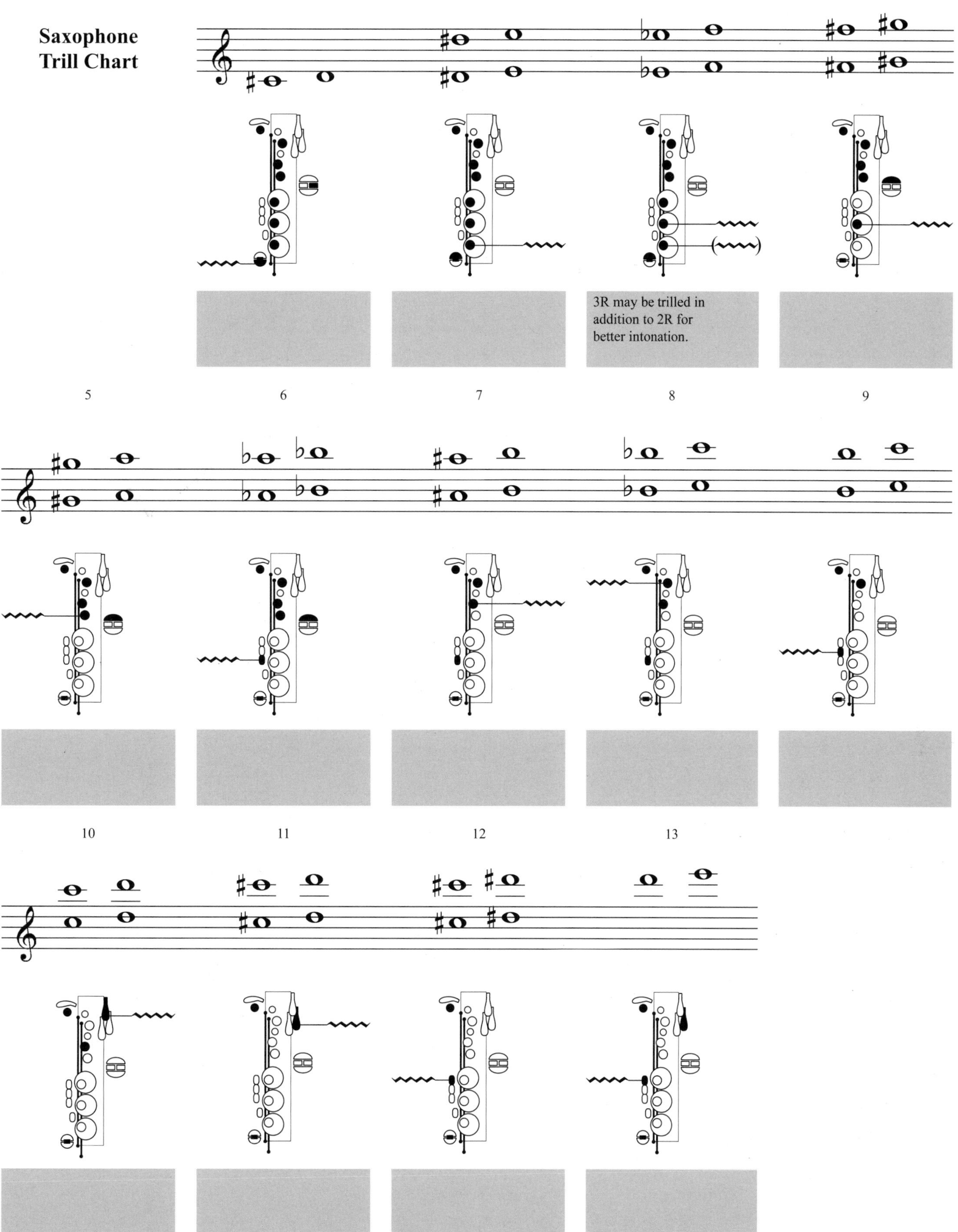

Note: upper octave is same fingerings as lower octave with octave key added.

SECTION 2

SEQUENTIAL EXERCISES

1. First Sounds #1

See the first page of each fingering chart

2. First Sounds #2

3. First Sounds #3

Notes:

1. Flute: Notice in the fingering chart that you have two main fingerings for B♭ on the flute. Teach the first one (Fingering no. 12) first, and "Thumb B♭" (Fingering no. 13) later. Thumb B♭ is wonderful if you are solidly in a flat key, but young students often forget to release the B♭ key and you will hear B♭ instead of B♮. The teacher cannot see the student's thumb from the podium and hearing an inexperienced player, the teacher might not recognize that one is hearing a B♭ and not just a flat B♮.

2. Oboe: All of these F's are "Regular F" (Fingering no. 9). We will use "forked F" (Fingering no. 10) in a future lesson.

3. Bassoon: You have two fingerings for B♭. The "back" fingering, (no. 15) with the right thumb is the common or default fingering and the key on the front between R2 and R3 replaces the thumb key for the alternate. Teach it this way so that the sequence B♭, A♭, G♭ played diatonically will alternate back-front-back, avoiding lateral motion with any one finger.

4. First Sounds #4

* See individual fingering charts for complete fingerings

** This is the first exercise in which the oboist uses “Forked F” (Fingering no. 10). Forked F is used when the note on either side adjacent requres 3R to depress its regular key. Examples would be C♯, D or D♯ in either register, any note below low D♯, and certain very high notes. Using Forked F removes the need to move 3R laterally up and down the instrument, pressing two different keys consecutively with the same finger.

The tone quality and pitch of Forked F are inferior, however, to Regular F, the default fingering, and thus Forked F is only used when using Regular F creates a lateral motion situation.

The tone quality of Forked F is very poor and the pitch is flat on very inexpensive oboes: on oboes with more elaborate mechanism, an “F Resonance Key” is present, making the tone and pitch considerably better. Most oboes with this mechanism will also have a “Left-hand F” lever for 4L, mounted above the low B and B♭ keys. While both Forked F and Left-hand F solve the lateral motion problem, most professional oboists will use Left-hand F the vast majority of the time instead of Forked F.

5. Largo from "New World" Symphony (No. 9)

Dvořák

Slur – passing from one note to another without articulating with the tongue.

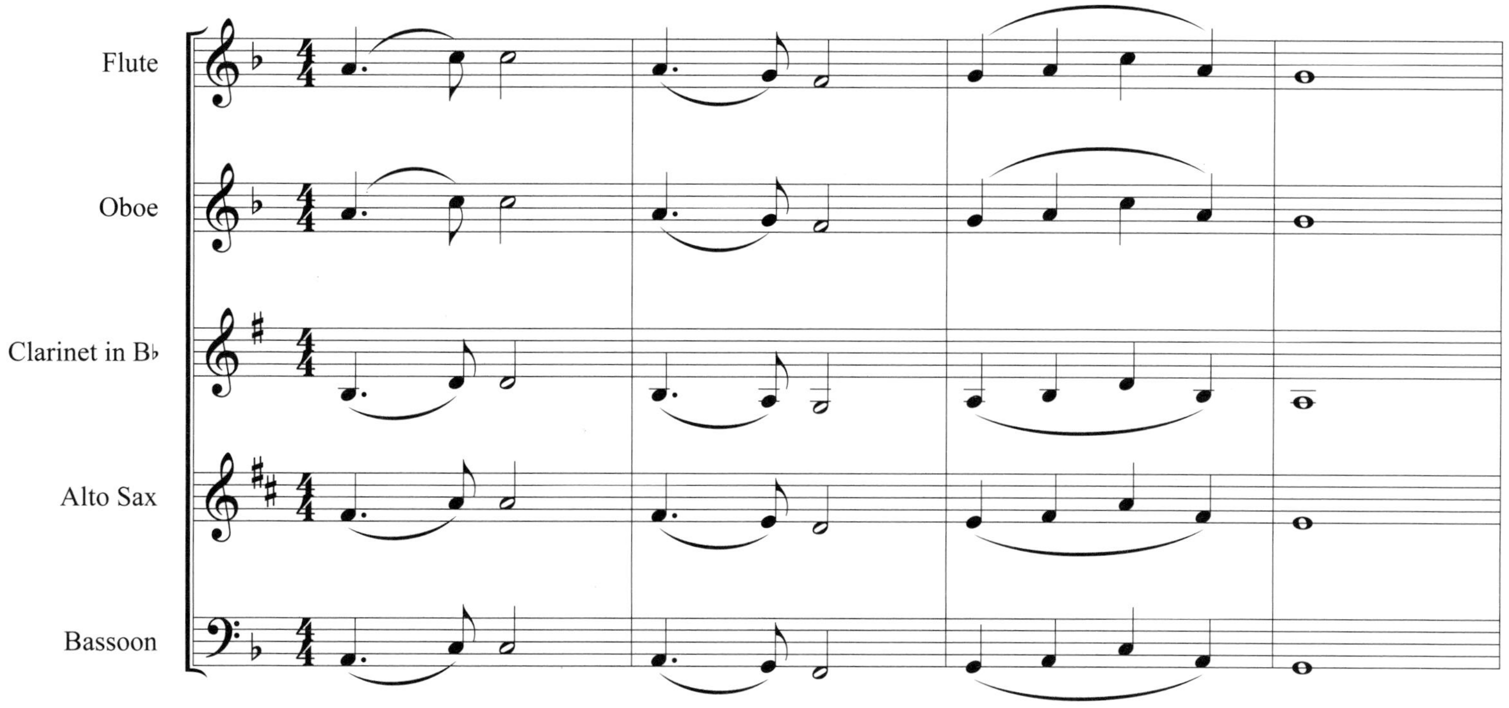
Flute
Oboe
Clarinet in B♭
Alto Sax
Bassoon

Fl.
Ob.
B♭ Cl.
A. Sx.
Bsn.

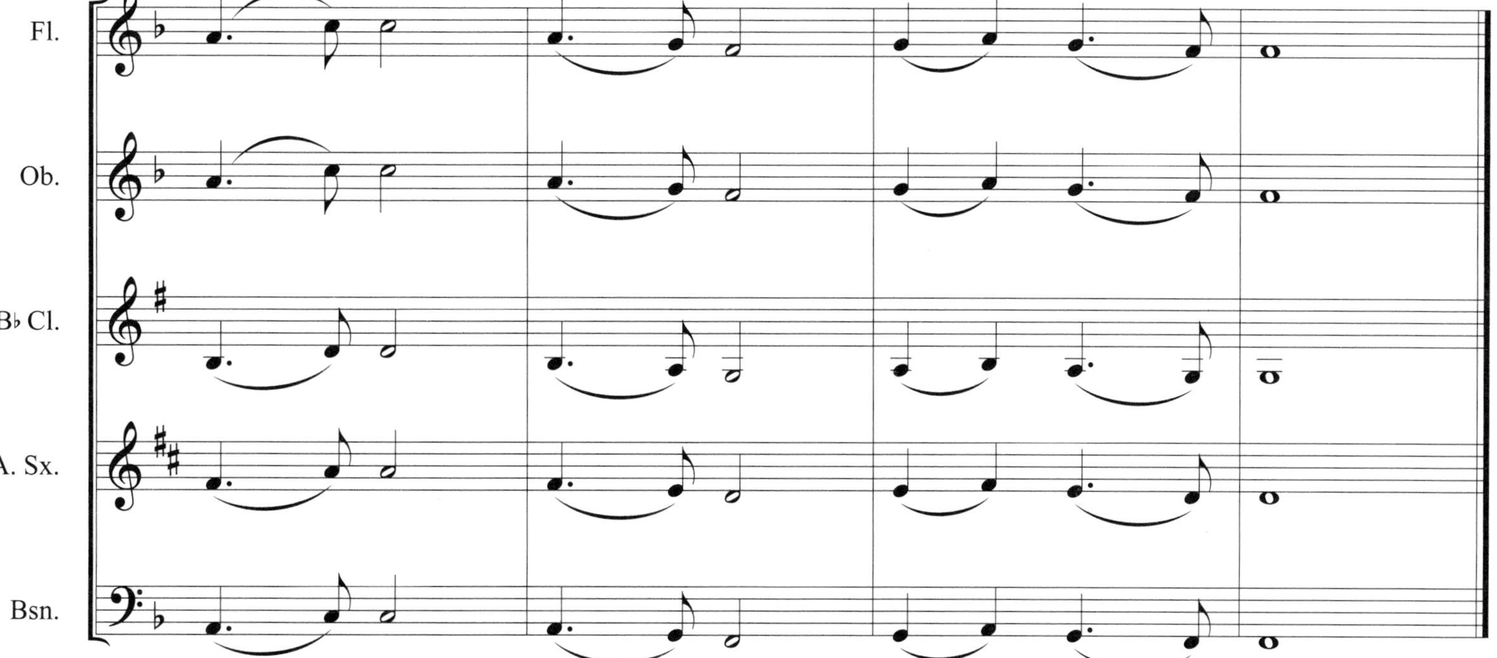

6. F Scale Studies

* On saxophone, any or all right hand fingers (R1, 2, 3) may be left down when playing C♯ if the C♯ is located between two notes that require the right hand to be down (for example, D or D♯).

7. Extending Range #1

* The default fingering (L4) for clarinet low E should be played with the F/C key (4R) unless there is an adjacent note which requires the use of 4R, in spite of the fact that the F key goes down automatically with the low E key. Slurring from low E to F without doing so causes a strong likelihood of the slur having an unwanted low G natural between the E and F.

The upper register B and C (same fingerings but with the register key) follow this same procedure for the same reason.

8. Extending Range #2

9. Extending Range #3

10. Orpheus

Can-Can

Offenbach

11. America

God Save the Queen

12. Polovetsian Dance

from "Prince Igor"

Borodin

13. Symphony No. 1

Finale

Brahms

14. Going Higher

In flat keys, oboists will use forked F a great deal because F is so often preceded or followed by E♭ or D.

15. Ah, vous dirai-je, Maman

(Twinkle, harmonized)

16. Clarinet Upper Register

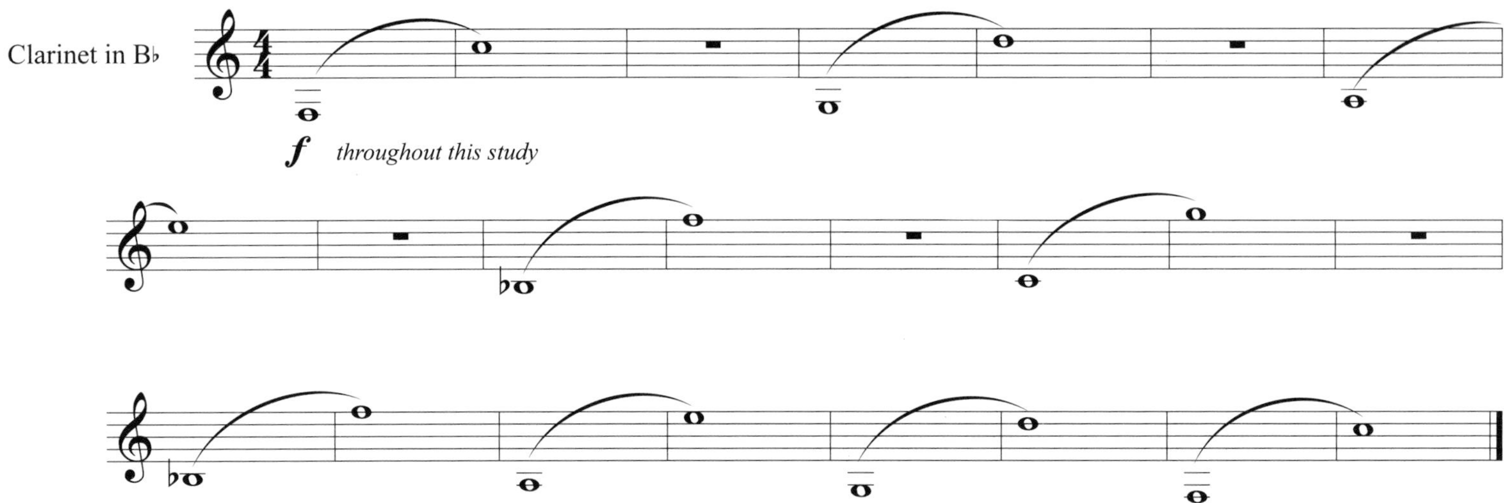

For the first attempt at the upper register, the student with the clarinet holds the lower note with a full, solid sound and a second person (either teacher or another student) reaches around to open the register key for the student who is playing the low note. This procedure reduces or eliminates two major variables: (1) in reaching for or squeezing the register key, sometimes the thumb hole or another finger hole will inadvertently open, and (2) many students, especially those with a brass playing background, will squeeze the reed and blow much harder, choking off the upper notes. Just knowing what the upper register feels and sounds like (and that it is possible!) is extremely helpful in succeeding at this challenge.

Remember, when playing in both registers, place the tone toward the front of your mouth by arching the tongue in a "ee" or "eh" position.

17. E♭ Major Scale Study

18. Symphony No. 9 Theme

Beethoven

18. Symphony No. 9 Theme

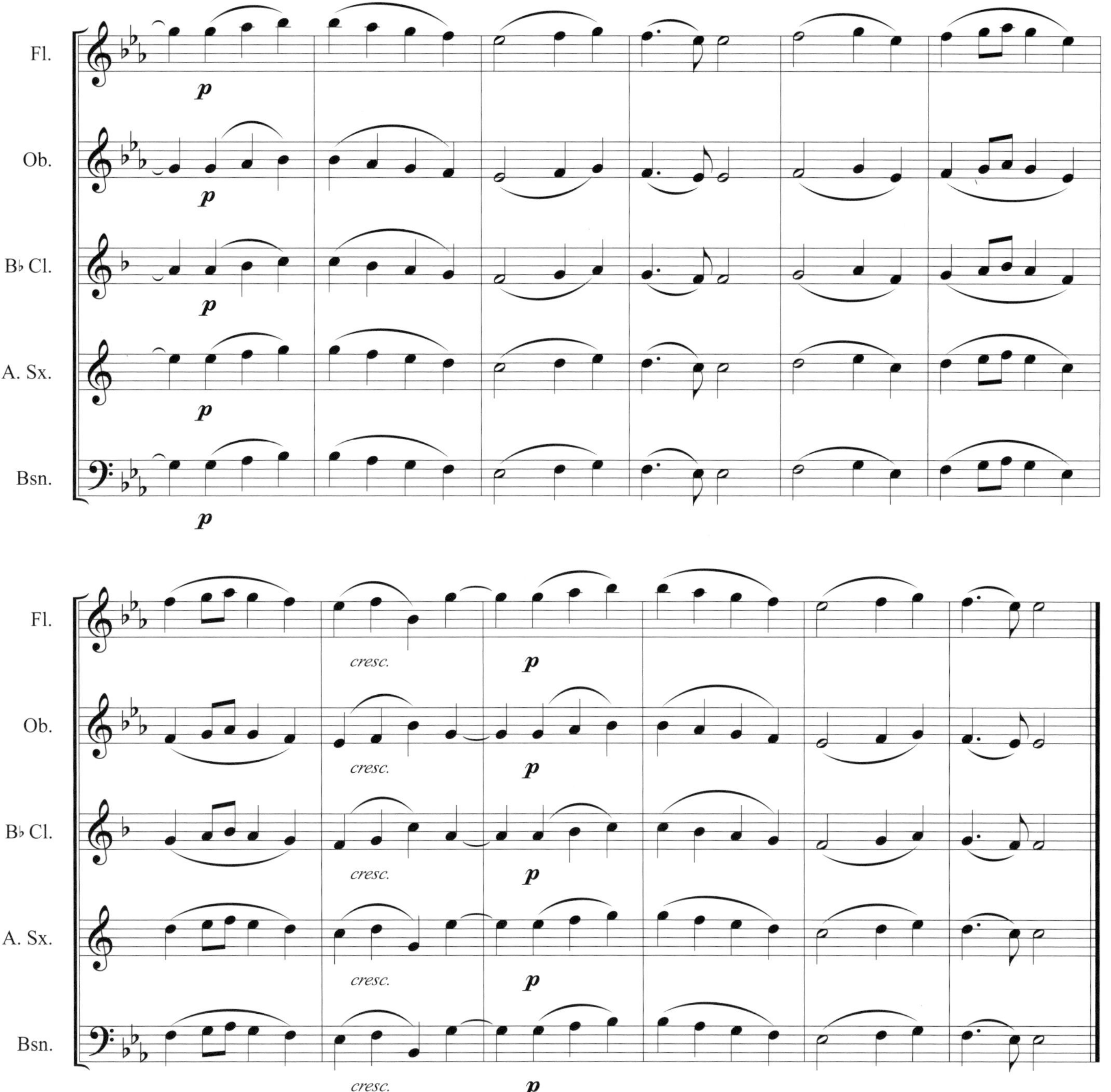

19. Unfinished Symphony (No. 8)

Schubert

20a. Flute Tone Development

Long Tones • Harmonics

Play the first note of each series focusing on creating a pure, centered sound. In the next measure, finger the lower note (in parentheses) but aim for the original pitch, or example, G, and then the same G pitch, played as a harmonic of the low C fingering. The note played as a harmonic will be more resistant and will require a more refined air speed and embouchure than the standard fingering. The sound that you make with the standard fingering will improve because the harmonic fingering teaches you to hit the very center of the target note – the "bull's eye," so to speak. Repeat this series several times on each pitch before moving on to the next pitch.

For more advanced study, this pattern may be continued up to high A♭.

20b. Oboe Tone Development

Long Tones • Octaves

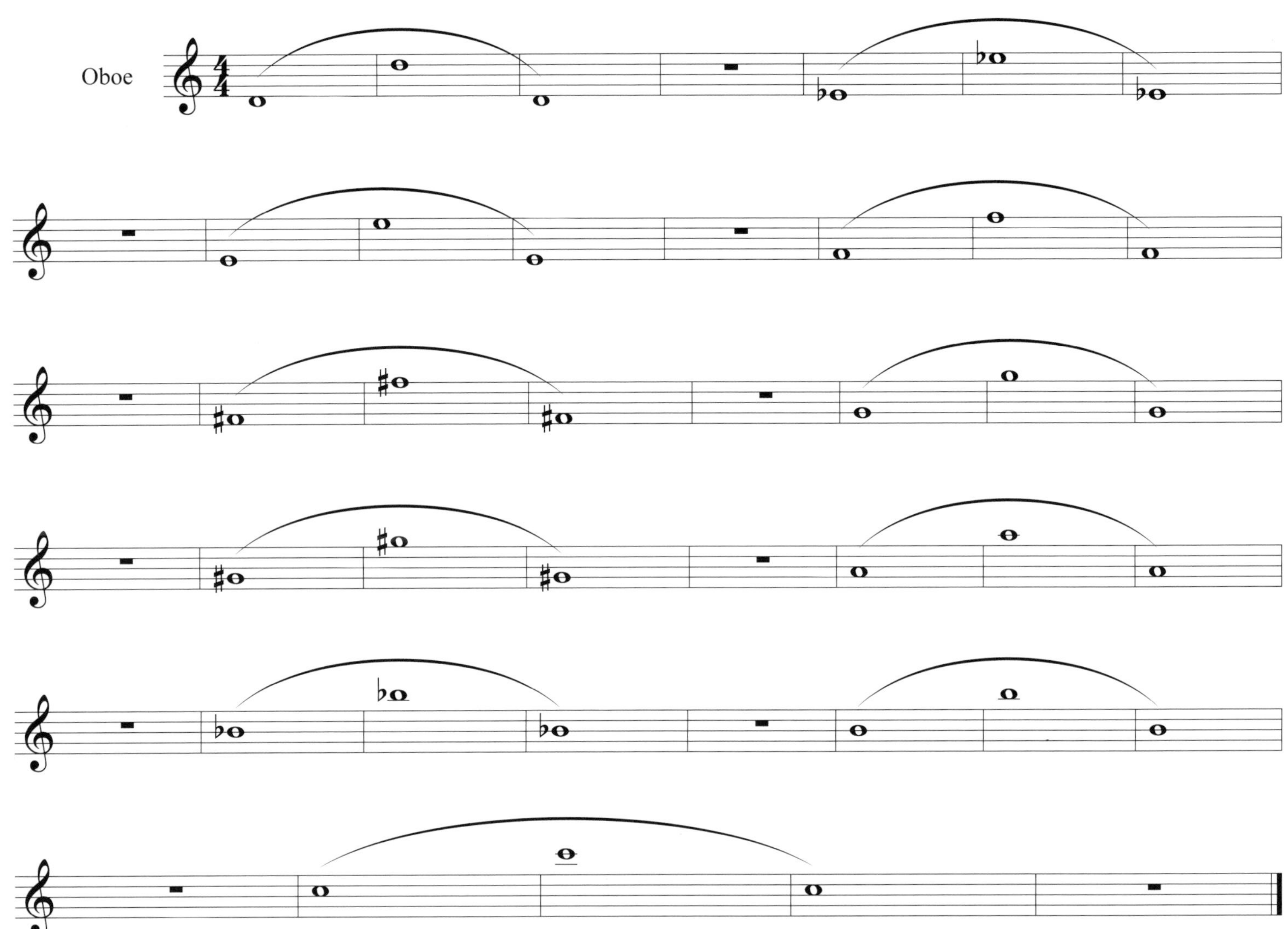

To produce a beautiful, clean attack on a low note, the oboist must have the tip of the reed in contact with the lower lip and very little reed inside the mouth. The reed is pushed into the mouth slightly for the upper note, but the same spot on reed remains in contact with the same spot on the lip at all times – thus, the lips follow the reed into and out of the mouth. Additionally, the back of the tongue moves higher into an "eeee" vowel position for the upper note, and drops back down to its original position for the lower. The extent to which the reed moves in and out and the degree to which the tongue arches into an "eeee" vowel position is governed by the ear, since the goal is to play the upper octave in tune with the lower. Doing this exercise with an electronic tuner is helpful.

20c. Clarinet Tone Study

Voicing

Slur up with the register key, release register key in the second measure and hold the tone with air pressure and tongue position.

This study requires a very arched tongue position and a very fast air speed. Holding the upper register note without the register key will become more difficult with lower notes, but with proper embouchure and air speed it will be possible.

■ *Flicking: What it is*

Flicking is a technique used to aid in producing the following notes, particularly when slurring from the lower register:

By opening an appropriate vent key, the response of these notes can be improved dramatically, especially on low quality student instruments. Below is a diagram of the left thumb keys and the notes that are associated with each.

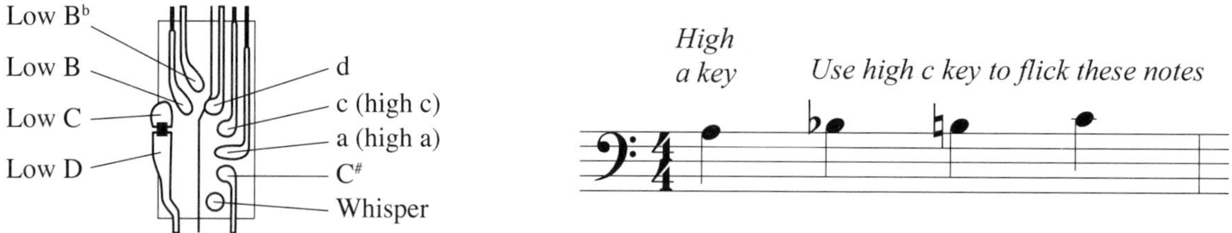

The proper use of this technique is a controversial topic for some bassoonists. Many believe that the "flick" keys should be used at all times with these notes, in effect, making them part of the regular fingering. This has the advantage of insuring that the response for these notes will be consistent and predictable. The disadvantage is an increased burden on the left thumb and a subsequent complication of the technical challenges already present. Many successful bassoonists have found the advantages to far outweigh the disadvantages and therefore, employ these keys at all times when playing these pitches.

However, many other bassoonists prefer to use the "flick" keys only in certain situations where the response of these notes is particularly troublesome. Some typical examples are shown below:

Generally all slurs from from open f and below, up to our "flicked" notes, will require the use of the appropriate flick key to aid in response. Additionally, slurs down to these notes from high eb and above will require the same treatment.

How To

The technique of flicking is a four stage process. From the low register, begin the note with the whisper key on. Then, lift your thumb, but maintain the pitch you are on. This is important! If the pitch jumps to the higher note prior to flicking then the embouchure/air coordination is incorrect. While holding the original pitch, find the desired "flick" key with your left thumb. Once prepared, the thumb (and other fingers) and embouchure/air will be ready to make a coordinated move to the new pitch. At first, it is easiest to put the flick key down with the new pitch and then release after the pitch has been stabilized. With practice, the thumb will briefly tap the flick key to help the new pitch speak.

20d. Bassoon Flicking Exercise #1

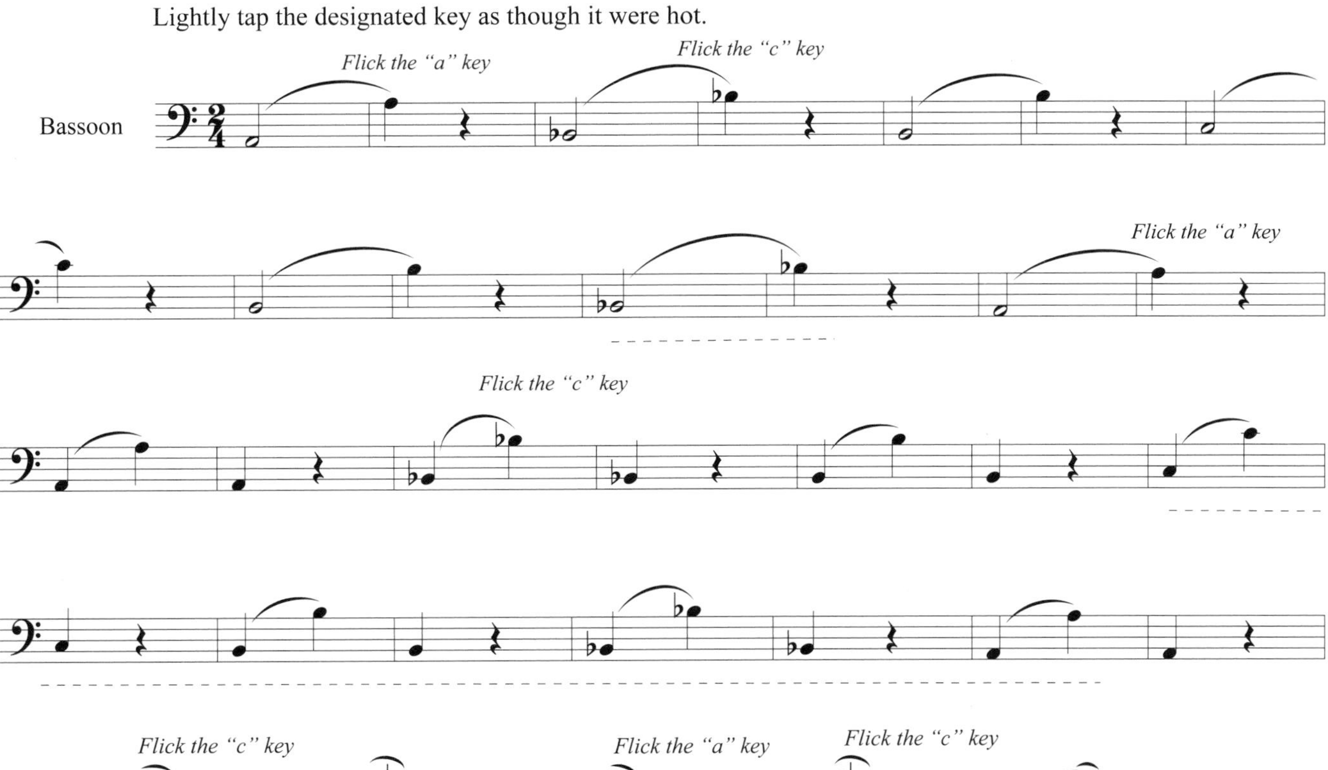

20e. Saxophone Embouchure Exercise

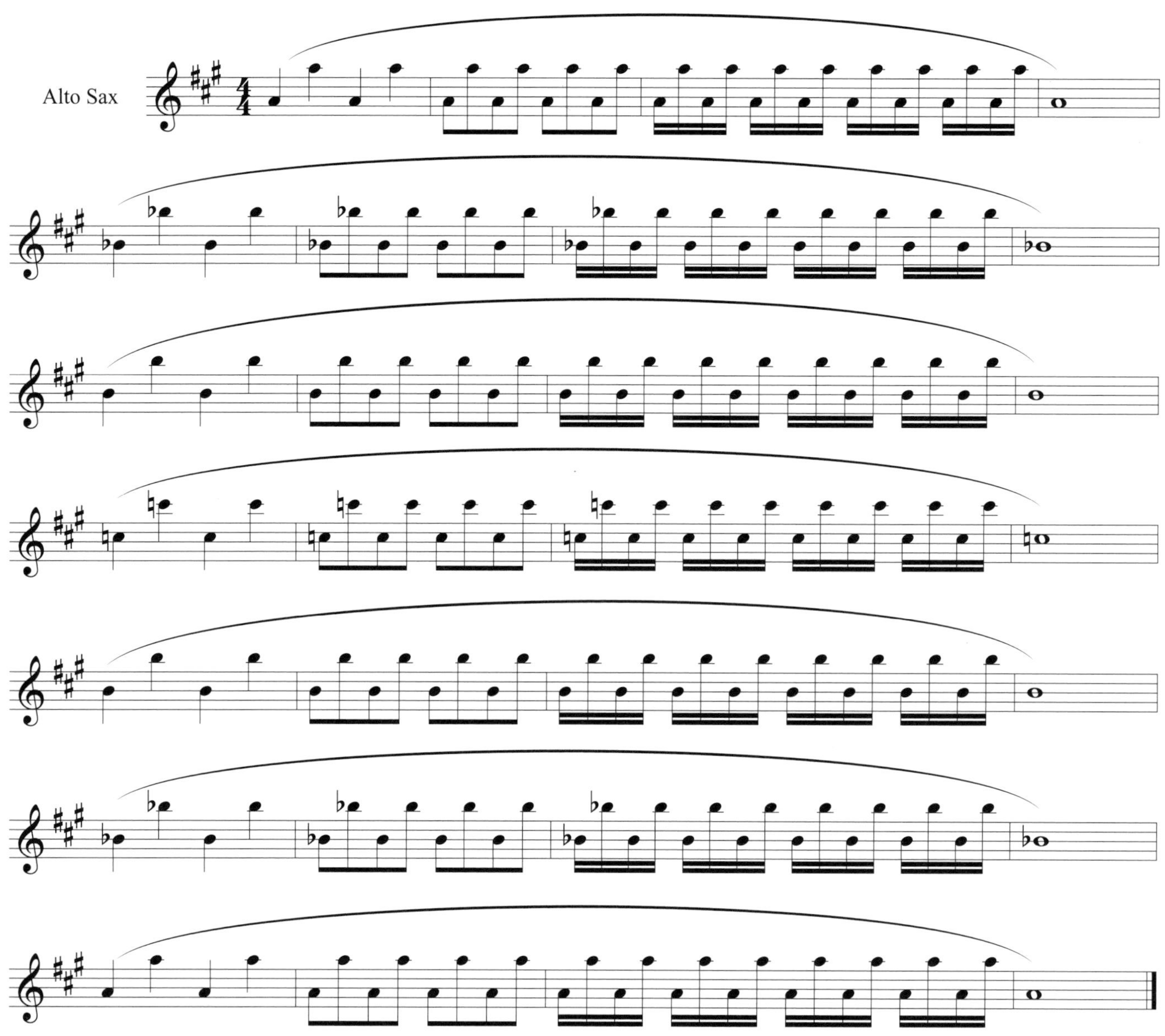

Slur quickly without adjusting the pressure that the embouchure applies to the reed. Find the center of the tone, be sure the lower lip is standing up by its own strength, and blow a steady stream of air.

21. Chromatic Scale Study #1

Basic Range

22. Chromatic Scale Study #2

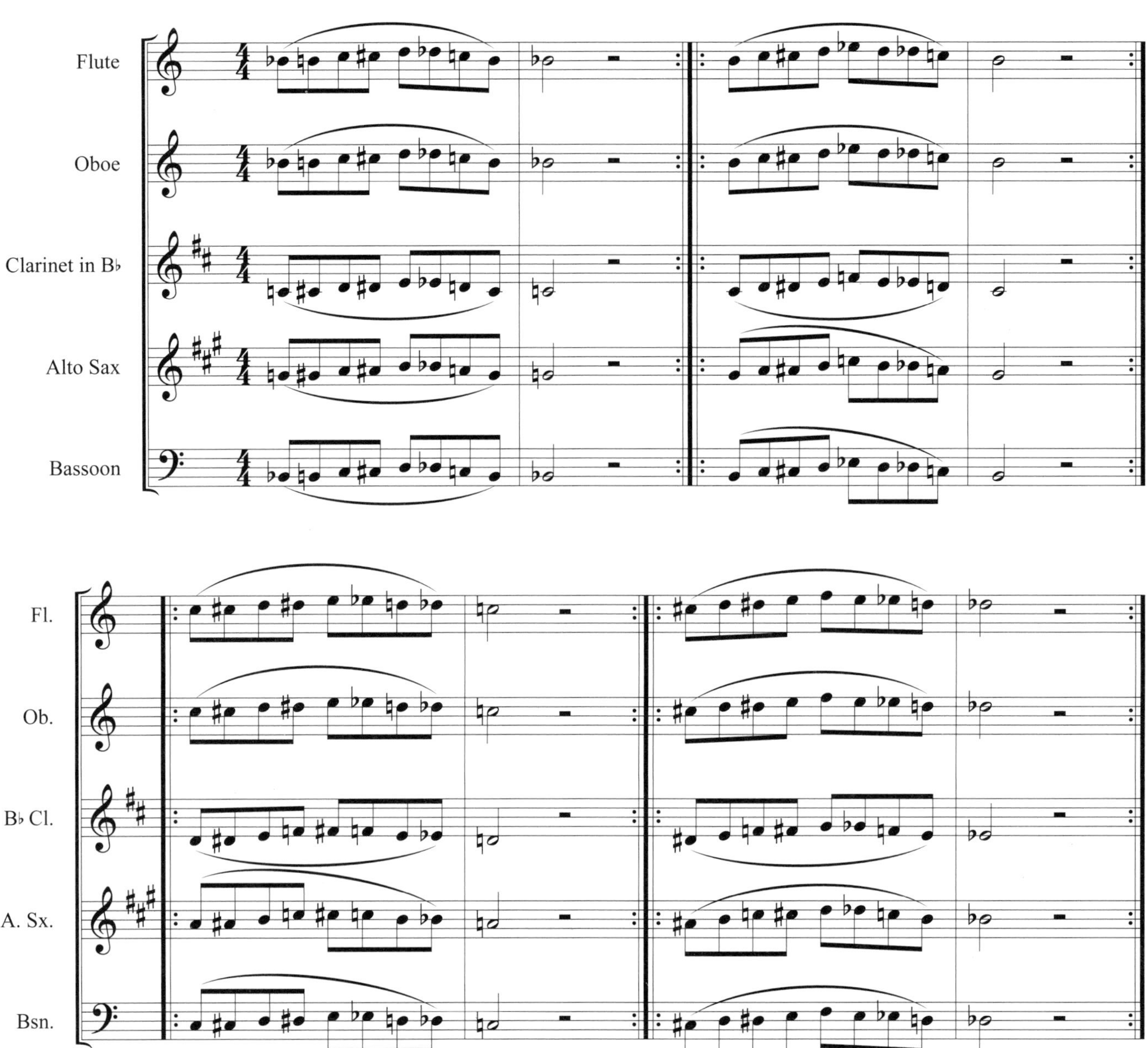

22. Chromatic Scale Study #2

23. Symphony No. 7, Second Mvt.

Beethoven

Certain articulations are perpetually confusing to the wind player, because the effect that the wide assortment of dots, lines, ties, slurs, etc. has no tangible effect on the wind player's technical execution of the articulations. To the string player, on the other hand, the slur indicates that the bow does not change direction, and the line beneath the slur or tie indicates a very gentle break between the notes. Ideally, particularly in music of this era which was written with strings were foremost in the composer's mind, the wind player is best advised to understand the bowing technique and imitate the articulation that the string player accomplishes as a result of the specific bowing directions.

23. Symphony No. 7, Second Mvt.

* A bass clef part may be played on an E♭ instrument by simply changing the clef to treble clef and adding three sharps. Given that cancelling a flat accomplishes the same thing as adding a sharp (moving one step the sharp direction on the circle of fifths), the alto or baritone saxophone key signature for this piece becomes "one sharp," or concert G minor because two flats were cancelled and one sharp was added to move three spaces toward the sharp side of the circle of fifths. The third space of the bass clef is concert E♭, and in the treble clef, the alto saxophonist plays a third-space C, which sounds concert E♭. So only the key signature need be changed – no transposition is necessary.
This is particularly useful information when one has a contralto clarinet or baritone saxophone in the ensemble and a band piece – especially an older publication – might not have a part for one or the other instrument. In this case, a bass clef part such as tuba may be substituted, asking the contralto clarinetist to change the clef, add three sharps, and read everything else as printed. Remember that this adjustment will affect certain accidentals.

24. Alma Mater and F Major Scale Study

Traditional

* Oboe: remember to switch to Octave Key 2 for high A and B♭

■ *Trills*

A trill is the rapid alternation between the written note and the note above it within the key signature, unless otherwise indicated. The common deviation from this rule is when an accidental is appended to the trill sign (tr), which alters the upper note according to that accidental. The speed of the alternation varies in accordance with the musical style.

Most trills on woodwind instruments—especially those in the lower octaves—can be done by alternating between the standard fingerings for each note—especially if moving only one (or at most two) fingers renders the desired pitches. For that reason, only trills that deviate from standard fingerings are listed in the trill charts at the end of each instrument's fingering chart. When there are specific trill fingerings, the upper auxiliary note may be slightly out of tune or the quality of the note itself may be less than ideal. For this reason, these specialized fingerings are limited to trills only.

The trill charts in this text are highly selective—there are often many possible trill fingerings for each combination of notes. Sometimes there are trills for which there is no totally satisfactory fingering. The Internet is a rich resource for other trill possibilities, for example: http://www.wfg.woodwind.org.

The execution of trills varies from one style period to another, such that the authentic performance of these ornaments can be a very involved study within the broader subject of *performance practice*. For that reason, only the technical aspect of trilling on woodwind instruments will be found in the trill charts. (When two trills a twelfth apart are given for clarinet, add the register key for the upper register.)

For clarity, both notes involved in each trill are given above the fingering in the trill charts. On flute, when the trill fingering is the same in two octaves, both sets of notes are given above the same fingering, making these common trill fingerings easier to memorize.

Bassoon trills are considerably more complicated than the other four woodwinds, since the instruments themselves vary so widely. As with the other trill charts, the bassoon chart suggests trills that are not done with regular fingerings. In addition to books by Cooper and Toplansky and others, there are several very good websites, especially http://www.wfg.woodwind.org/bassoon/basn_tr2_2.html and http://www.wfg.woodwind.org/bassoon/basn_tr2_2.html

25. Trill Study

"TK" indicates Trill Key. See Trill Chart.
No Indication = regular fingerings

Flute 1
Thumb
tr
TK
tr
tr
tr

Flute 2
Thumb
tr
L2
tr

Oboe 1
tr
TK
tr
tr
tr

Oboe 2
tr
L2
tr

Clarinet in B♭ 1
tr
tr
tr
tr

Clarinet in B♭ 2
tr
R1/TK
tr

Alto Sax 1
tr
tr
tr
tr

Alto Sax 2
tr
tr

Bassoon 1
1&2R
tr
tr
tr
tr

Bassoon 2
tr
Finger B♭, Trill 3R
tr

25. Trill Study

26. Baby Blues in C

* Change clef and add 3♯ to the key signature. Accidentals in parentheses apply to E♭ instruments reading bass clef parts.

26. Baby Blues in C

For E♭ instruments reading by changing clef, all B♭'s become G♮'s, E♭'s become C♮'s, and A♯'s become F×'s.

More troublesome to the classically-trained musician, however, is the placement of the accent – often off the beat instead of on the beat. Here, accent suggestions are notated for you.

27. Habanera from "Carmen"

Chromatic Study

Bizet

27. Habanera from "Carmen"

28. Bassoon Flicking Exercise No. 2

Habanera from "Carmen" with Bass and Harmony

Bizet

28. Bassoon Flicking Exercise No. 2

29. Alternate Fingering Study #1

Before studying exercises 28, 29, and 30, please read "The Principle of Alternate Fingerings, " page 178

30. Alternate Fingering Study #2

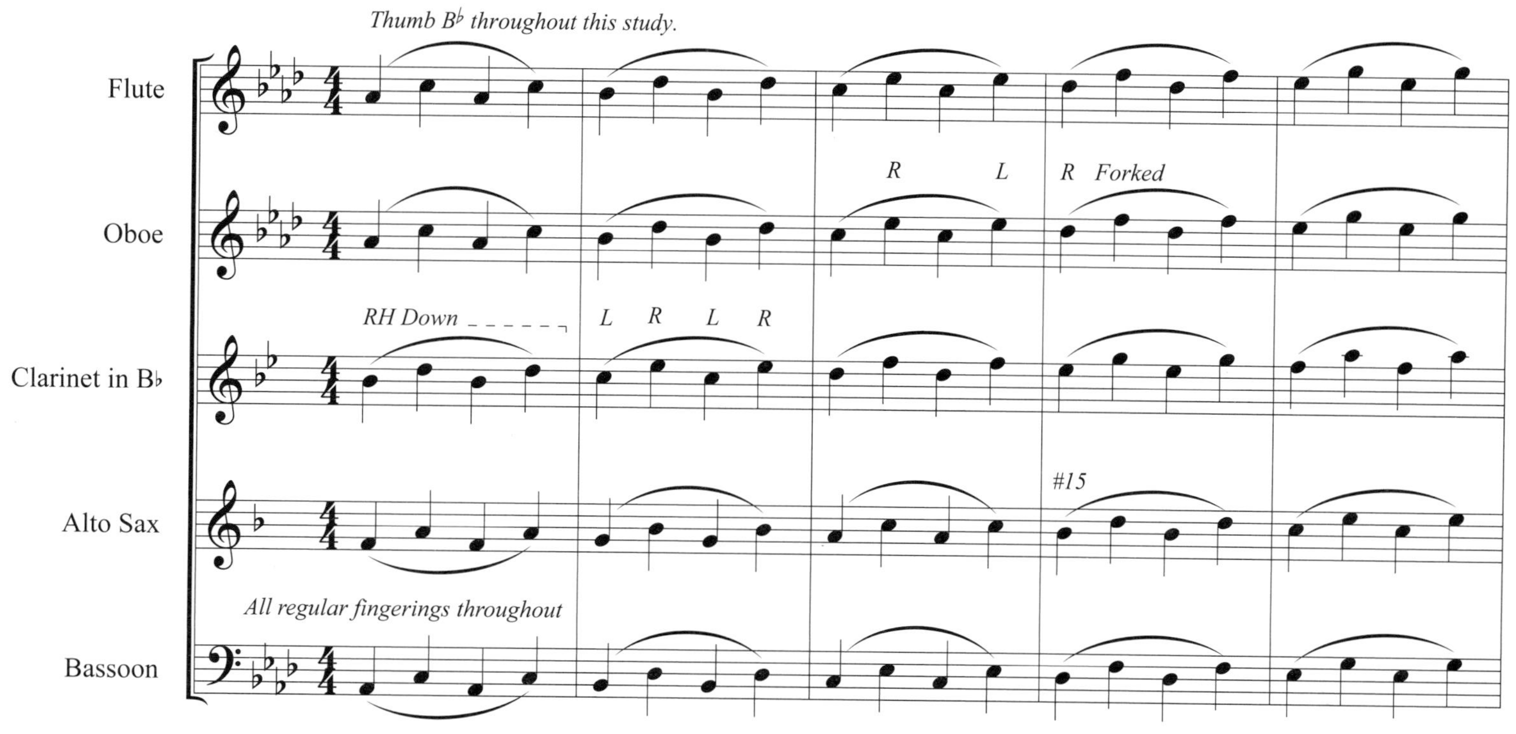

30. Stars and Stripes

Trio

Sousa

30. Stars and Stripes

* Use the F♯/C♯ key on the left, but be sure the F/C key on the right is down at the same time. This avoids an extraneous note between the D♭ and the C when the F/C key might momentarily open.

32. G Major Scale Study #1

33. G Major Scale Study #3

* Clarinet plays B on the left and C♯ on the right throughout.

34. G Major Study #3 and Joy to the World

Traditional Carol

The 1st parts may be practiced separately in unison – *Joy to the World*. The 2nd parts may also be practiced as a scale study for each instrument, and all parts may play together for a harmonized, compete version of the carol.

34. G Major Study #3 and Joy to the World

35. Symphony No. 2, Third Mvt.

Brahms

35. Symphony No. 2, Third Mvt.

SECTION 3

DIRECTOR'S GUIDE

Similarities and Differences Between the Woodwinds

Similarity—***The First Cardinal Rule of Woodwind Fingering***: When there is more than one key that produces a particular note, *the one which is under the hand is the principal fingering*. This is especially useful information when dealing with certain harmony instruments—bass clarinets, for example—for which there is no standardized low note fingering system, and is especially critical information for solving technical problems on clarinet and bassoon, the instruments which have the widest choices of fingerings.

Similarity—***The Second Cardinal Rule of Woodwind Fingering***: We use alternate fingerings to *avoid lateral motion*. This means that we do not play two adjacent notes by sliding the same finger up or down the instrument from one key to the other unless there is absolutely no alternative.

- Cases do occasionally exist on all woodwinds where sliding laterally is necessary. Whenever you see a "roller" key (as on bassoon, saxophone and sometimes on flute), you will know that the rollers are there to facilitate lateral motion on those keys.
- When lateral motion is absolutely unavoidable, slide down the instrument (toward the bell or toward the palm of the hand) rather than up the instrument (toward the mouthpiece or by straightening the finger).

Similarity: All embouchures need to be "set" before the player attacks the first note of a phrase. Adjusting an embouchure "on the fly" never works as well as having all factors under complete control prior to making a sound.

Similarity: All woodwind instruments "overblow," or play in more than one octave with the same basic fingering. Thus, all woodwinds have a "break," where in an ascending scale, one puts most or all fingers back down to play notes in a higher octave or "register" in the same basic fingering sequence as before.

Similarity: On the double reeds, *only one form of venting is used at a time* in the second register—never two. One uses either the half hole or one opens the vent hole (octave key or whisper key) but not both at once.

Difference: The bassoon is the only instrument whose vent hole, at the base of the bocal and covered by a pad operated by the whisper key, is sprung open and is thus closed by pressing the touchpiece. All other vent keys (octave or register keys) are spring closed and opened by pressing the touchpiece.

Similarity: There are THREE half-hole notes immediately above the break on all double reed instruments—oboe, English horn and bassoon.

Difference: There are only TWO notes on flute above the break with the first finger of the left hand up.

Similarity: All reed embouchures require the engagement of the facial muscles—especially the lips. The lips are dynamic, supported by their own musculature and functioning as a spring, rather than merely as a pad being pushed by the teeth.

Similarity: To articulate, the tongue touches the reed on all reed instruments.

Similarity: Lower notes become difficult if not impossible to produce if there are leaks in pads anywhere on the instrument.

Similarity: On all woodwinds, grasping the instrument at a point not designed to accommodate the hand is dangerous and will easily throw the instrument out of adjustment. This is especially true of grasping over the rods on the narrow end of a saxophone, and the lower part of the lower joints of clarinet and oboe.

Similarity/Difference: All woodwinds *except oboe* have an "open" note. While the open tone (all fingers up) on oboe gives approximately a C#, the tone is ugly and the pitch is unreliable.

Similarity: The G# key is in the same place on all woodwinds except bassoon—played with the little finger of the left hand (4L).

Similarity: Oboe, English Horn, all saxophones, alto and bass clarinet and most other low clarinets have an "articulated G# key." This means that the touchpiece and key cup for the G# key are on separate axels, with a point where the motion is transferred from the touchpiece to the key cup. When 4L is depressed to open the G# key and left down, putting fingers down in the right hand closes that pad on any instrument with an "articulated G#," facilitating trills to G#.

Difference: The middle finger of the right hand works well for F# on the single reeds but it is too flat for F# on the flute.

Transposition

The woodwinds are designed so that the player can use the same basic set of fingerings on all of the instruments of a particular family. Otherwise, an obstacle would exist if someone who played one instrument such as alto saxophone were asked to play another such as tenor or soprano saxophone to fill out an instrumentation and had to learn a different fingering for each note on the staff.

Transposing is changing the position of the notes on the staff to accommodate the pitch differential produced by building instruments with lower (and thus longer tube length) or higher (and thus shorter tube length) voices.

"Concert Pitch" means the pitches that the piano plays. "C natural" on the piano is thus "Concert C." So on piano or any "C" instrument (such as flute or oboe), the pitch "Written C" is also the pitch "Concert C."

When a written "C" is played on any instrument, the concert pitch that is heard is the name of the instrument. Thus, "C" played on a B-flat clarinet sounds "Concert B-flat," and "C" played on an E-flat alto saxophone sounds "Concert E-flat." This will always be true, such that if one is not familiar with an instrument but knows the "key" in which the instrument is built, one can figure out what transposition is appropriate to achieve the desired Concert pitches.

In order to use the same fingerings on all instruments of a type (for example, clarinet or saxophone), an instrument whose actual sound may be in or below the bass clef will still read a part written in the treble clef. Thus, written "C" will sound a major second lower on B-flat soprano clarinet or saxophone, a major sixth lower on an E-flat alto clarinet or saxophone, an octave plus a major second lower on B-flat tenor sax or bass clarinet, and so forth as shown below. With only very rare exceptions all players with any kind of clarinet or saxophone will still read treble clef. (You will sometimes see "BB-flat contrabass clarinet" on published parts—this indicates not one, but two octaves plus a major second lower than written.) Here are the sounding pitches of written "C" on the various clarinets and saxophones:

Transposing instruments could also sound higher than written. For example, the E-flat soprano (sometimes called *sopranino*) clarinet sounds a minor third above the written pitch. The only other common woodwind instrument that sounds higher than written is the modern piccolo, sounding a whole octave higher than written. The common piccolo is a "C" instrument, but its octave transposition means it still is a transposing instrument.

After some time teaching band, you will become very adept at transposing "on the fly." You will ask a clarinetist to play a "G," a flutist to play an "F" and an alto saxophonist to play a "D" and you will hear everyone playing concert "F" in unison. Apply the same principles to figure out what to have some less familiar instrument play. English Horn and French Horn, for example are in "F," and so you would ask these players to play their "C" for the resulting pitch to be concert "F."

Teaching "Breath Support"

Breath support is taught in a variety of ways, but virtually all approaches involve some form of forceful exhalation and some form of resistance to that exhalation. Regardless of approach, all would likely agree that "breath support" and "blowing hard" are not the same thing.

To illustrate the concept of "support," consider that a long wooden board may be "strong," but unless it leans on something else, it is not likely to stand vertically on its own. However, if two boards were leaning against each other with each resisting the other's tendency to be pulled over by the force of gravity, then the force of gravity pulling each board in an opposing direction would create stability. It would be less likely that they would fall over because one board would be *supporting* the other.

In the same way, the mechanics of breath support involves diaphragm muscle resisting the strong pushing action of the muscles of the abdomen.

The *Diaphragm* is a powerful muscle laying horizontally between the chest and abdominal cavities, functioning as the floor of the chest cavity and the ceiling of the abdominal. When relaxed and the lungs are relatively empty, it is dome-shaped, attached around its perimeter to the inside of the ribcage. When the diaphragm tightens, the dome flattens and creates a vacuum in the lungs and air rushes in from the mouth and/or nose. When it relaxes, we "sigh," and the air escapes from the same opening through which it entered. *Generation after generation of wind teachers have propagated the misconception one pushes the air out with the diaphragm while playing, and that the diaphragm is located somewhere mid-abdomen. Physiologically, this is simply not true.*

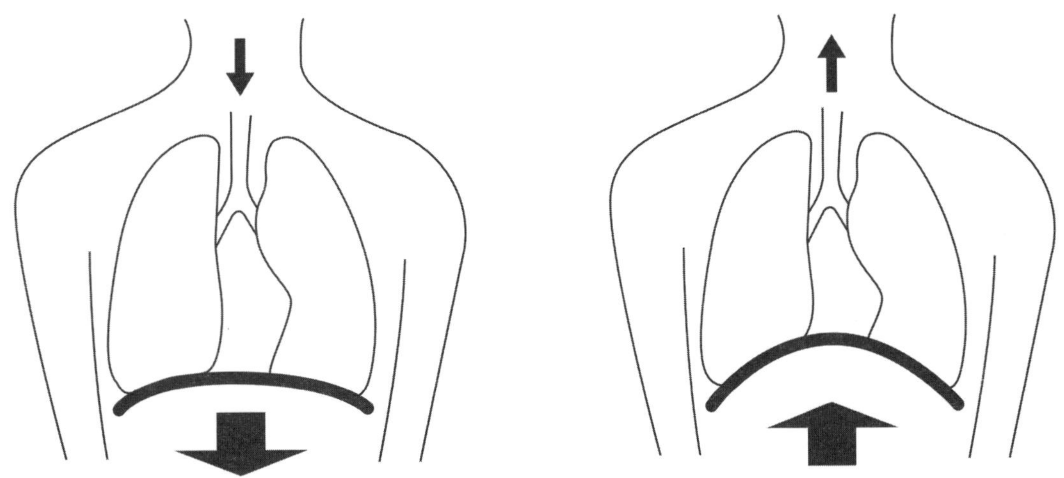

Action of diaphragm in inhalation (L) and exhalation (R)

The mechanics of inhalation involves flattening the diaphragm to pull the lungs downward and create negative pressure. Ideally, the exterior of the abdomen expands to its maximum distention, and then the middle and upper parts of the thoracic cavity follow in smooth succession until the lungs have been filled, stretching them both vertically and horizontally in all directions.

Exhaling, the diaphragm muscle provides resistance to the abdominal muscles' efforts to push the bottom of the lung upward. This resistance results in pushing the air out of the body firmly and with stability. While consciously pushing upward with the abdomen, engage the diaphragm by spreading the ribcage to stretch the diaphragm like a drum head. Pushing upward abdominally with diaphragmatic resistance utilizes the player's strength much more efficiently. Here are some techniques of illustrating this to students:

- To inhale, put a hand on your abdomen over the naval and inhale by pushing outward on the hand first and then filling the upper part of the chest with air.
- To exhale, pull the naval upward while pushing downward from the bottom of the rib cage. Or . . .
- Imagine that there is a grapefruit wedged between the bottom of the sternum and the naval and you are squeezing out the juice. Or . . .
- Imagine that you have filled a basketball behind the naval with air. As you exhale, shift the basketball upward into the ribcage, spreading the ribcage as the basketball ascends.

Keep the diaphragm fully engaged by keeping the ribcage as large as possible. It may help to imagine (or to actually use) a belt loosely around the bottom of the ribcage. As you blow outward, keep the ribcage large so that the belt does not fall, until the very end of the breath.

So . . . "blowing hard" is only the beginning of "breath support.

Teaching students to inhale the maximum quantity of air is a perennial challenge. Here are two suggestions for illustrating maximum inhalation:

- Take one full breath, and then before attacking the first note of the phrase, without exhaling, take another breath on top of the first. The sound will usually improve and the length of phrase possible usually enlarges considerably.
- Rather than taking one breath before a phrase, take twenty very short ones, never exhaling. Then begin the phrase—ideally one which has been impossible heretofore.

Tuning

When tuning in an ensemble, always check more than one note, and always tune in the middle of the dynamic range. Because dynamic affects the pitch of all woodwinds differently, tuning at the soft extreme (which is generally the tendency) and playing at the other end of the dynamic range does not yield the best results. Remember that "Tuning note C" (Concert B-flat) is especially unreliable on clarinet, where the note is naturally sharp. Bringing clarinetists' "Tuning note C" into tune by pulling at the barrel will most likely leave the throat tones flat.

Wind instruments play sharper when they are warm and flatter when they are cold. Woodwind instruments are built to play at or very near a specific level of pitch—either A=440 or slightly higher. Our standard in the United States since the early Twentieth Century has been A=440 or very nearly so, but in Europe orchestras regularly play somewhat higher

On all wind instruments, shortening the tube makes the instrument sharper and lengthening it makes it flatter. Lengthening the tube near the source of vibration flattens the short fingerings (notes which have the fewest fingers down) more than it flattens the longer fingerings (those with more fingers down) because the size of the extension is a larger percentage of a short tube fingering than one with more fingers down.

Applying this principle to a real instrument, pulling the flute headjoint out will flatten open C# more than any other note on the flute since the highest open hole is very near the blowhole, and the effect on low D or C will be considerably less. The same is true of pulling the mouthpiece out on saxophone, and pulling at the barrel on clarinet. As will be discussed below, because the clarinet is built in separate sections (in contrast to the flute), pulling out between the hands is useful to keep the short notes from being disproportionately flat to the longer fingering notes.

Beyond the adjustments that can be made to the whole instrument as described above, often the simplest solution to a problem is the best one. Be aware of how high pads lift off of instruments and how dirt in tone holes affects individual notes. A considerable amount of accumulated dirt inside a tone hole will make the note emitting from that hole (i.e. when that hole is the highest open hole on the instrument) flat. Pad height is also critical—most often one experiences a flat note which may also "wheeze" as a result of the pad not opening sufficiently. Sometimes this happens when a thin pad is replaced with a thicker pad in a repair shop or a striker cork is replaced with a thicker cork, stopping the pad from lifting sufficiently. The other common reason for this problem is that a key may have been bent, either by rough handling or by dropping, in which case carefully re-bending the key is the solution.

Finally, remember that without conscious adjustment to counteract the instrument's natural tendency, the dynamic at which a woodwind instrument is played affects the level of pitch at which it plays. One often hears students tuning at a very soft dynamic and then playing *mezzo forte* and above. If flutes tune softly, they will push in and if clarinets and saxophones tune softly they will pull out to match the tuning standard—then when they play louder, flutes will be sharp and clarinets will be flat. Tune with a full sound in the middle of the dynamic range—not at the soft end of the range.

Articulation

Articulation in music and consonants in speaking have similar functions. On a woodwind instrument, the tongue functions as a valve, starting and often stopping notes and in so doing, proving clarity, emphasis, and contributing style to music.

Articulation develops best with thoughtful practice. Students must understand that there is a difference between playing a note "short" and tonguing it "hard." A helpful analogy is that of a light switch—in the "off" position, there is no light coming from the bulb. Pushing the light switch more forcefully does not make the light any more "off."

Good tonguing exercises exist in many method and etude books at many levels for all instruments. Such etudes allow students to focus on articulating cleanly while developing speed and a variety of articulation styles.

In the early years, most teachers prefer to teach articulation by starting notes with the tongue and stopping them with the breath. Once a student's sound has matured, there are instances when stopping staccato notes with the tongue is desirable. Flutist and colleague of C.P.E. Bach, J.J. Quantz recommended it nearly 300 years ago—it is not a new idea.

The reed instruments are different in tone production mechanism from the brass and flute. *Good advice for flute and brass is not necessarily good advice for the reeds.*

The source of vibration on all reed instruments is behind the lips, rather than at the lips (brass) or in front of them (flute). Thus, "voicing," or the vowel sound associated with the tongue position becomes particularly critical to the formation of the tone. *Whenever possible, apply something which is known to something which is unknown.* So teaching the formation of a vowel sound on the reed instruments is much less abstract than instructing the student to move the tongue into some specific position, since the student will already know how to form the vowel. On the double reeds this vowel sound will vary from upper to lower register in an "eeee—-ahh" manner. On clarinet the tongue and thus the vowel sound remains more constant. Thus "eee" or "eh" sounds in which the back of the tongue remains arched will produce the best focus. The voicing of the saxophone tone is similar to that of clarinet, though a vowel sound closer to "eh" with the tongue slightly lower will produce a more characteristic saxophone tone. On all reed instruments, *advising a student to "keep and open throat" often encourages the student to vocalize "ahhhh," which is the antithesis of what is desirable, especially on clarinet.*

Instrument Selection

No one does superior work with inferior equipment. An experienced teacher insists on the best possible equipment in the best possible working condition for his or her students.

Music store owners often refer to the Fall as "Instrument Season," because they sponsor numerous events for schools where prospective band students—generally fifth or sixth graders—can try several instruments and pick the one with which they seem to have the most success and attraction. Often, older students assist in these events explaining embouchures and hand position and the educational experience for all involved can be quite positive.

Your local music store may carry instruments made by one or two specific companies and may not have as convenient access to others. Since most of the major instrument manufacturers produce entry-level instruments of reasonable quality, it is recommended that school directors develop strong working relationships with the local merchant. There are distinct advantages to working with a local professional music dealer.

That said, a preferable woodwind instrument will have the following qualities:

- It will make an appealing sound
- The scale will be even—some notes will not be muffled with others that are bright.
- The scale of the instrument will be true or nearly true to an electronic tuner. (Always take a tuner when buying an intermediate or professional instrument.)

- The tone focus and quality can be retained at both high and low dynamic levels.

Other considerations such as resale value, repair record and serviceability may have an influence as well, especially for step-up instruments. You do not want a student to appear with a new professional model instrument that he or she has fallen in love with (perhaps because it is shiny) but plays unmanageably flat or sharp in one or all registers. Unfortunately, this does happen.

Flute

Generally, beginning flutes have closed tone holes (as opposed to open or French model), and C foot joints (as opposed to B). Optionally, some makers such as Jupiter will supply a curved head joint, a "wave" head joint, or a straight one—curved in a U-shape or bent with a "wave" so that a young student with very short arm reach can play the instrument. The argument for starting students on open-hole flutes is that the open holes automatically force good hand position. An open-hole flute will likely be supplied with plugs for the tone holes, which makes the instrument easier to play (though possibly with poorer hand position). The in-line or out-of-line G key is also an option—the advantage of the out-of-line G is that L3 does not have to reach as far to close the key. Some students leave the plug in the G key only, so that L3 closes more easily with slight inadequacies of hand position.

Recommended student flute brands include the following, with multiple options at different price points:

Yamaha, which offers both closed and open-hole student flutes

Gemeinhardt, which offers several student flutes including Model 3, 2SP and 2SH

Jupiter, which offers 515S with curved head joint available, 511 with B foot joint, and 515RS and are usually somewhat less expensive than the above

Armstrong

Oboe

Student oboes may be found at a wide variety of price points with a variety of options, but generally one should expect to pay more for a student oboe than for a student clarinet or flute. The very least expensive plastic oboes will lack low B-flat keys, LH F lever, and F resonance key and may feel somewhat unstable—especially on Forked F. Unless a compelling financial reason exists to shop the "bargain basement," consider the importance of your oboist to your instrumentation and strive for the best possible plastic instrument. Recommended brands:

Renard—Student models from the Fox Company offered at several price points. (The Fox Company generally dominates this market.)

Yamaha

Clarinet

Unlike oboes and flutes, student model clarinets will all have the same options—seventeen keys, six rings, Boehm fingering system. Plastic is much more stable and durable than wood for student clarinets, so virtually all modern student clarinets are plastic. Recommended student clarinet brands:

Buffet, B-12

Yamaha, YCL255

Conn-Selmer, including Vito 7212PC and Selmer

Bassoon

Like oboes, bassoons have numerous variations, including location of whisper key lock, and number of keys for either thumb. "Short reach" may be an advantage for a student with small hands, especially in middle school—a touchpiece for L3 is provided so that the ring finger doesn't have to reach beyond its potential. The Fox Renard dominates this market, with four basic acoustical options. It features "Long Bore" instruments with a rounder tone as well as "Short Bore" bassoons which are somewhat more flexible and more open in tone quality. Expect to pay considerably more for a student bassoon than any other student instrument.

Renard—Student models from the Fox Company offered at several price points

Saxophone

More than any other wind instrument, hand-me-down, estate sale or pawn shop saxophones seem to find their way into students' hands. The absence of an articulated G# key, a low B-flat key, a high F palm key or the presence of a marking "high pitch," "low pitch," or any abbreviation "hp," "h," "lp," or "l" are indications of an obsolete and thus unusable instrument. If the instrument looks like a tenor saxophone but is small, it may be a "C Melody," which is also obsolete.

New student models vary widely in price and quality, with the instruments at the very low end of the price range frustratingly inadequate. Always recommend that an instrument be procured from a knowledgeable music dealer and not from a discount or "big box" store.

Yamaha (model 1295)

Jupiter (model AL769, which at the time of this writing offers a unique warranty until the original owner graduates from high school)

Reeds

Oboe Reeds

Recommended Suppliers for Oboe Reeds:

- Forrest's, the Double Reed Specialists
  1849 University Ave.
  Berkeley, CA 94703 U.S.A.
  (510) 845-7178
  sales@forrestsmusic.com
- RDG Woodwinds, Inc.
  589 North Larchmont Blvd., 2nd Floor
  Los Angeles, CA 90004
  (323)463-4930

About Oboe Reeds:

Good reeds are absolutely essential for your oboe students' success. While many excellent texts exist which discuss making and adjusting oboe reeds in great detail, I regard the following to be essential bits of knowledge for the non-oboist music teacher.

- Get your oboe students to a good private teacher as soon as possible. That teacher will either be able to supply oboe reeds or to adjust ones that have been bought.
- All cane (organic) reeds react to changes of altitude, barometric pressure, humidity, and weather. So do not be surprised if a reed made in Florida and sold as "medium" feels too hard when played in Colorado.

Physical Characteristics

- Generally oboe reeds are made on a 47mm staple (the metal part of the reed, wrapped with cork on the bottom end), and are 70mm in overall length. One can make a shorter reed to play sharper, but it should be on a shorter staple, for example 45mm, otherwise the tone and response will suffer.
- The threads that hold the cane on the staple should go exactly to the end of the staple, so you can be fairly certain that the exterior measurement from the bottom end to the top thread is the length of the staple.
- The two blades of cane need to seal all the way to the strings. Plug the open end of the staple with your finger, draw a vacuum into the reed with your mouth and pull the reed out of your mouth quickly. You should hear a "pop" as the reed flies open a short time after you have drawn the reed out of your mouth. If your reed leaks, soak is some more to see if it was not wet enough. Beyond that, reeds that leak, even slightly, near the staple might be salvageable with a small amount of plastic wrap or "fish skin" (also called "Goldbeater's skin") wrapped around the area where the cane meets the tube. But don't bet on it—air escaping from the reed itself can easily be the sign of an unsalvageable reed.

- An oboe reed needs to have a discernable tip—a thinner area in the last 4-5mm of the reed. Avoid commercial reeds that have a gradual slope, more like a clarinet or saxophone reed.
- An oboe reed needs to have a heart—a somewhat thicker area behind the tip—and a spine. Both of these features can be seen by holding the reed between a light source and your eye. The back of the reed should have a scraped shape that looks like the letter "W." These are features of a well-engineered reed.

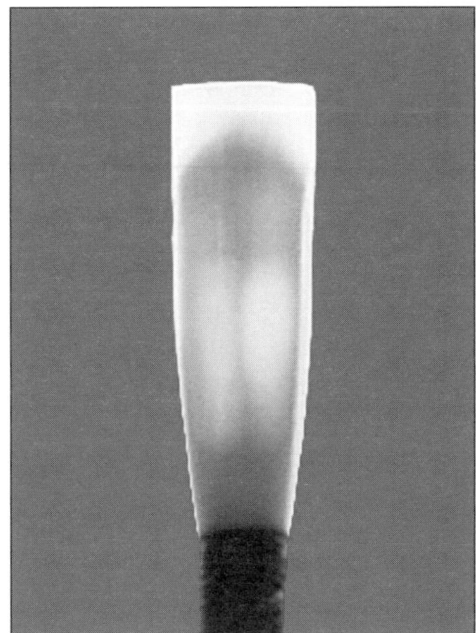

Oboe reed, showing spine, "W," tip and heart

General Information

- If the staple fits too tightly into the oboe, or if it does not go down all the way into the tube, roll the tube between a flat surface and a reed knife or table knife to compress the cork slightly. Do not use cork grease on the reed, as the inadvertent transfer of cork grease to the blades of the reed will waterproof the outside of the reed, making the reed much more closed.
- If the staple does not fit tightly enough, soak the cork until it expands sufficiently to fit securely into the tube. Heating the cork will also cause it to expand, but only temporarily.

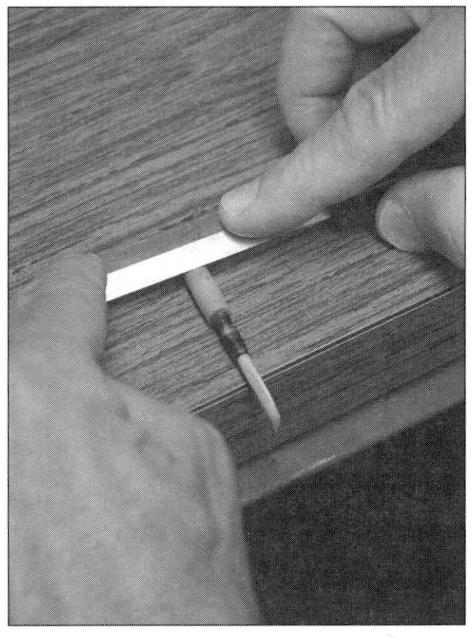

Compressing staple cork

- The wood part of the reed should be soaked in water (as opposed to saliva) a small distance past the strings. Since wood expands toward moisture, mouth soaking will cause the reed to be excessively open. A new reed will absorb water quickly; an older one will take longer to soak, and warmer water will soak a reed more quickly than cold. Generally avoid ice-cold water from a drinking fountain.
- A reed should produce a "double crow" when inserted all the way into the mouth to the strings, with no contact between wood and lip. *This is not an oboe embouchure*—it is merely a way to know that the reed will produce both high and low sounds when allowed to vibrate in an uncontrolled fashion. It may be necessary to open a reed by gently squeezing it sideways near the strings, or it may be necessary to close it by squeezing it shut at the tip before it will crow. You should hear both high and low sounds in the crow—if you only hear high sounds, for example, the lower notes of the oboe will respond poorly, if at all.

- Very often, one side of an oboe reed will play better than the other. Test the reed with both blades uppermost and remember which way it plays best. Usually putting the more arched blade uppermost works best.
- Sometimes reeds develop a split in one of the blades. If the split is toward the center of the blade, the reed probably is ruined. Sometimes a reed which is split closer to the side of the blade will continue to function. Most likely, however, the split will get worse and the reed will not last much longer.
- Before removing wood with a reed knife, an oboe plaque should be gently placed between the blades of an oboe reed. Do not push the plaque in very far, or you run the risk of tearing a hole in the side of the reed, between the blades. Remember, the knife is used for scraping rather than cutting or carving, and is thus held more or less at a perpendicular to the reed than at an oblique angle.

Bassoon Reeds

Recommended Suppliers for Bassoon Reeds:

- Forrest's, the Double Reed Specialists
  1849 University Ave.
  Berkeley, CA 94703 U.S.A.
  (510) 845-7178
  sales@forrestsmusic.com
- RDG Woodwinds, Inc.
  589 North Larchmont Blvd., 2nd Floor
  Los Angeles, CA 90004
  (323)463-4930

About Bassoon Reeds

As is true of any reed instrument, good reeds are absolutely essential to your bassoon students' success. Many excellent texts discuss bassoon reeds at great length: the following are essential bits of information for the non-bassoonist music teacher:

- Get your bassoon students to a good private teacher as immediately as possible. That teacher will either be able to supply bassoon reeds or to adjust ones that have been bought.
- All cane (organic) reeds are subject to changes of altitude, barometric pressure, humidity and weather. Do not be surprised if a reed made at low altitude becomes very hard at high altitude.
- Simple adjustments may be made with a minimal tools. Begin with a bassoon mandrel, a guitar pick or bassoon plaque, a round file, a reed knife and a pair of needle-nosed pliers. While a reamer is preferable to a round file for enlarging the bottom opening of a bassoon reed, reamers vary widely in price and the less expensive ones may be inadequate. Reed knives also vary widely in price, but a knife is more likely to be used on reeds other than bassoon, making it a wiser investment.
- If using store-bought reeds begin with a medium soft strength. Bassoon reeds must be soaked completely before playing or adjusting. They will vary in length and width, and these dimensions can have significant impact on the overall pitch of the instrument.

- Like an oboe reed, a bassoon reed must "crow" when blown by placing the lips past the blades onto the wires. One should hear at least two tones in the crow.

Common Problems and Solutions

The reed is too hard to blow (too resistant)

- If the tip opening is large (over about 1/16 of an inch), gently close the reed at the first wire with pliers. If it remains too resistant, put the mandrel in the back end and the guitar pick or plaque between the blades of the fully-soaked reed and take a little cane off both sides with sandpaper or a reed knife.

The reed doesn't fit onto the bocal or falls off while playing.

- Use the round file or reamer to enlarge and round the opening at the bottom of the reed. Reaming should be done when the reed is dry.

The string binding (Turk's Head knot) has come loose or moves up or down the reed.

- Shrink tubing (found in a hardware store or home center where electricians' supplies are located) makes an adequate substitute if the string is completely off the reed, but remember that reed cane makes very good kindling and ignites easily. If the knot is only loose, usually soaking the reed long enough for the wood to swell is all that is needed to tighten the knot. Secure the knot with clear fingernail polish.

The wires don't stay in place.

- If the wires are loose when the reed is wet, they need to be tightened with pliers. With the mandrel in the reed, carefully lift the twisted ends of the wire, pull on them and then twist it slightly tighter. Be sure to lift the wire while twisting or it will break. Playing without the first wire will cause the reed to play flat and be unstable on E.

Tip opening is too large or too small.

- Squeezing the wire closest to the tip on the sides of the fully soaked reed with pliers perpendicular to the reed opening will open the tip. Squeezing the second wire from the tip on the sides with the pliers perpendicular to the tip will close the tip.

The pitch sags on third space E.

- Move the top wire a little closer to the tip. If this does not solve the problem, clip a very tiny amount off of the tip of the reed with a single-edged razor blade.

Clarinet and Saxophone Reeds

Recommended Brands

- Vandoren. Industry leader for many years. The "blue box" Vandoren is the basic product, and many other options are also offered, for example "Java Jazz" for jazz saxophone use, and V-12 and V-l21 for clarinet.
- Rico: Reserve, Reserve Classic and Grand Concert
- D'Addario: Reserve and Reserve Classic

- Mitchell Lurie (clarinet only)
- Fred Hemke (saxophone only)
- Legere: This currently leads the synthetic reed market. Available for all clarinets and saxophones, this semi-transparent polymer reed is considerably more expensive than cane reeds, but outlasts cane reeds and never warps. Especially convenient for large instruments—contralto and contrabass clarinet, bass saxophone.

Reed Strength

- The higher the number, the more resistant (i.e. "harder") the reed.
- Recommend a number 2 for the first reeds your beginners purchase. Then adjust the strength number as you notice how the first reeds are working.
- A reed that is too resistant (hard) will have a very fuzzy, "airy" sound and the student will tend to bite.
- A reed that is too soft will blow very easily, but will produce a flat pitch if it speaks at all in the upper register. So as a student's embouchure and air stream grow stronger and as the upper register becomes more necessary, the strength number can be adjusted upwards. (i.e. from no. 2 toward no. 2 1/2 or 3).
- Do not assume that the better the player, the harder the reed. The reed must be of an appropriate strength for the player *and the mouthpiece*. Many students play reeds which are inappropriately resistant because they believe it is a mark of an advanced player.
- Not all mouthpieces are equally resistant (see the discussion on selecting mouthpieces)—some are much more resistant and others blow much more freely. Therefore, the same reed strength will not be appropriate for all mouthpieces.
- There are two broad categories of reed problems: organic and mechanical. If the material from which a reed (cane) is made is of inferior quality, no amount of adjusting will make it into a good reed. If the cane is of high quality, the reed may be improved by adjustment.
- A quick way to recognize a poor piece of cane is to write on the back of the reed with a ball-point pen. The more the pen digs into the cane, the less likely it is that it will ever be a good reed, no matter how skillfully one adjusts it.

Reed Care And Adjustment

- Many reeds work better when placed slightly off the center of the mouthpiece facing one direction or the other. If one works best placed slightly to the left, it does not follow that all reeds will work best placed to the left. When a reed improves when pushed to the left, the right side is too resistant.
- Moving a reed upward on the mouthpiece increases the resistance (makes it seem "harder"), and moving it downward does the opposite. One may need more resistance to control the sound in the upper register.
- All other factors being equal, the wider the reed, the more difficult it is to focus the sound.
- A reed will almost always sound and respond better after it has been rubbed smooth and sealed. This can be done with writing paper or the back of a sheet of sandpaper.

Understanding Warpage

Virtually all single reeds warp when wet and dried a few times. The two kinds of humidity-related warpage are: (1) convex, when the sides of the flat back reed pull off of a flat surface and the center stays in contact, and (2) concave, when the sides touch a flat surface and the center arches off the surface. To see the warpage clearly, use a piece of glass and a small drop of water. One can decide quickly by where the water is in contact whether the reed is convex or concave. When a reed is convex, it is telling us that it has dried too quickly, and when it is concave, it has dried too slowly or has been over-soaked. Regularly check the backs of single reeds and adjust the storage humidity as needed, possibly by using a more air-tight reed container or by using a sealable plastic bag with the reed holder that you have.

Many clarinetists make the common error of pinning a reed down to a flat surface—*especially a non-porous flat surface like glass.* Unfortunately, this encourages rather than discourages convex warpage. When the back of a wet reed is pinned to a nonporous surface, the thin edges of the reed dry first, trapping water between the nonporous surface and the thicker center of the reed. The cane warps toward the water resulting in much more pronounced convex warpage than if the reed had been left flat side-up in the same atmosphere.

The tip of a reed sometimes becomes wavy, especially when it has been allowed to dry for a long time and then just barely wet again. This waviness is of little concern—soaking and playing restores the flatness to the tip.

Reed Width and Overall Reed Shape

The width of a single reed affects the way in which it responds and the ease with which the sound will focus. While a "spread" sound can be due to many factors such as a loose ligature, leakage in the upper joint, embouchure or tongue position, it is also often due to a reed which is too wide for the mouthpiece. Any cane which hangs over the side of the facing can be removed with light sandpaper on a flat surface such as glass. However, if a little narrowing is good, much narrowing is not necessarily better. The point at which the sides of the reed exactly match the sides of the mouthpiece facing is the ideal width—removing more cane will cause the reed to become bright and thin-sounding.

Tip thickness

There is only a very small range of thickness measurements that can work for the tip of any reed. Just under five thousandths of an inch seems to be best. One becomes sensitive to the feel and sound of the reed clipper as it cuts through the tip—thinner than .0035 hardly makes a noise at all, and more than .005 makes an audible "snap." When a tip is thicker than .005 inch, the tone is bright and edgy and altissimo register becomes sluggish. With tips much thinner than .0035, one begins to run the risk of producing very high-pitch whistles or "pressure squeaks."

Thinning the tip—especially toward the center of the tip—of a single reed often darkens the sound, all other factors being left alone

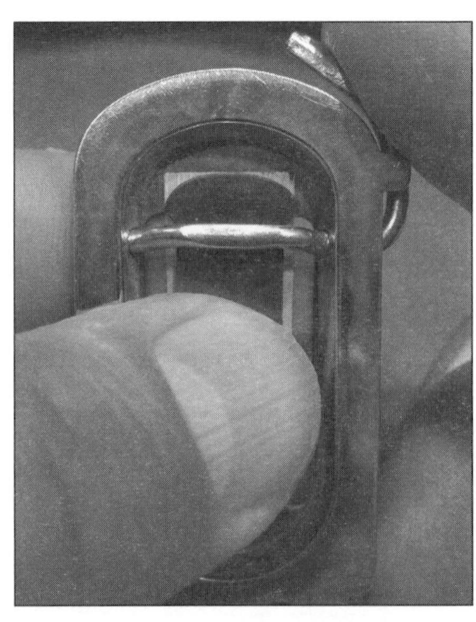

Correct alignment & use of reed clipper

The obvious application of this knowledge is to the practice of clipping reeds to regain a desirable resistance. The reed gets "soft" because it bends inward, decreasing the tip opening. We feel too little resistance, and so we clip a small amount from the tip of the reed to slide a thicker part of the reed up over the facing curve of the mouthpiece. This provides more resistance, but it also leaves the tip thicker than .005 inch. The tone is bright and ugly, and the altissimo no longer responds. Thin the very tip after clipping—especially in the center—to regain darkness and upper register response. *Resistance does not come from the tip of a single reed—it comes from the area over and behind the curve of the mouthpiece facing.* Thinning the tip will not change the resistance.

Balance

There is no such thing as a reed which is balanced for all mouthpieces. *Balance* simply means that the resistant areas of a reed match the less resistant parts of the mouthpiece facing *for that player.* Briefly stated, *in order to be balanced, the reed must be a mirror image of the mouthpiece facing*.

There are two very good tests to determine whether a reed is balanced or not. First, rolling the mouthpiece on its axis in the mouth while playing a short-tube note (like open G on clarinet or third-space C on saxophone), one might notice that a more colorful sound is found slightly off center one direction or the other. The side that the lip is pressing when the tone is most colorful and perhaps louder is the resistant side. Secondly, one might move the reed very slightly to one side of the facing or the other. When the reed responds best moved to the left, the right side is too resistant, and vice versa. With a well-shaped reed, removing some wood from the more resistant side of the vamp between the beginning of the cut to about halfway to the tip will balance the reed. Avoid thinning one corner of the tip or the other to balance the reed. This will only make the tone dull.

Summary: Reeds in General

Think of problems with reeds in two categories: mechanical and organic. Organic problems cannot be repaired mechanically—bad cane makes bad reeds. Mechanical considerations include warpage, balance, tip-to-heart relationships, tip center-to-corner relationships, vamp length and reed thickness and width. Understanding the function of each of these considerations leads to greater control of reeds.

While maintaining an elevated humidity level to prevent warpage of single reeds makes a great deal of sense, remember that a double reed is warped intentionally—either around a mandrel or around a staple. Elevating the humidity in storage of a double reed makes less sense and elevating it to excess can cause a double reed to mildew.

Regardless of how good one's best reed is, the only real safety comes in numbers. Players who rely on just one good reed are often not aware that the reed has worn out, and typically continue to play on inadequate equipment.

An accomplished player wouldn't trust something right out of the box to last through a whole concert. Reeds must be "broken in" carefully. This includes limiting the time that a new reed is played to just a few minutes for the first several days, and it includes carefully sealing and polishing the vamp (cut part) and the back (flat part) of single reeds.

Reed players frequently make the statement that a new reed has gotten "soft." Players perceive "softness" not because the density or strength of the cane has changed, but because the distance between the tip of the reed and the tip of the mouthpiece (or the tip opening on a double reed) has decreased as a result of the reed warping inward.

Mouthpieces

A student clarinet will be supplied with an injection-molded plastic mouthpiece. If a replacement is needed and the price is a major issue, the following are recommended:

Pyne Polycrystal

Fobes Debut

The mouthpiece is the least expensive and most effective upgrade that one can make on a clarinet or saxophone, and certainly should be the first upgrade to be sought. Professional model mouthpieces divide themselves into two groups—machine made- and hand-made, with numerous wonderful hand-made mouthpieces considerably more expensive. Be very careful if you are shopping for hand-made mouthpieces—they need to be reed-friendly and then must tune well on your instrument. Of the machine-made mouthpieces, Vandoren has dominated the clarinet mouthpiece market for many years with the older 2RV, B45 and 5RVlyre the most prominent, and Selmer and Vandoren have dominated the classical saxophone mouthpiece market with the C* (C-star) and V2 respectively. In more recent years, Vandoren has made some major improvements in both the clarinet and classical saxophone mouthpiece markets and Rico and D'Addario have made worthy contributions to the market, so the following recommendations are made as of the publication date of this volume.

Recommended entry-level professional clarinet mouthpieces:

- Vandoren: (Series 13 or otherwise) BD5, CL6, M30, M15, M15lyre, M13, B40lyre, M30lyre, recommended approximately in that order. "Series 13" on a Vandoren mouthpiece refers to "American pitch," or A=440, whereas without the oval "13" stamp on the side, the mouthpiece will play at a higher pitch.
- D'Addario Woodwinds: Reserve X10 or X10E, with the X10E slightly more open.

Bass Clarinet

- Vandoren: B50, B44 or B40

Saxophone

- Vandoren: Optimum AL3 (alto), TL20 (tenor)
- Selmer C*, S 90 C* (all saxophones)

The jazz saxophone market is considerably more diverse, with the type of tone quality varying widely. See the discussion below for details. Recommended jazz mouthpieces for young (through high school) players:

Alto Saxophone

- Meyer 5
- Vandoren Jumbo Java

Tenor Saxophone

- Otto Link
- Berg Larsen
- Vandoren Jumbo Java

Baritone Saxophone

- Dukoff
- Vandoren Jumbo Java

General Information

Clarinet and saxophone mouthpieces are commonly made of plastic, hard rubber, crystal, or metal. Plastic mouthpieces are inexpensive, injection-molded and are generally beginners' mouthpieces. Hard rubber is the material of which the vast majority of high-quality clarinet mouthpieces and a very large number of quality classical and jazz saxophone mouthpieces are made. Crystal (glass) is used as well—it feels colder and harder to the player and it is heavier than hard rubber, but it never warps and is virtually impervious to wear on the facing. Metal—generally surgical steel, sometimes plated with gold—is also impervious to wear but it also weighs considerably more than hard rubber. So although some very famous metal clarinet mouthpieces have been made, because the weight of the clarinet is supported by only one thumb, the weight issue is the reason why metals are not commonly used for clarinet mouthpieces. Because the weight of a saxophone is supported by a strap or harness, the small bit of extra weight is of less consequence. Since many jazz mouthpieces are metal, it is commonly thought that if a mouthpiece is metal it is therefore a jazz mouthpiece—however, this is not always true.

Resistance (the feeling that the instrument is blowing back at the player) varies from mouthpiece to mouthpiece, and is largely but not solely a function of the facing curve. Appropriate resistance is absolutely necessary on all woodwinds for a controllable upper register. *All other factors being equal, the more open a woodwind mouthpiece facing is, the more resistant it will be and the more closed, the less resistant. Again, all other factors being equal, the shorter a woodwind facing is, the more resistant it will be and the longer, the less resistant.* "Open" and "closed" refers to the distance between the tip of the mouthpiece and the tip of the reed, and "short" and "long" refers to the distance between the tip of the mouthpiece and the point on the facing where it begins to curve away from the mouthpiece's flat table (upon which the reed sits).

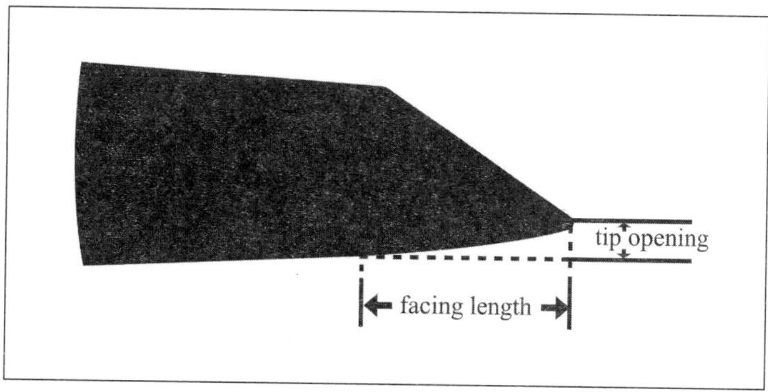

Mouthpiece facing length and tip opening

Most major mouthpiece manufacturers and some suppliers will publish a chart which compares the opening and facing length of the mouthpieces that they are merchandising. Interior dimensions also affect resistance, but the facing is the major variable since it affects the leverage exerted upon the reed when it attempts to vibrate.

When buying a clarinet or saxophone mouthpiece for use in classical music, look for a sound that is pleasing to the performer and listener, ease and cleanness of articulation, evenness of sound from bottom to top, and reliable intonation. The problem of general flatness is especially critical on clarinet because the mouthpiece can only be pushed into the barrel joint to a certain point. The saxophone mouthpiece can usually slide onto the neck to whatever location is needed, even if the neck cork needs to be sanded. Of greater concern, however, is the mouthpiece which causes the short fingerings (with few fingers down) to be out of tune with the longer fingerings. Eliminate mouthpieces which do not tune well with themselves throughout the range of the instrument.

Saxophone mouthpieces are either designed for jazz or for classical use. Generally, a classical mouthpiece is designed with a woodwind paradigm—to be controllable in all ranges with reliable response and compared to a jazz mouthpiece, a sweeter, even, more blending sound. Most, but not all, of these mouthpieces will be hard rubber. Jazz mouthpieces are made for greater projection and/or volume so that the player can be heard in balance with brass and rhythm sections. Most importantly, be sure the jazz mouthpiece selected produces an acceptable sound for the situation at hand, be sure the intonation is reliable, and be sure the player can control the mouthpiece. Do not assume that the mouthpiece that a famous jazz saxophonist plays or has played is therefore appropriate for a young student!

Jazz mouthpieces generally have wider tip openings than classical mouthpieces. It will be difficult if not impossible to produce acceptable tone quality with a jazz mouthpiece in a classical ensemble or vice-versa, so saxophonists who play both styles usually carry two mouthpieces and change for each style. There are excellent (and very loud) hard rubber jazz mouthpieces as well as metal mouthpieces.

Ligatures

Clarinet and Saxophone Recommendation:

- Bonade (Screws under)
- Vandoren Optimum
- Rovner (Vinyl)

There are many ligatures on the market at a wide variety of price points. They do make a difference in the way the player perceives the sound and response. The greatest question that must be answered, for the clarinetist especially is, "does this ligature hold the sound at loud dynamics?"

Ligatures with screws either have the screw mechanism above the mouthpiece or over the reed. Ligatures are right-handed, so if the screws cannot be turned by the right hand when the mechanism is below, then it is designed to be played with the screws on top of the mouthpiece.

Materials from which ligatures are made vary widely—metal, leather, plastic, nylon, string or vinyl among other possibilities. The variation that one achieves by changing ligatures is not as significant as that of changing mouthpieces or instruments, but at a very refined level it is worth consideration. Also at a very refined level is the question of stability of a ligature, as some may be inclined to become loose by themselves or when the mouthpiece/reed/ligature assembly is removed for swabbing or switching to another clarinet (such as an A clarinet from a B-flat). The level of audible difference a ligature makes pales by comparison to the level of difference a mouthpiece or an instrument makes.

Barrel Joints

There are numerous after-market barrels existing in the marketplace. Generally, the only reason an instrumental teacher would need to seek an alternative barrel joint is if the clarinet and mouthpiece combination is chronically flat or sharp. In these instances, a longer or shorter barrel of the brand of clarinet upon which the barrel is to be used is probably the best recommendation. The interior of the barrel is an inverse cone, and dimensions affect the width of the twelfths (overblow), so the wrong barrel might allow a "tuning note" to be in tune with an electronic tuner, but the scale of the instrument might become erratic. This is the reason to "stay with the brand name." At a very high level, an artist teacher might have a different recommendation, but that person should have sufficient experience and knowledge to make a reasonable recommendation.

Equipment Problems

There are various options that allow teachers to test a student's equipment without risk of exposure to the viruses and germs that frequently incubate in schools. The best option is to own oboe and bassoon reeds, and clarinet and saxophone mouthpieces and reeds in which we have 100% confidence. The other option is to own one of the available mouthpiece disinfectant sprays that are used for instrument demonstrations when elementary school students are recruited for the middle school band program. These may be ordered from music tool suppliers such as Ferree's.

■ *All woodwind instruments*

The instrument can be played from the shortest (or "open") fingering downward only to a certain point and won't go any lower

- A pad is either missing or not sealing the tone hole at about the location of the lowest finger in the last successful fingering. Sometimes this is due to a bent bridge key as on clarinet or oboe, an adjustment screw inadequately adjusted as on saxophone, or a bent key on any woodwind.

Flute

The pads all seat but it's difficult to produce a tone and/or the tone is just not controllable.

- See if the head joint cork is in the right place. When a head joint cork gets very old it becomes loose and will slide up the headjoint toward the crown, and if it has really shrunk badly, it will leak. Also, be sure the metal face plate at the end of the cork opposite the crown is snug against the cork itself.

Oboe

Low notes do not speak. The reed does not crow when inserted all the way to the strings in the mouth and blown.

- Insufficient soaking can cause the tip to be too closed and thus the reed will only have high pitches
- If the tip is too open, squeeze the top half of the cane part of the reed closed between your thumb and index finger and try it again. Over-soaking can cause the tip to be too open.
- Is there a wire on the reed? If so, the wire very possibly could be keeping the back part of the reed from vibrating, and the reed will have no low pitches in the crow. Remove the wire from the reed by untwisting it with a small pair of needle-nosed pliers.
- Dirt may have accumulated inside the reed. Use a clean pipe cleaner, insert it in the bottom end of the reed and pull it through without reversing directions.
- If the reed does not have low pitches in the crow regardless of soaking or even manually opening the reed by squeezing it sideways, insert a plaque and remove some wood from the back 1/3 of the reed between the center and the sides.
- Other "fixes" for a reed that does not crow require the experience and tools of a specialist. Change reeds

The reed crows, but many or most notes don't speak.

- Be sure the reed is not leaking air near the strings. This can happen if the reed is not sufficiently wet, if it was tied poorly, or if the plaque was inserted forcefully and a hole was created where the blades should seal. Sometimes, putting Goldbeater's skin or plastic wrap at the base of the cane part and covering over some of the strings will seal the reed

The reed responds poorly in general.

- There may be dirt accumulation inside the reed. Clean with pipe cleaner.

Clarinet

The instrument squeaks, but the pitch of the squeak is very high and whistle-like, unlike the more common accidental "quack" most often heard.

- Could be a thin spot or a split in the tip of the reed.
- If all reeds "whistle" in this way, the mouthpiece facing may be worn or damaged. First, clean the rails of the mouthpiece so you're not looking at accumulated plaque on the rails. Light reflected off the rails should not show

an obvious inward tilt at the fulcrum point (about a half inch from the tip). Reface or replace the mouthpiece.

- Some mouthpieces have very thin rails and for that reason are more inclined to whistle in this way. (This is especially true of certain jazz saxophone mouthpieces).

The tone lacks focus—"spreads" and perhaps sounds a bit saxophone-like.

- The tongue position is represented by an "ahhh" vowel sound rather than "eh" or "ee."
- There is leakage in the upper joint, especially on the higher trill keys.
- The ligature is too low or is too loose to hold the stock of the reed firmly.
- The reed is too wide and needs to be gently sanded on the sides to narrow it.
- The reed is much too soft.

Pitch is generally flat.

- Different mouthpieces tune differently. If you are thoroughly committed to a particular mouthpiece and it is flat overall, the solution is to get a shorter barrel.

Pitch is generally sharp.

- See comment above. A longer barrel or a different mouthpiece can adjust for this. If the barrel needs to be pulled out a long way, inserting a tuning ring between the barrel and upper joint will allow the increase in bore length without exaggerating the flatness of the throat tones.

Pitch of upper clarion register is very sharp or flat to the rest of the instrument.

- The wider the bore of the barrel joint, the wider the twelfths (overblown fingerings) will be. Try different barrels.

Pitch of short fingerings (many open holes) is flat or sharp to long fingerings (many holes closed).

- A mouthpiece issue. Be sure the mouthpiece tunes well with the instrument before you buy it. Do not fall in love with a mouthpiece because of its sound if it cannot be played in tune.
- Pulling between the upper and lower joint will flatten the long fingerings without flattening the short fingerings—i.e. the notes which emit from holes above the middle tenon. For this reason tune open G first by pulling (if necessary) at the barrel. Once open G is in tune, the longer notes (including "tuning note C" on the fourth space, which is sharp on most clarinets) may be adjusted downward by pulling between the hands.

Pitch of one particular note is unusually flat and perhaps "wheezes" more than the notes around it.

- Be sure the pad clears the highest open hole sufficiently. A key may have been bent, or a pad or striker cork that is too thick may have been installed, decreasing the clearance of the pad from the clarinet.
- Check the highest open hole for accumulated dirt.

Numerous acoustical compromises have been made in the design of the clarinet. Certain problems have been minimized but cannot be fully eliminated. The placement of the register key hole forces the twelfth (overblow) between low E and low F and their overblown notes B and C to be too wide—to solve this problem would require considerably more mechanism which would bring with it a completely different set of problems.

Remember also that low C# and G# a twelfth above (Fingerings 16 and 44) will both wheeze somewhat because the hole is too high and too small to be acoustically correct. It's designed that way so that the instrument can be broken down into and upper and a lower joint, allowing more pitch flexibility than if the whole body of the instrument were one piece. One can use a cork or other solid pad and bevel the sides to minimize the issue but it is unlikely that it will go away completely.

Bassoon

Low notes do not speak.

- A pad or several pads are leaking or missing somewhere on the instrument.
- The reed is too heavy, especially in the center and back.
- Whisper key pad is not seating on the bocal.
- If someone has bent the bocal, there may be a tiny hole in it where the metal has crimped.

Most notes do not speak.

- Be sure the reed "crows." If the reed does not crow, notes will not speak
- Whisper key pad is missing
- Leakage between the reed and the bocal. Take the reed and bocal off of the bassoon, plug the end of the bocal and the whisper key hole, suck the air out of the reed and bocal and draw it quickly out of your mouth. The reed should "pop" soon after drawing it out of your mouth.
- Bocal may have a hole in it, caused by a crimp or bend. Replace the bocal.

Tenons too loose.

- Bassoon tenons are wrapped with string. Add string to the tenon and secure it with paraffin.

Stuck swab.

- This happens to everyone at some point. Buy swabs that have a piece of cord that follows the cloth part through the instrument so that if it does get stuck (and it will always be in the wing joint), the swab may be drawn out the large end. Never try to force it the rest of the way up the narrow end, never try to push it with a baton or a stick, and never try to work it out through a tone hole. Most likely it will need to go to the repair shop. (To be absolutely sure this does not happen, insert the swab from the narrow end of the wing joint—where the bocal is inserted.)

Bocal clogged or air flow impaired.

- Bocals need to be cleaned periodically. Use a bocal brush and warm flowing water.

Saxophone

Lower notes do not speak.

- A pad or pads are leaking or missing. Check with a leak light.
- The octave key on the neck is not seating because it has been bent in the assembly process.
- Reed is warped. See the Single Reed section to read about warpage.
- The student is using a reed that is too hard.
- If low C speaks but low C#, B and B-flat do not (or they are much more difficult to produce), the adjustment screw over the articulated G# pad might not be holding the G# pad down when the C#, B and B-flat keys are depressed. Sometimes this happens because the cork bumper on the end of the screw has fallen off.

Turning the adjustment screw on the G# key

Common Repair Problems

Woodwinds in General

Rod-axels or pivot screws loose.

- As long as tightening the pivot screw all the way does not cause the key to bind, it should be tightened all the way. Do not confuse a pivot or rod axel with an adjustment screw, as shown in the photo above.
- If a screw continues to work its way loose, put some beeswax on the threads of the screw.

Adjustment screws misaligned.

- When closing one pad ("master") causes a pad above it ("slave") to also close, both must rest on the seating ring with equal pressure. Test with a small strip of cigarette paper (oboe, clarinet, flute, bassoon) or a leak light (saxophone).

Needle springs unhooked.

- Use a spring hook or crochet hook to restore the needle spring to its saddle.

Needle springs broken.

- A rubber band can provide a nearly adequate temporary solution, but a technician needs to replace the spring.

Flat springs loose or fallen off.

- Tighten or replace the screw that holds the flat spring on the key.

Pad has fallen out.

- If the pad was held in by glue, the glue behind the pad melts when the key is heated, and then sets firmly when it cools. Replace the pad in as nearly as possible to the original position (you can often tell when the seating ring that has pressed into the pad matches the tone hole) and holding the key closed, carefully heat the key cup to melt the glue using an alcohol lamp, butane lighter or Bunsen burner. Hold the key nearly vertical as pictured below, allowing the flame to heat the key cup without actually touching the pad or the instrument. When it cools, test all the way around the pad with a long, pointed piece of cigarette paper to be sure the pad seats in all places. [On a saxophone, the keys may have lacquer on them which will melt, and the buttons on the keys can burn or melt with heat, so leave this to a qualified repair technician.]

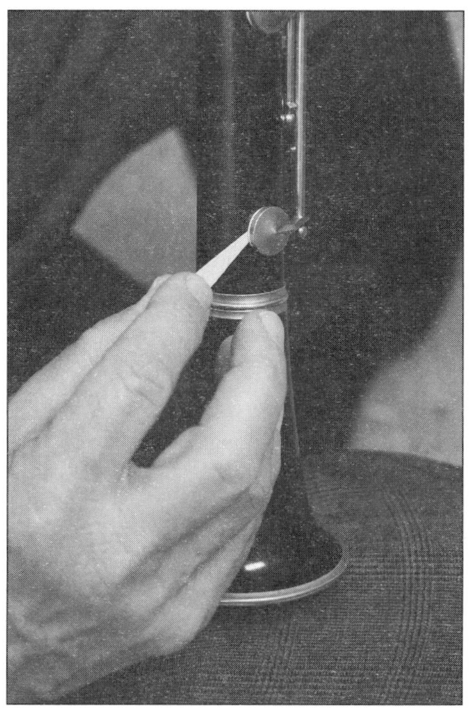

Checking a pad for even seal around circumference of the seating ring

Pad seats poorly and leaks.

- A pad will leak when the cigarette paper pulls tightly in one part of the circumference of the seating ring and not in others. It is usually simpler to replace the pad with one that has no seating ring pressed into it.

Pad has split or the skin has come off.

- Replace the pad. If you do the repair yourself, poke a hole in the very side of the pad to allow expanding air to escape when the pad is heated, melt a little French Cement or stick shellac from the stick and apply enough of it to the back of the new pad to fill the space between the key cup and the pad, put the pad in the instrument and follow the procedure above. The cigarette paper must resist being pulled out at every point around the circumference of the pad (as shown above). When finished, moisten the pad and gently pin it in closed position overnight so that a seating ring develops on the new pad.

Heating a pad from the side to avoid burning the pad or the instrument

Sticky pads.

- Pads occasionally stick to the instrument, either causing the pad to lift too slowly (as for example articulated the G# key on saxophone) or eventually to stick to the instrument. Insert a clean piece of paper (for example, non-gummed cigarette paper) between the pad and the instrument, hold the pad down to the instrument, and pull the paper out. It may be necessary to use a small amount of rubbing alcohol to clean the seating ring on the instrument. If the pad continues to stick, a small amount of talcum powder on the pad may solve the problem.

A tenon cork or saxophone neck cork has fallen off or torn or is too loose.

- For a temporary repair, wrap the tenon or saxophone neck with waxed dental floss, to serve until the instrument arrives at the repair shop.
- Re-gluing the old cork is rarely satisfactory. Replace with a new cork by measuring the correct size, beveling the end, applying contact cement, wrapping the cork around the tenon or neck, and sanding down to size with sandpaper.
- Sometimes wrapping a small strip of paper around the cork and putting the mouthpiece over it makes a satisfactory temporary saxophone repair.

Cork bumper has fallen off.

- Striker corks and felts are held on with contact cement—follow the instructions on the tube or bottle or tube. Best to replace the cork with a new one, as re-cementing a dry, old cork is rarely satisfactory. Cement a larger piece of cork onto the key and then trim to size with a single-edge razor blade.

A wood instrument (oboe, clarinet, piccolo) has cracked.

- Stop playing the instrument and mark the crack with a pencil—draw a line over the crack and perpendicular lines at the ends of the crack showing its total length so that the crack can be identified if it closes before the technician sees it. *The crack should be pinned and not flush-banded.* Pins are screws embedded in the wood across the crack at a diagonal to stabilize the instrument and prevent further movement. Pinning allows the instrument to swell and contract at that point, whereas flush banding does not, causing the relationships of bore dimension to change with the weather and season.
- If the crack goes into a tone hole, have a plastic tone hole bushing inserted and a new pad installed. Without the bushing, there will always be the potential for leakage if the crack opens even slightly.

Flute

Head joint cork in the wrong place.

- The position of the head joint cork affects the intonation of the flute's scale. The line on the end of the cleaning rod should be in the middle of the blowhole or very slightly past the middle toward the crown. If the cork has shrunk

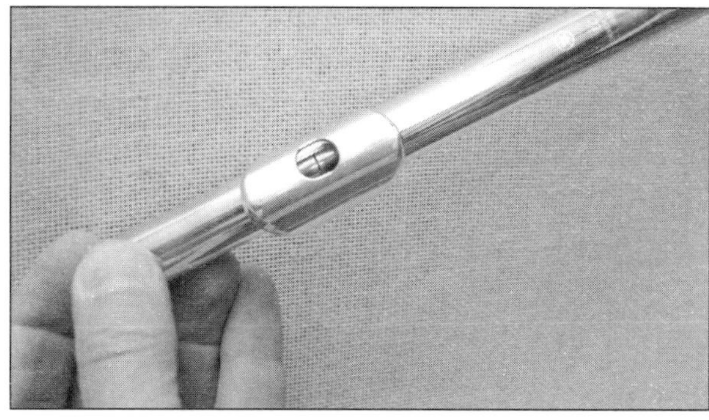

Headjoint with cleaning rod line in the middle of the blowhole considerably and moves easily, it most likely is leaking and needs to be replaced.

Tenons do not fit together.

- Probably the student has dropped the head joint or body and the male tenon has been damaged. This requires special tools that a good repair shop will have. These tools can expand or contract the male end as well as restore the roundness.

Male tenon has dirt and corrosion.

- Lightly clean the male end with very fine steel wool.

Bent keys, causing pads to seat on one side but not the other or to bind.

- Unless you have considerable repair skills, send the flute to a quality repair shop.

Pads seat on one side but not the other.

- Since all but three flute pads are screwed in (closed holes) or snapped in (open holes), adjusting them is done with paper shims inserted behind the pad. This is tedious work and best left to a technician. [This problem is found very frequently on the E-flat key on the foot joint, because the player has pushed directly on the pad while assembling the instrument.]

Pads which should seat together do not—one pad seats more lightly than the other.

- On student flutes, you will find adjustment screws that will change the alignment of the two pads (the "master" below, and the "slave" above). These may be in different locations on different brands of flutes.
- Often, professional model flutes do not have adjustment screws, and so these adjustments are made by a technician by adjusting cork thicknesses at the points where the motion transfers from the "master" pad to the "slave" pad.

Oboe

Stuck swab

- The swab should be pulled back through the large end of the instrument. Ideally, use a swab that has a piece of cord that trails beyond the end of the swab so that if stuck, it can be easily pulled backwards out of the larger end of the bore.
- Better yet, insert the swab from the narrow top end and pull it out the large end, which completely eliminates the possibility of the swab getting stuck.
- Never try to work the swab out by inserting a tool in any tone hole.

Adjustment screws

- This is a more complicated issue on oboe than on flute or saxophone because the first pad of the lower joint raises pads in the upper joint which are then put down again by left hand fingers. This task may be best left to a repair shop or to an oboe specialist. However, to check for problems, always start checking master-slave combinations from the top of the instrument.

Missing pads, felts, corks.

- See "All woodwind instruments," above.

Clarinet

Stuck Swab.

- This usually happens if there was a fold in a cloth swab when it was inserted, and the fold gets stuck on the register key tube. If possible, pull the swab out the direction from which it came.
- If pulling it backwards is not possible, remove the barrel and work with the upper joint alone, pulling alternately on one side and then on the other and on the middle of the swab. Usually this dislodges the swab or at worst tears the swab as it is pulled through.
- Do not push the swab with a baton or stick as this will merely compress the swab and scratch the inside of the bore.
- Small chamois swabs can be more problematic than larger cloth swabs. A larger cloth swab can be more easily pulled backward in the direction from which it came.

Bent bridge key.

- This happens because of careless assembly of the upper and lower joints. The left hand notes probably all work but none of the right hand notes work. The bridge key needs to be bent back into position.
- If you do this bending yourself, the low E-flat (R1 & L1) needs to speak securely, but if the upper ("slave") pad pushes too tightly, it will not be possible to play smoothly from low C to B or Bb. Master and slave pads must pull evenly on the cigarette paper being used to adjust the pads.

Low E and F pads misaligned.

- This happens because the player's hand was over the lower end of the lower joint rather than over the finger holes during assembly. These keys are finicky, so if you are not confident with your repair skills, it's best left to a qualified technician.

The tenons of a wood clarinet stick together.

- This happens most often in more humid times of the year and to newer instruments that are suddenly being played heavily. No amount of cork grease solves the problem. The wood in the tenons swells and wood binds against wood, creating the danger of causing part of the male tenon to break off. The female portion of the tenon must be enlarged by rolling a piece of sandpaper into a tube shape and carefully sanding so that the cylindrical shape of the socket is retained.
- As a precaution, when applying cork grease, rub some cork grease into the wood at the end of the tenon and even for a small distance up the inside of the bore to prevent water penetration into the wood.

Bassoon

Whisper key pad has fallen off the key cup.

- The whisper key pad is oblong, leather, and is specifically designed for this one key. Re-attach with French Cement or stick shellac.

Whisper key pad does not contact the bocal as the same time the pancake (low E) key contacts the butt joint.

- Usually, this is a matter of changing the position of the wing joint with slight clockwise or counter-clockwise adjustments.
- If twisting the wing joint in the butt does not fully correct the problem, the bridge key may need a thicker cushion. A good temporary spacer is shrink tubing, found in the electrical section of a hardware store.

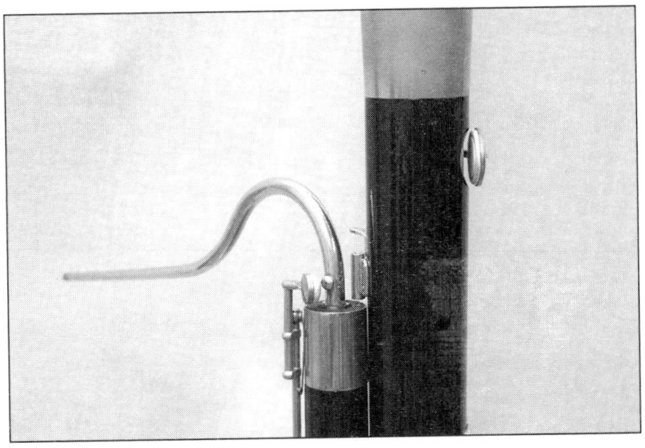

Whisper key pad and bocal with pad in open position

Stuck swab

- This usually happens in the wing joint. The best swab to use is one with a piece of cord which trails the actual cloth so that, if stuck, it can be easily drawn out of the wide end. Otherwise, it must be pulled—not pushed—out of the wide end.
- Do not insert a tool in a tone hole and push the swab.
- Better yet, insert the swab in the narrow end of the instrument and pull the cord out the wide end.

Broken tenon.

- The male end of either tenon at the butt joint end can be the object of a considerable amount of torque or sideways bending, and the tenon may break off. A qualified technician will need to back-drill the tenon up into the joint and replace the wood with a properly-tapered bore section that serves the bassoon acoustically as well as mechanically.

Pad fell out.

- Bassoon pads often cover holes that are bored slantwise through the body, causing the seating ring imprint to be oblong rather than round. The exact position of the seating ring must be rediscovered before heating the glue and reattaching the pad. Hold the instrument so that gravity holds the pad in the key cup and test the pad with cigarette paper in may positions of rotation until a quality seat is found around the whole circumference. Then, close the key and heat the pad as shown above under "General."

The gasket which seals the U-shaped tube at the bottom of the butt joint has developed a leak.

- If the gasket is cork, it may rot and develop leakage, causing the lowest notes to be very unresponsive. Have it replaced.

Saxophone

The octave pad on the neck does not seat or does not raise.

- Probably the key on the neck was bent to an incorrect position during careless assembly, and must be returned to its original position by carefully bending the key back. Torque on the neck can also bend the key, throwing the pad out of position and causing a leak. The lower register will hardly work, if at all. The key needs to be bent back, and most likely the pad should be replaced.

Low Bb, B and C# do not respond but low C does.

- The G# pad does not go all the way back to the instrument when the Bb, B, C# or G# keys are depressed. On most saxophones, there is an adjustment screw right above the G# pad that has worked its way loose or has compressed or lost its soft cork bumper. Turn the screw so that it stays down when the G# key is pressed with 1R held down.

Low notes do not respond or respond with great difficulty.

- There is a leak under one or more pads somewhere on the instrument. A technician will discover the location of the leak by inserting a leak light, and then will adjust as necessary.
- An old "trick" is to put a wine bottle cork or cork grease tube down the bell so that it rests in the lowest part of the saxophone's curve. Often this helps the lowest notes to respond more easily.

The saxophone is generally flat or sharp.

- If sharp, the neck cork is probably too thin or compressed such that the mouthpiece slides all the way onto the neck. Have the cork replaced.
- If flat, the neck cork may be too thick and the neck will not fit far enough into the mouthpiece. Sand the cork.

Maintenance

Water Removal

Swab the inside to remove moisture before returning the instrument to the case. Do not store the wet swab inside the bore of the instrument. Generally, long, cloth swabs are safer than shorter ones or chamois ones because it is easier to remove them from the direction from which they came if they become stuck in the instrument.

- Flute—insert the corner of a handkerchief into the eye of the cleaning rod as shown in the picture at the beginning of the flute section in this book. Drape the handkerchief over the end of the cleaning rod to prevent it from scratching the inside of the flute and swab each joint individually.
- Clarinet—Remove the mouthpiece and invert the instrument so that the bell is uppermost. Check to be sure the cloth or chamois swab is not folded to ensure that it will not become stuck on the register key tube. Drop the

weighted end of the swab into the bell and pull it through to the other end. Swab the mouthpiece separately.

- Saxophone—Swab each piece individually. Drop the weighted end of a saxophone swab into the bell, invert the instrument and jiggle gently so that the weight comes out the narrow end. Pull the swab through.
- Oboe and bassoon—Either try to find a swab that has a bit of cord trailing the cloth so that a stuck swab may be pulled back out the larger end, or use swabs on a rigid rod, with one of a smaller size for the narrow bore of the upper or wing joint and a larger size for the larger bores. Dropping a swab in the narrow end ensures that the swab will not get stuck in the bore.
- Bassoon—To clean the butt joint, drop the weighted end of the swab into the larger open end of the bore, invert and jiggle the joint until the weight comes out the other end and pull the swab through.

■ *Oiling Keys*

Oil the keys periodically to lubricate moving parts and to protect the rods and pivot screws from becoming rusted. Oilers made specifically for woodwind instruments are available and can be a very good investment, or a small drop of key oil or clean motor oil on the end of a toothpick can be applied to every point where one piece of metal moves against another. Wipe the excess oil off of the keys with a tissue. Do not over-oil the keys—a small amount two or three times a year should be sufficient. Keys that make an annoying amount of noise (especially on larger instruments) may be quieted by using a heavier motor oil.

■ *Polishing keys*

Chemically-treated polishing cloths designed for woodwind instruments may be purchased in a music store. Do not apply liquid or cream silver polish to a woodwind instrument because these products contain an abrasive which can wear the mechanism of an instrument.

■ *Tenon corks*

Apply cork grease to tenon corks periodically. Do not put cork grease on cork pads, on an oboe reed staple, or on a flute headjoint cork.

■ *Oiling wood instruments*

(Grenadilla is the African black wood used in the manufacture of clarinets, oboes and piccolos.)

- This is a subject upon which there is considerable disagreement. Some people play a wood instrument for years and never oil it, and others oil their instruments regularly, especially in the Fall as the air becomes drier. If you choose to oil the wood, use commercial bore oil purchased in music stores or sweet almond oil. Dedicate one chamois swab to oiling and keep it separate from swabs that would be used for cleaning and drying the bore. Apply a few drops of oil to the swab, run it through the bore several times until the shine of the oil without dry streaks is visible inside the bore. Use the same swab to oil the outside of the instrument everywhere except where the oil might run onto the pads. Oil the very ends of the tenons as well. Place the instrument in the case overnight. The next day, if there is oil still sitting on the instrument, dry it with a tissue and return to playing the instrument. Those who advocate oiling a wood instrument do so because oil is absorbed and lost by the instrument much more slowly than water, so the presence of the oil in the wood stabilizes the wood by maintaining a more-or-less constant moisture level. Removal of all keys and oiling thoroughly is the best oiling practice if time allows.

- Wood bassoons also need oil occasionally. Most repair people use either light mineral oil or linseed oil for this purpose. It is advisable to remove all of the keywork from of the instrument to protect the pads.

Basic Woodwind Toolbox

Many of the following items are available in various local markets. Specialized tools are easily found under *Woodwind Instrument Repair Tools* on the Internet.

Waterproof (Wetordry) sandpaper, 400 grit

Small swivel-top screwdrivers (flat)

Pair small toothless pliers

Small crochet hook or spring hook

Piece of one-quarter inch thick glass or plexiglass with edges smoothed

Cork grease

Roll of waxed dental floss

Small bottle or tube of contact cement (avail. in hardware store—for cork replacement)

Stick of French cement or stick shellac (for pad replacement)

Package of non-gummed cigarette paper

Single-edged razor blades

Source of heat such as an alcohol lamp with denatured alcohol or a butane lighter, (which unlike matches, will not leave a carbon deposit on the key).

Scissors

Woodwind key oil or an oiler with clean motor oil

Bore oil and a chamois swab dedicated to oil (Once it is used to oil an instrument, it can no longer be used for cleaning).

Clear finger nail polish (to stabilize unraveling string on oboe or bassoon reeds)

Pad slick (pad leveling tool)

Needle or safety pin

Tweezers

Cork Grease

Flute cleaning rod

Mouthpieces and reeds for all common woodwinds, so that the teacher may test an instrument without risk of catching communicable diseases

More advanced:

Reed knife

Oboe plaque

Bassoon plaque or guitar pick

Repair kits which include the bulk of the above already supplied are available from Ferree's Tools, Inc (www.ferreestools.com). Often, ready-made repair kits also have a supply of clarinet, saxophone and flute pads, flute shims, pivot screws, springs, corks, and many tools used for brass repair. Consider whether you have the knowledge and skills to attempt more complicated repairs and whether it is wise in your situation to create an expectation that you are the "go-to" person for every small repair. A good repair shop is a tremendous ally for your instrumental program.

Recommended Methods and Studies

Of all of the beginning band method books available as of the time of this writing, the most widely-used in the market as of this writing are:

- Essential Elements Interactive (Hal Leonard)
- Accent on Achievement (Alfred)
- Band Expressions (Alfred)

These books come with interactive CD's, mp3 access, and/or a great deal of support through the internet, and are designed to be used by full band.

The following are recommendations for private lesson study:

All Woodwinds

- Pares Scales, Pares & Whistler, (Hal Leonard) For individual or like-instrument study—not playable by bands or by mixed instruments). Much of this is duplicated in Voxman & Gower Rubank Advanced Method.
- Rubank Advanced Method, Vols. 1 & 2, Voxman & Gower (Hal Leonard). These are for individual instrument study—not useable in a heterogeneous class or band.
- Odd Meter Etudes, Everett Gates, (Alfred) For all treble clef instruments—outstanding introduction to asymmetrical meters. Use after Voxman Advanced Methods.

Flute

Beginning Methods:

- Rubank Elementary Method, A.C. Petersen, (Hal Leonard)
- Eck Method, Vols. 1 & 2, Emil Eck (Alfred) Books 1 &2
- Breeze-Easy Method, Vols 1 & 2, Valentine Anzelone (Alfred)
- Belwin Flute Method, Books 1, 2, 3, Gekeler & Hovey (Alfred)
- A Tune a Day for Flute, Herfurth & Stuart (Boston)
- Learn to Play the Flute! Books 1, 2, 3, Frederick Jacobs (Alfred)
- Suzuki Flute School, Vols. 1 & 2, Alfred Publishing Staff (Alfred)

Other study material:

- Rubank Intermediate Method, J. E. Skornicka & A. L. Petersen (Hal Leonard)
- Rubank Advanced Method, Vols 1 & 2, Gower & Voxman (Hal Leonard)
- Intermediate Studies for Developing Artists on the Flute, Shelley Jagow (Meredith Music Publications)
- Supplementary Studies, R. M. Endresen (Hal Leonard)
- First (and Second) Book of Practical Studies for Flute, Ralph Guenther (Alfred)
- Beginner's Book for the Flute, Parts 1 & 2, Tervor Wye (Novello)
- Flute Class—A Group Teaching Book for Students and Teachers, Trevor Wye (Novello) duets, trios and quartets, with CD's
- Complete Daily Essentials for Flute, Trevor Wye (Novello)

Oboe

Beginning Methods:

- Rubank Elementary Method, Nilo Hovey (Hal Leonard)
- Gekeler Method for Oboe, Books 1, 2, Kenneth Gekeler (Alfred)
- Breeze-Easy Method, Vols. 1 & 2, Valentine Anzelone (Alfred)

Other Study Material

- Rubank Intermediate Method, Skornicka & Koebner (Hal Leonard)
- Rubank Advanced Method, Vols. 1 & 2, Voxman & Gower (Hal Leonard)
- Supplementary Studies, R.M. Endresen (Hal Leonard)
- Intermediate Studies for Developing Artists on the Oboe, Shelley Jagow (Meredith Music Publications)
- Studies for Oboe, Sellner (EM Budapest) daily technical studies
- 48 Famous Studies, Ferling (Kalmus)

Clarinet

Beginning Methods:

- Rubank Elementary Method, Nilo Hovey (Hal Leonard)
- Modern Course for the Clarinet, Books 1-6, James Collis (H. Elkan)
- Breeze-Easy Method, Vols. 1 & 2, Valentine Anzelone (Alfred)

Other Study Material:

- Rubank Advanced Method, Vols. 1 & 2, Voxman & Gower (Hal Leonard)
- Supplementary Studies, R.M. Endresen, (Hal Leonard)
- Intermediate Studies for Developing Artists on the Clarinet, Shelley Jagow (Meredith Music Publications)
- Practical Study of the Scales, Stievenard (G. Schirmer)
- Melodic Etudes: A Lyric Approach to the Clarinet, Ted Hegvik, (Northeastern)

Bassoon

Beginning Methods:

- Primary Handbook for Bassoon, Richard Polonchak (Meredith Music Publications)
- Rubank Elementary Bassoon Method, Skornicka (Hal Leonard)
- Practical Method for the Bassoon, J. Weissenborn, augmented and adapted by W. F. Ambrosio (Carl Fischer)
- Breeze-Easy Method, Vols. 1 & 2, Valentine Anzelone (Alfred)

Other Study Material:

- Rubank Advanced Method, Vols. 1 & 2, Voxman & Gower (Hal Leonard)
- Intermediate Studies for Developing Artists on the Flute, Shelley Jagow (Meredith Music Publications)

Saxophone (Remember that saxophonists may also use oboe etudes)

Beginning Methods:

- Rubank Elementary Method, Nilo Hovey (Hal Leonard)
- Learn to Play the Saxophone! Books s1 & 2, Frederick Jacobs (Alfred)
- Breeze-Easy Method, Vols. 1 & 2, Valentine Anzelone (Alfred)
- Belwin Saxophone Method, Vols. 1 & 2, Gekeler & Hovey (Alfred)
- A New Tune a Day, Vols 1 & 2, Ned Bennett, (Boston Music) with CD
- Do It! Play Alto Saxophone, Books 1 & 2, James O Froseth, (GIA Publications)

Other Study Material:

- Rubank Intermediate Method, Skornicka (Hal Leonard)
- Rubank Advanced Method, Vols. 1 & 2, Voxman & Gower (Hal Leonard)
- Supplementary Studies, R.M. Endresen (Hal Leonard)

- Voicing: An Approach to the Saxophone's Third Register, Donald Sinta (Sinta)
- Intermediate Studies for Developing Artists on the Saxophone, Shelley Jagow (Meredith Music Publications)

Books particularly useful to instrumental music teachers

- *Tuning for Wind Instruments: A Roadmap to Successful Intonation* by Shelley Jagow (Meredith Music Publications)
- *The Woodwind Player's Cookbook: Creative Recipes for a Successful Performance*, West and others (Meredith Music Publications)
- *Clarinet Fingerings: A Guide for the Performer and Educator*, Thomas Ridenour
- *Essentials of Bassoon Technique*, Cooper & Toplansky

Advanced Techniques

Vibrato

The mechanism by which a vibrato is achieved is not the same on all woodwind instruments. Saxophonists (and occasionally clarinetists) produce a vibrato by moving the jaw up and down, and the vibrato produced is known as a "jaw" vibrato. Flutists and double reed players produce a vibrato by varying the air pressure, with a vibrato that some call "diaphragmatic," though the actual mechanism has been proven to function otherwise. Generally, one can introduce vibrato to a saxophonist earlier in the player's development than flutists and double reed players. In fact, vibrato exercises reinforce proper embouchure habits for a saxophonist, whereas adding a vibrato to an insufficiently-developed flute or double reed sound can be a distraction and an annoyance.

Singers' vibratos develop naturally with good vocal habits, and so there is no intentional formation of vibrato in conventional vocal pedagogy. On string and wind instruments, a vibrato must be taught and developed. There is no one "best" way to introduce vibrato, but a few proven strategies are described below:

Saxophone

The lower lip stands up by its own musculature and the tone quality itself remains consistent while the jaw moves up and down to vary only the pitch. When the lip supports the reed fully, the jaw movement affects only the pitch and not the tone.

Begin on the mouthpiece alone, producing a "siren" sliding smoothly on an alto mouthpiece between concert A-natural on top and concert F# on the bottom or on a tenor mouthpiece slide from concert E-flat to concert C . It is possible to produce a pitch as high as concert C-natural or slightly above on alto or F# on tenor, in which case it's clear that the jaw is biting into the back of the lip and the lip is only being used as a cushion for the teeth. Usually when a student gets "stuck" around C-natural, there will be great difficulty sliding down even as far as A-natural, and they will need to "find" the feeling of pushing with the lip rather than the teeth. Sometimes it helps to think about what a small child does when someone offers a spoonful of some food the baby does not want, and pushes the lips tightly together.

Once the A-F# siren is developed, replace the mouthpiece on the instrument and play a long tone on written A-natural above the staff. The mechanism learned from the siren becomes the vibrato.

Flute, Oboe, Bassoon

Again, many different pedagogical approaches that can be very effective exist. Regardless of the approach, remember that the vibrato is made by intermittently adding intensity to the sound—not by subtracting it. One can start with a "hissing" sound, "sssssssss." Listening carefully to avoid "jerks" in the undulation, make a series of crescendi and decrescendi, accelerating to a speed expected of a vibrato. When a successfully undulating "hiss" is accomplished, transfer it to the instrument, playing long tones in patterns like those suggested on the tone development pages of this text.

Another very common approach is to simply produce an accelerating crescendo-decrescendo pattern on a long tone and to sustain the undulation. Regardless of approach, a set of exercises is necessary to transfer the vibrato from something intellectual to something which is internalized and habitual.

No vibrato should ever be rhythmic—i.e. a consistent number of undulations per beat, such as four for a quarter note, two for an eighth, etc. The vibrato operates independently of the rhythm of the music being played.

In the flute culture, Marcel Moyse's book *De la sonorite* is a widely-used series of long tone exercises, and can be an effective tool for oboe and saxophone vibrato development.

The Principle of Alternate Fingerings

The two "cardinal rules" of woodwind fingering are (1) avoid lateral motion, and (2) the common, or regular fingering is the one which falls under the hand. We use alternate fingerings for one of three reasons then:

- to make technique smooth by avoiding lateral motion (most common)
- to improve intonation on an exposed or longer note
- to make fast technical passages more playable even though pitch or sound might be slightly compromised

Alternate fingerings that avoid lateral motion are relatively rare on saxophone and flute, and the few examples that do exist are discussed in the Fingering Chart Commentary sections. The flute mechanism is quite simple, with only "regular" and "thumb" B-flat as the major choices in the lower two octaves. Thumb B-flat is useful when playing in a solidly flat key, with no B-naturals in the immediate area. The L4 and R4 touchpieces on oboe are designed for some sliding, and because most of that sliding is isolated to the very lowest notes (which are used considerably less than the notes above low D), the only alternate choices are E-flat and A-flat. Again, the fingering chart and commentaries explain these choices.

Alternate fingerings on clarinet are perhaps the most baffling of all woodwind instrument fingerings for the non-clarinetist for a variety of reasons, not the least of which is that any band is likely to have more clarinetists without private instruction than oboists or bassoonists, putting a very large responsibility on the shoulders of the band teacher. Low G# and D# a twelfth above (fingerings 10 and 38) are the pivotal notes that dictate the sequence of L4 and R4 fingerings on either side. Since there is only one fingering for either of these pivotal notes they will be done on the right. Thus, the note on either side will be done on the left, and the one beyond that on the right and so forth, alternating until the series of little finger notes ceases. Marking the first note of the sequence with the correct fingering is the most important point.

The principles that apply to bassoon fingering choices are the ones that apply to oboe and clarinet, but the application differs. Instead of alternating between left and right, the bassoonist alternates between the front and back of the bassoon with the right fingers and thumb respectively.

There are very few alternate fingerings on the saxophone, but understanding two particular ones will save great stress in your teaching. These are (1) the G# coupling with three keys for the lowest notes on the instrument and (2) the three options for B-flat. See the Fingering Chart and Commentary.

GLOSSARY

Adjustment Screw A screw on a key which regulates the alignment of two pads or the rise of a pad from the instrument

Alcohol Lamp A source of clean flame consisting of an alcohol reservoir, a wick, and a guide for the wick

Altissimo The highest register of a woodwind instrument

Articulated G# A G# mechanism in which the touchpiece and the key are on different axels. Closing 1R closes the G# key whether the touchpiece is down or not.

Axel (Rod Axel) A rod running from one end to the other end of a woodwind key upon which the key pivots

Backbore The interior area of a mouthpiece farthest from the tip of the mouthpiece

Barrel Joint The part of a clarinet between the mouthpiece and upper joint

Bladder Pad A pad made of a cardboard ring and a felt ring, covered with a very thin, semi-transparent membrane

Bocal The curved metal piece between the reed and the body of the bassoon itself

Bore The hollow interior of a woodwind instrument

Bore Oil An organic oil used to stabilize the wood of a grenadilla instrument

Bridge Key An extension of a woodwind key that transfers motion from one joint over a tenon to another joint

Bunsen Burner A source of clean flame using natural gas

Bushing A plastic replacement for a tone hole seat, used after the wooden seat was compromised by a crack in the wood

Chalumeau The first octave of a clarinet's lowest register

Chamber The hollow interior of a mouthpiece closest to the tip

Clarion The second register on clarinet consisting of third partials

Concert Pitch The sounding pitches on a piano or any "C" instrument

Cork Grease Lubricant designed for cork, usually organic in origin

Cork Pad A woodwind pad made of high-quality cork

Crown The metal piece on the very end of the headjoint, screwed onto the flute headjoint cork assembly

Denatured Alcohol The type of alcohol used in an alcohol lamp. (In contrast to isopropyl or grain alcohol)

Diaphragm The dome-shaped muscle that separates the thoracic and abdominal cavities

Embouchure The manner in which the facial muscles and lips are formed to correctly produce a tone on a wind instrument

Facing (curve) The curved part of the table of a woodwind mouthpiece

Flat Spring A flat piece of metal attached to a key which causes a key to return to its original position

Flush Band A metal band shrunk around a woodwind instrument for the purpose of holding a crack closed

French Cement A solid adhesive which becomes malleable when heated, used to secure woodwind pads to key cups

Head Joint Cork Plate The round plate attached to a threaded screw in its center, snug against the end of a flute headjoint cork

Joint An individual piece of a woodwind instrument, often with holes and keys

Key Cup The part of a woodwind key in which a pad is attached, that covers a tone hole

Key Oil A lubricant, usually petroleum-derived, used to lubricate keys on a woodwind instrument

Leak Light A small light which is inserted in the bore of a woodwind instrument which discloses the location of leaks around the seat of the pad

Master Pad The pad that is touched directly when a two-pad combination moves at the same time

Neck The curved part of a saxophone between the mouthpiece and the body of the instrument (sometimes called "gooseneck")

Needle Spring A slender piece of metal mounted between a key post and a saddle which causes a key to return to its original position

Octave Key The key on oboes and saxophones that open a vent hole, causing the pitch to jump to a higher octave

Overblow Causing a woodwind pitch to shift to a higher harmonic, often by opening a vent hole or changing air direction

Pad Slick A flat piece of metal used to adjust the position of a pad while the adhesive is malleable

Pancake Key The low E key on a bassoon butt joint

Paraffin A petroleum derivative wax used to secure and lubricate string on bassoon tenons

Performance Practice The study of stylistically authentic performance

Pinning Using small pieces of threaded wire (like screws) to stabilize a crack in a woodwind instrument

Pivot Screw A small screw at the ends of a solid key upon which the key moves freely

Plaque A flat piece of metal used to separate the two blades of a double reed when scraping with a reed knife

Rails The sides and tip part of a woodwind mouthpiece that touch the reed when the reed is pushed into the mouthpiece

Reamer A tool used to remove wood from the end of a bassoon reed that attaches to the bocal

Refacing Changing the facing curve by adjusting the rails of a mouthpiece. Done with fine sandpaper

Register All notes of a single partial, such as fundamental or first overtone

Register Key The clarinet key operated by the left thumb that causes the instrument to produce partials above the fundamental

Resistance The feeling that the instrument is "blowing back" at the player

Rod axel see **Axel**

Saddle The perturbation on a woodwind key into which the end of a needle spring is secured

Seat A pad seats when it touches the instrument evenly around the circumference of the tone hole

Seating Ring The ring that an instrument's seat presses into a pad

Shoulder The area of a single reed where the bark ends and the cut part (vamp) begins

Shrink Tubing Plastic tubing used by electricians which shrinks when heated

Slave Pad The pad of a two-pad combination that moves when the master pad is depressed

Sopranino An instrument of high soprano range sounding above concert pitch

Spine An area of thicker cane running down the center of an oboe reed between the strings and the heart

Staple The metal tube upon which an oboe or English horn reed is tied

Stock The part of a single reed with bark on it. The ligature touches this part of the reed.

Striker The part of a woodwind key which strikes the body of the instrument, limiting the distance the pad rises

Table The flat part of a clarinet or saxophone mouthpiece

Tenon The ends of a woodwind joint which attach two joints together. Called "male" and "female."

Throat Tones The seven clarinet notes from bottom-space E through B-flat

Touchpiece The part of a woodwind key that the finger touches

Tuning Ring A flat washer that fits between joints of a clarinet to occupy airspace caused by pulling the joint apart for tuning

Vamp The part of a single reed from which the bark has been removed

Vent (hole) A hole near the mouthpiece or reed, covered by a key which is opened in order to produce a higher register

Whisper Key The bassoon key with the pad closing a hole on the bocal, used to facilitate overblowing to a higher partial

Xiphoid Process The cartilage at the bottom of the sternum

ABOUT THE AUTHOR

Recipient of the Award of Excellence, the Virginia Commonwealth University VCUArts' highest faculty honor, Charles West has taught all five woodwinds on the university level and has performed professionally on four of five woodwinds for four decades. He has been a Fulbright Scholar, President of the International Clarinet Association, and Principal or Bass Clarinetist in six professional orchestras on two continents. He holds two Bachelor's degrees in Music Education and Performance from the University of Northern Colorado and the Master of Fine Arts and Doctor of Musical Arts degrees from the University of Iowa. He studied all five woodwinds with Loren Bartlett, and his further flute study has been with Watler Smith, Keith Pettway and Evelyn Tyrell, his oboe study with James Lakin, his clarinet study with Himie Voxman, Robert Marcellus and Leon Russianoff among others, and his bassoon study with Ronald Tyree.

West has held professorships in three North American universities, and guest professorships or residencies in South America, Taiwan, Hong Kong, Australia and China. He has recorded repertoire on the Klavier, Wilson Audiophile, Centaur, CRI and Crystal labels and on a Grammy Award-winning Telarc CD and has played flute, piccolo, oboe, English Horn, clarinet, bass clarinet, and all saxophones as a first call doubler in Richmond, Virginia and El Paso, Texas. He is Coordinator of Winds & Percussion at Virginia Commonwealth University, artist-clinician for the Buffet Group, and Conductor of the Youth Orchestra of Central Virginia. His other publications with Meredith Music Publications are *The Woodwind Player's Cookbook: Creative Recipes for a Successful Performance* and *Woodwind Instruments: Purchasing, Maintenance, Troubleshooting, and More.*